# Screens Without Screams

# Screens Without Screams

## A Family Plan for Phones and Tablets: Set screen rules kids follow without daily battles

**Reema Sanzari**

**Mindful Pages**

Published in 2026

ISBN: 9789376551200 (PB)
ISBN: 9789376550937 (eBook)

*Published by*

**Mindful Pages**
*Imprint of Alpha Editions LLC*
312 W. 2nd St #1834
Casper, WY 82601, USA



This book was developed using advanced writing tools to support the drafting and ideation process. All content has been thoughtfully curated, refined, and reviewed to ensure quality and relevance.

# Content

# Introduction

On 9 January 2007, at the Moscone Center in San Francisco, Steve Jobs held up a small rectangle of glass and promised a "revolutionary" phone. The room erupted. The applause had that dry, sharp sound it gets in a big hall when thousands of palms hit at once, a kind of weather. Under the stage lights, the device looked almost damp, as if it had been lifted from water rather than a pocket. Glass glowed in his hand. In that moment the object was not yet a domestic problem, not yet the cause of a Tuesday-night argument about homework or a Sunday morning spoiled by a sulk. It was simply a new tool, sleek enough to invite belief. What was harder to see—what most of us could not see, because it had not yet become ordinary—was that the tool would arrive with its own gravity, tugging at attention with the quiet persistence of a charging cable left across the floor: easy to ignore until someone trips.

The modern family did not choose a moral battlefield; it inherited a design problem. A screen can steady a child after a hard day, translate a confusing maths worksheet into something solvable, carry a shy friendship across the awkwardness of adolescence. The same screen can, minutes later, turn a kitchen into a negotiation chamber, where every request is treated as an opening bid and every boundary becomes, by default, a debate. It is tempting to frame this as character: children lacking discipline, parents lacking backbone. Yet the more honest diagnosis is architecture. Many households are running on policies that were never written, enforced with emotions that were never meant to be the enforcement mechanism.

Consider what the devices themselves are optimised to do. A phone is not a neutral book that politely stays shut when the reader closes it. It is a door that does not like being shut, because other people are knocking, because the handle is warm, because behind it there is always another room. Designers have a name for the way rewards arrive at unpredictable intervals: variable reinforcement. The brain reads that unpredictability as possibility, and possibility is sticky. A child in the middle of a game level is not merely "playing too long"; the game has been built to suspend completion, to keep the next little burst of success just out of reach. A teen waiting for a reply in a group chat is not merely "being rude"; the social loop is live, and social loops are older than civilisation. The household argument that follows is rarely about minutes. It is about being pulled away mid-flight.

The friction shows up in small, repeatable scenes. A parent calls from the hallway, voice already tired, "Time to stop." The child answers without looking up, "In a minute." The minute multiplies. The parent returns, now louder, and suddenly the request is a threat—because it has to be, because the parent has no other tool in their hand. The child, who has learned that delay is a bargaining chip, pushes for another concession, and the parent, who has learned that concession buys temporary peace, gives it. Everyone feels faintly foolish. No one has solved anything. What has been rehearsed, instead, is a conflict pattern: vagueness, delay, escalation, explosion. Families repeat it because it is easy to slip into, and because the alternative—clear rules, calmly held—requires decisions made ahead of time, not in the heat of the moment.

What screens replace is often misdiagnosed because it hides in ordinary life. They do not only displace "family time" in some sentimental sense; they crowd out measurable things. Sleep slides later. Morning routines get brittle. Movement shrinks to the walk between sofa and fridge. Chores become a war of attrition. Boredom, which once forced invention, becomes something to be extinguished at the first itch. Casual talk thins out. A home can still look functional from the outside—packed lunches made, uniforms ironed, everyone technically present—but inside the day has lost its soft spaces, the informal moments where children casually admit what is bothering them because there is nothing else competing for their attention. Screens do not cause every problem, but they make certain problems easier to avoid, and avoidance has a cost.

The simplest way to understand the cost is to look at the times of day when arguments flare. After school is one of them. A child arrives home carrying the exhausted self-control of a day spent behaving, learning, coping. The screen offers immediate decompression: no conversation required, no homework demanded, no awkward feelings named. The parent sees the homework undone, the shoes kicked off, the blank stare. The child is not necessarily addicted to entertainment; they are often avoiding the difficult transition between public effort and private responsibility. Name the concept and it becomes less personal: transition friction. The implication is not that the child is lazy, but that the household needs a better bridge between "home" and "responsibility" than a device can provide by default.

Night-time is another flashpoint, and it behaves differently. When a phone is used in bed, the negotiation is not only about time. It is about privacy, identity, and the fact that late night has fewer natural stopping cues. There is no bell. There is only the internal promise of "one more", whispered by an endless feed that is designed never to end. It is not surprising that "just five more minutes" expands most at night; those minutes are surrounded by fatigue, loneliness, and the sharp intensity of teenage social life, which often blooms after adults have gone quiet. The visible behaviour—screen in bed, phone under the pillow, a face lit in the dark—is only the surface. Underneath are needs: connection, belonging, distraction, relief. A plan that ignores those needs will be enforced with force. A plan that recognises them can be enforced with structure.

This is why willpower, on its own, fails so reliably. Willpower is a scarce resource, and families spend it carelessly when they rely on improvisation. A child is asked to stop at a random moment, to do a less rewarding task, with no clear boundary that was agreed when they were calm. The parent is asked to be judge, jury, and emotional shock absorber after a day of work and care. Everyone's self-control is already depleted. The result is predictable: either the boundary collapses, or the household pays for the boundary with a blow-up. Better design changes the question. Instead of "Will everyone behave perfectly?", the question becomes "Can the environment make the sensible choice the easiest one?" A charging station in a shared place, for example, is not a moral statement. It is architecture. The cable is a reminder that devices live somewhere, and that somewhere is not under a duvet at midnight.

Governments and institutions have, in their own blunt ways, recognised the same design problem. In July 2018, France passed a law restricting mobile phone use in primary and lower secondary schools, a move widely reported at the time as an attempt to protect attention and reduce distraction in classrooms. It was not a perfect solution—schools vary, children vary, and enforcement is never as simple as legislation imagines—but it revealed something important: when the adults who run an institution decide what they are protecting, they do not ask eleven-year-olds to negotiate the policy in real time. They build defaults. They create clear zones and times. They make expectations public. The implication for home is uncomfortable, because it suggests that many households are trying to operate a complex system with fewer boundaries than a school can tolerate.

Companies have also acknowledged the pull, though often in the careful language of "wellbeing" rather than "we built this to be irresistible". In September 2018, Apple released iOS 12 with Screen Time, a set of tools intended to make usage visible and limits easier to set. Visibility matters. Metrics change arguments. A family that can compare actual hours spent on video apps against sleep patterns is no longer debating feelings alone; it is debating data, and data has a calming effect when used honestly. Still, the existence of a tool does not guarantee its usefulness. A limit set in a menu is only as strong as the family's agreement to treat it as real. Tools can support a plan; they cannot substitute for one. The implication is sobering: the solution is neither banning devices nor surrendering to them, but building a culture of boundaries that technology can reinforce rather than undermine.

And yet, a credible counter-example haunts any attempt to talk about limits with confidence. In March 2020, when COVID-19 lockdowns began reshaping daily life across the UK and much of the world, screens became a social prosthetic. For some children—especially those isolated by geography, anxiety, disability, or circumstances—video calls, online games, and group chats were not distractions but lifelines. A teen who might have eaten lunch alone at school could find a community online that felt safer than the physical world. A child with a specialist interest could meet others who shared it, breaking a loneliness that family love alone could not solve. It would be dishonest to deny this. Screens can widen a life as well as shrink it. The challenge is that a lifeline can also become a leash. The same channel that carries support can carry drama, comparison, sleep disruption, and the slow erosion of attention. The honest reconciliation is that boundaries are not a rejection of screens, but a way of protecting what screens are best at—connection, learning, creativity—while limiting what they are worst at: endless consumption, spiralling social feedback, and sleep theft.

So the household problem is not "screens" in the abstract, but the grey areas where screens become the default response to every gap in the day. Grey areas create arguments because they force constant interpretation. Is homework "done enough" to earn the tablet? Does a rainy Saturday count as a special occasion? If the child is upset, is a video a comfort or an avoidance? Without shared expectations, every moment becomes a miniature trial. Children, being excellent students of incentives, learn to push at ambiguity. Adults, being human, respond with inconsistency. Inconsistency teaches negotiation. Negotiation becomes the household sport. The behavioural metric that matters is not only screen hours, but the number of times per day the question is raised: "Can I have it now?" When that question becomes constant, even generous screen allowances feel like deprivation, because the device is always mentally present, always contested.

A workable family plan begins where arguments usually end: with values made practical. "We protect sleep" is not a slogan; it becomes a concrete behaviour—devices charge in a shared place, notifications are quiet at night, music is available without scrolling. "We protect kindness" is not a poster; it becomes a rule—no messaging after curfew, no posting in anger, no group chats that turn cruel without adult involvement. "We protect attention" is not nostalgia for a quieter era; it becomes a metric—phones away during homework blocks, feeds trimmed, auto-play disabled, breaks built in. Values are the only reason rules survive adolescence. A teen can out-argue a parent's preference; it is much harder to out-argue a household principle that has been lived consistently.

The shape of the plan must also respect a hard truth that parents often whisper to each other with weary relief: families have different capacities. A household with shift work, multiple jobs, caring responsibilities, or a child with neurodiversity will not run the same routines as a household with spacious evenings and predictable weekends. Any system that demands perfect consistency in a messy life will collapse and produce shame. Realistic design tolerates pressure. It assumes busy weeks. It expects exceptions and builds them in, rather than letting exceptions become the loophole through which every boundary escapes. The most elegant plans are often modest ones, because modest rules can actually be enforced. A child can tell when a boundary is performative. They can also tell when it is real.

Age changes everything, not because younger children are morally better and teens morally worse, but because the tasks are different. A six-year-old needs practice starting and stopping without drama, and they learn through routines that are simple enough to repeat. An eleven-year-old needs a sense of agency, because autonomy is part of healthy development, but they still need guardrails around sleep and school focus. A teenager needs privacy and identity respected, because humiliation is poison at that age, yet they also need protection from the social mechanisms that can destroy sleep, reputation, and mental space in a single weekend. The plan that works is one that makes responsibility grow gradually, with check-ins that treat mistakes as information rather than evidence of permanent failure. It is not a graduation ceremony; it is an apprenticeship.

What children accept, even when they grumble, are rules that feel like defaults rather than punishments. A dinner table that is always device-free becomes a place with its own atmosphere; after a while, reaching for a phone there feels odd, like wearing shoes in the bath. A bedroom that is never a charging location becomes, in a quiet way, a protected space. A car ride that is sometimes conversation, sometimes music, sometimes simple staring out of the window becomes a buffer zone rather than a delivery system for constant stimulation. These are not moral victories. They are design wins. They also reduce the need for surveillance, which is one of the most corrosive dynamics in family life around technology. When rules are clear and environments support them, monitoring can be transparent and proportionate rather than secretive and anxious. Trust becomes a behaviour: devices are used in shared spaces, expectations are stated upfront, reviews happen regularly, not only after a disaster.

There will still be meltdowns. That is not a sign the plan has failed; it is a sign that change is uncomfortable, especially when a child has been using screens to manage feelings they do not yet know how to manage differently. The goal is not to eliminate all conflict but to change its texture. A household can move from daily battles—long, exhausting, personal—to shorter moments of disappointment that are held calmly, repaired quickly, and understood as part of learning. Repair is not indulgence. It is the mechanism by which boundaries stop becoming wounds. A parent can apologise for shouting without apologising for the rule. A child can be helped back into dignity without being rescued from consequence. The relationship, not the screen, becomes the centre of gravity again.

It helps to admit, without dramatics, that adults are not outside the system. The child sees the parent glance at notifications during dinner, scroll while saying "just a second", respond to work messages late at night with the same urgency the parent criticises in their teen. Hypocrisy is not a philosophical issue in a family; it is a practical one. Children use it as evidence. Parents feel it as shame. The plan becomes sturdier when adults make small visible changes, because those changes remove an entire category of argument. They also model the deeper skill: that attention is something a person can choose to protect. No child learns calm boundaries from speeches. They learn from what is normal in the room.

The question, then, is not whether screens are good or bad. That debate is too blunt to be useful, like asking whether rain is good or bad. The question is where the household wants friction to live. Friction will exist either way. A family can pay for friction in daily arguments, in eroded sleep, in anxious secrecy, in constant low-grade negotiation. Or it can pay for friction upfront, in a few deliberate decisions that feel awkward at first and then quietly make life easier. Every boundary is a trade-off. Every freedom is too. The charging cable across the floor is still there; the only difference is whether it is a hazard everyone trips over, or a line everyone has agreed to route neatly, so people can walk without bracing for impact.

What matters most is not the perfect rule, but the ability to ask a diagnostic question and answer it honestly: which part of family life is being protected, and what is being traded away to protect it? That question has no universal answer. It changes as children mature. It changes with school demands, friendships, mental health, and the strange weather of adolescence. Yet it is the question that turns screen time from a daily quarrel into a family decision—one that can be revised without chaos, held without humiliation, and measured in something more meaningful than minutes.

# Chapter 1
# Why Screens Create Daily Friction

A parent stands at the kitchen doorway and hears it: the faint, insistent tapping of thumbs on glass, the tiny clicks that say someone is somewhere else. The evening smells of warm food and detergent. The child on the sofa does not look up. Homework is half-open on the table, a pencil balanced like a surrendered flag. The parent speaks, gently at first, and the child answers with that maddening calm that belongs to people who know they have time: "Just a minute." A minute becomes a mood. The room tightens. The request becomes a demand. The demand becomes a fight. Later, everyone will remember the argument, not the original problem, and the device will sit there, perfectly innocent, as if it had not pulled invisible strings.

The oddity is that the conflict does not always correlate with the obvious things. Some children can spend a long time on a screen and hand it over without a tremor. Others erupt after what looks, to an adult, like a modest session. Sometimes the same child is cooperative on Tuesday and explosive on Thursday, as if the rules have changed when they have not. It is tempting to call this manipulation. It is also tempting to blame the parent: too strict, too soft, too inconsistent, too distracted. Those explanations contain slivers of truth, but they miss the more useful reality: the screen itself is a kind of environment, and environments shape behaviour far more reliably than moral lectures ever will.

If this were only a matter of entertainment, families could treat screens like sweets: a treat, a limit, an occasional complaint, then life goes on. Yet screens do not behave like sweets. They behave more like doors. Behind them are friends, games, humour, status, novelty, and the possibility of relief from whatever feels difficult in the room. A child is not only losing a cartoon; they are being pulled away from a stream of social belonging or a task that offers constant feedback. An adult is not only asking for compliance; they are asking for a sudden switch from a bright, reactive world into a slower one where effort is required and the rewards are delayed. The friction is not a character flaw. It is a collision between two tempos.

The chapter's central tension is simple and sharp: the home needs predictability, while most screens are designed to resist it. A household runs on rhythms, on transitions, on the small social agreements that let people share space without constantly renegotiating who controls it. A device runs on immediacy, on prompts, on the invitation to stay a little longer because the next thing is always waiting. When those two systems overlap without clear boundaries, the family ends up doing something no one enjoys: improvising governance in real time, with tired bodies and frayed patience, while a child learns that the loudest feelings set the rules.

This tension matters because it reaches into places families often treat as separate problems. Sleep loss is not only about tiredness; it changes emotion regulation, attention span, and how easily a child tips into tears or rage the next day. A home with constant screen conflict tends to develop a background hum of vigilance, the sense that any calm moment might be interrupted by another demand, another refusal, another escalation. That hum is exhausting. It shapes how adults speak to children, how siblings relate to one another, even how parents relate to themselves. A person who spends the evening enforcing a boundary with rising anger is not only managing a device; they are managing their own shame at not being calmer, their fear of being outmatched, their worry that something important is slipping away.

The stakes are also long-term, in a quieter way. Children learn the rules of reality by watching what repeatedly happens at home. If the pattern around screens is that the first "no" is negotiable, that delay is rewarded, that volume changes outcomes, then those lessons leak into other domains. If the pattern is that boundaries appear suddenly and unpredictably, then children adapt by scanning for weakness and resisting as soon as a request is made, because resistance is part of how they keep a sense of control. None of this requires a child to be malicious. It requires only that they are human, that they learn from reinforcement, and that they prefer a rewarding activity to an unrewarding one. Adults do too. The home becomes a training ground, whether anyone intends it or not.

There is another reason this matters, and it is less dramatic but more intimate. Screens can quietly thin out the ordinary conversations that make families resilient: the after-school ramble about who sat next to whom, the grumble about a teacher, the half-formed worry that comes out sideways while buttering toast. When a child goes straight from the front door to a screen, the day is not only being "decompressed"; it is being sealed. A parent may feel shut out not because the child is secretive, but because the day has no doorway into speech. Later, when a serious issue arrives, the family may find it harder to talk, not because of a single device session, but because of a repeated habit of avoidance. Still, it is important to concede something: not every screen moment is an erosion. Sometimes a child uses a device to regulate after a hard day, to connect safely, to create something they are proud of. The friction is not proof of harm; it is a signal that the system is unmanaged.

The path through this chapter begins with the mechanics of capture: not as a villain story, but as an explanation of why stopping can feel like a small loss or even a small injury, especially when the activity has no natural ending. From there the focus shifts to the home as an ecosystem, asking what screens quietly displace and why certain parts of the day become vulnerable. Then the lens tightens again, not on screens but on arguments themselves, tracing how families accidentally teach negotiation and escalation through the way limits are delivered, delayed, and defended.

A useful way to hold the whole problem is to picture that kitchen doorway again, not as a stage for a recurring battle but as a diagnostic point. What exactly is happening in the second before the request to stop lands? What is the child doing on the screen, what are they being pulled away from, and what has the family trained each other to expect when the boundary arrives? The friction begins somewhere specific, not in a general dislike of rules. If the first protest sounds inevitable, almost rehearsed, it is worth asking a sharper question: what, precisely, is the device offering in that moment that the room is failing to offer, and why does ending it feel like a rupture rather than a routine?

## How attention gets captured

In the 1950s, in a laboratory at Harvard University in Cambridge, Massachusetts, B. F. Skinner refined an idea that would outlive his pigeons. In 1957 he published *Verbal Behavior*, but it was his earlier work on reinforcement schedules that quietly altered the way people would one day live with machines. The apparatus was plain: a box, a lever, a reward delivered on a pattern. When the reward arrived on a fixed schedule, the behaviour stabilised and, crucially, it stopped when the reward stopped. When the reward arrived unpredictably, behaviour became stubborn. The organism kept trying. It kept hoping. Decades later, the glossy phone in a child's hand would be vastly more complex than a lever in a box, but the underlying bargain would feel strangely familiar: act, wait, maybe receive. The next reward is unknown.

That is the first reason devices are hard to put down: they do not behave like tidy activities with a natural ending. They behave like open loops. The screen offers a stream of small possibilities that arrive on irregular timing: a message, a funny clip, a new comment, a level completed, a friend joining, a surprise item. Each possibility is individually trivial. Together they form a pattern the brain treats as urgent, not because the user is weak, but because the brain evolved to privilege uncertain rewards. This is not a defect. It is a survival feature, repurposed.

The second reason is more domestic, and more painful. Screens tend to capture attention at exactly the moments when a family most needs attention to be shareable: transitions, interruptions, and emotional edges. A child arriving home from school does not want a lecture on discipline; they want relief. A teen does not want a sermon; they want belonging. An adult does not want yet another decision; they want the evening to run. The screen is designed to offer immediate relief and easy belonging, and it does so with a kind of indifferent competence. The home, by contrast, is full of ambiguous tasks and delayed rewards. The competition is not fair.

To see how capture works, it helps to begin with a concrete behaviour rather than a moral judgement. A child is asked to stop a game. They resist. The resistance spikes when they are stopped mid-level, mid-match, mid-mission, mid-conversation. The protest softens when they are stopped after a natural break, such as a level completion or a clear pause. The visible difference is timing. The named concept is the open loop, and it is older than phones. In 1927, the psychologist Bluma Zeigarnik described what became known as the Zeigarnik effect: unfinished tasks tend to linger in the mind more than finished ones. The explanation is not mystical. An incomplete task keeps mental resources allocated because the brain has not yet marked it as safely stored. The implication for the family is immediate and often overlooked: stopping is not a single act. It is an interruption of a cognitive process that has not yet resolved. People resist interruptions. Children do it loudly.

The modern screen multiplies open loops with impressive efficiency because it reduces friction. A printed book ends a chapter. A film ends. A football match ends. A phone feed often does not. When a video auto-plays into the next, when a feed refreshes with fresh content, when a chat keeps moving, the user is denied the small psychological relief of an ending. The show is continuity. The concept is frictionless continuation: a design choice that removes the pause where a person might decide to stop. The explanation is mechanical as much as psychological. If stopping requires an internal decision every few seconds, and starting requires almost nothing, the balance is predictable. The implication is not that people are incapable of choice; it is that choice becomes expensive when it must be made repeatedly, especially when someone is tired or upset. Families tend to try to solve this with a stronger voice. The system responds with stronger pull.

There is a deeper neurobiological story underneath the pull, and it is useful precisely because it reduces blame. In 1997, Wolfram Schultz, Peter Dayan, and P. Read Montague published work in *Science* on dopamine neurons and what became widely known as reward prediction error. The show is a laboratory finding: dopamine activity reflected not simply reward, but the difference between expected reward and actual reward. When something better than expected occurred, the signal rose; when an expected reward failed to appear, the signal dipped. The named concept is prediction error. The explanation matters because it clarifies why novelty and uncertainty are so compelling. A predictable reward quickly becomes background. An uncertain reward keeps producing spikes and dips that make the brain pay attention. The implication is quietly unsettling: a device does not need to offer deep pleasure to hold attention; it needs to offer uncertainty. The user keeps checking not because they are continually delighted, but because they cannot reliably predict what will happen next.

This is why variable rewards feel like "just one more". "One more" is not a number. It is a hope. In a feed, the next item might be dull, but it might be brilliant, and the possibility of brilliance is enough to keep the thumb moving. In messaging, the next reply might be boring, but it might be the one that matters. In games, the next attempt might fail, but it might succeed, and success is never far away. Each moment is a wager, small enough to seem harmless, repeated often enough to reshape the evening. Here the abstraction is *efficiency*, but it becomes visible as a behaviour: the child does not walk away; they renegotiate. They stretch time because the reward structure teaches stretching.

Games, in particular, offer a clean demonstration of capture because they make the loop explicit. A game provides clear goals, rapid feedback, and escalating challenges. This is not inherently sinister. It is good design for learning and mastery. Mihaly Csikszentmihalyi's work on flow, popularised in the 1990s, describes the state in which a person becomes deeply absorbed when challenge and skill are balanced. The show is recognisable: a child who is not merely entertained but focused, solving, adapting, tracking outcomes. The concept is flow. The explanation is that the game offers the brain what school and home tasks often fail to offer: immediate feedback and an unambiguous sense of progress. The implication is tricky for parents because it cuts against the usual narrative. The child is not always escaping effort; they are often seeking a form of effort that feels coherent. Stopping them mid-level is not only stopping "fun"; it is stopping a process of mastery at a moment when the brain is primed for completion.

That completion hunger collides with another mechanism: sunk cost. The longer a person spends on something, the more they feel compelled to justify the time by reaching a satisfying endpoint. A child who has been grinding for a reward in a game, or waiting for a reply in a chat, feels the pull to stay until the loop closes. The abstraction is *investment*, but it becomes visible as a phrase: "I'm nearly done." The phrase is sometimes true in a narrow sense. It is also sometimes a cognitive trick. "Nearly" can expand indefinitely in a system designed without endings. The implication is that arguments about minutes are often doomed, because "nearly done" is not a time estimate; it is an emotional state.

Social feedback loops add another layer, and they make the capture feel personal. A notification badge, a vibration, a subtle chime: these are cues that something might have happened. The show is a hand moving towards a pocket before the mind has fully decided. The concept is cue-triggered checking. The explanation is partly conditioning: cues become associated with social reward, and the brain begins to respond automatically. But there is also a reputational dimension. A teen who does not reply may fear being seen as rude, uninterested, or excluded. A child in a group game may fear missing their chance to join. The abstraction is *belonging*, and it becomes visible as a decision: reply now or risk social cost. The implication is that phone conflict is rarely only parent versus child. It is often parent versus the child's peer world, a world that can be intensely unforgiving and relentlessly present.

A checkable example makes this less abstract. In September 2006, Facebook introduced the News Feed, prompting immediate public backlash from some users who felt surveilled or overwhelmed by the constant stream of updates. The show was not a family argument but a mass emotional response: a platform shifted from a profile you visited to a feed that visited you. The concept is ambient social information. The explanation is that a feed converts other people's lives into a continuous drip of updates, and the drip invites habitual checking because it is never complete. The implication is that the social internet is not simply a set of conversations; it is an environment of constant social visibility. For adolescents, whose social standing can feel like a daily referendum, that visibility can intensify the urge to monitor and respond. Adults are not immune. They are simply more practiced at pretending they are.

The same logic can be seen in the small mechanics of messaging: read receipts, typing indicators, streaks, group chat activity. These features are often treated as "fun". In practice they are timers attached to social expectations. The abstraction is *trust*, but it becomes visible as an anxious micro-behaviour: checking whether a message was seen, checking whether someone is typing, checking whether silence means rejection. The explanation is that these signals create a sense of real-time social accounting. The implication is that leaving a conversation is not merely closing an app; it can feel like stepping out of a room mid-sentence, with everyone watching.

Still, capture is not absolute, and it is important to say so plainly. There are counter-examples that do not fit the stereotype of mindless scrolling. Many people can engage deeply with digital tools that have clear endpoints and internal structure: a document editor, a music composition programme, a coding environment, a language lesson with defined modules, a long essay read without interruption. The show is different: the person can stop at a paragraph break, a saved file, a completed exercise. The concept is bounded activity. The explanation is that bounded activities offer natural stopping cues and meaningful completion. They often shift attention from reactive checking to sustained focus. The implication is that "screens" are not a single thing in the brain; the design of the activity matters. A family that treats every screen as equally capturing will misunderstand their own household dynamics, and may miss opportunities to favour activities that support agency rather than erode it.

Even the science of self-control contains a caution against simplistic narratives. Some popular claims about willpower have been contested over time, and debates about effects such as ego depletion have highlighted that human behaviour is shaped by context, motivation, and measurement choices, not just a single inner "muscle" of restraint. The honest limitation is that no single mechanism explains every child, every app, every evening. Temperament varies. Family stress varies. Sleep varies. The same design can hook one person and bore another. Reconciliation does not require giving up the framework. It requires using it as a map rather than a verdict. The map explains why certain designs predictably produce more friction and why certain moments of the day predictably magnify it.

The quiet motif worth holding here is the badge: that small red dot, literal or metaphorical, that claims urgency. It is a tiny thing with an outsized effect. It sits there on an icon and turns a neutral device into a pending task. It tells the brain there is something unfinished, something waiting, something that might matter. In family life the badge takes other forms: the half-finished level, the unread message, the unclosed loop. Each one makes stopping feel like loss. When a parent says "turn it off", they are sometimes unknowingly asking the child to tolerate a specific kind of discomfort: the discomfort of incompletion. Adults ask children to practise it daily. Adults often avoid it themselves.

Understanding capture does not soften boundaries by itself, but it changes the emotional tone around them. If a parent believes a child is choosing defiance, the parent escalates quickly. If a parent sees a predictable pull created by variable rewards, frictionless continuation, and social feedback loops, the parent can interpret protest as information rather than insult. The family can begin to notice patterns that are concrete enough to measure: protests spike mid-task, checking spikes when cues arrive, meltdowns cluster at transitions, late-night scrolling expands when there are no natural endings. Naming these patterns does not absolve anyone of responsibility. It relocates responsibility from moralising to design: the conditions under which attention is taxed, and the moments when stopping is hardest.

A final complication makes the problem feel so personal: devices are portable, intimate, and socially charged. A television in the corner is a shared object; a phone is a private world. When a child resists stopping, the parent is not merely contesting entertainment; they may be contesting a friendship, a status game, a moment of competence, a refuge from anxiety, or a simple sense of control. That is why arguments can feel disproportionate. They are often fights about autonomy disguised as fights about time. The badge, again, does its work: it makes the digital world feel pressing, and it makes the parent's request feel like an interruption of something urgent.

The unresolved tension is not whether attention can be captured. It can. The harder question is where a household chooses to place its friction: in constant, improvised interruptions, or in clearer structures that make endings easier to reach. When a child protests at the moment of stopping, is the protest a sign of entitlement, or a sign that the activity was designed to be hard to end, and the family has not yet built reliable landing places? The answer changes what a parent notices next, and what a child learns to expect when the badge lights up again.

## What screens replace at home

In April 2019, the World Health Organization in Geneva published guidance on physical activity, sedentary behaviour, and sleep for young children, placing screen time in the same sentence as movement and rest. The document was not a cultural manifesto. It was a sign of what had become visible across countless households: the question is rarely only what a screen adds, but what it quietly removes. That quietness matters. Screens do not storm the front door. They seep into the seams of the day, into the five minutes before dinner, the half-hour after school, the sliver of time that used to hold nothing in particular. Something else quietly disappears.

The strange thing about "replacement" is that it seldom feels like a swap. A child is not weighing sleep against a video clip like a careful accountant. An adult is not trading a family conversation for a scroll with full awareness. The exchange happens by default, because the screen is the most available tool in the room: portable, instantly gratifying, and socially backed. That is why families often talk about screens as if they were a substance, an outside force. Yet the more practical view is ecological. The home has a finite number of hours, a finite number of transitions, a finite supply of shared attention. When a screen occupies a space, it displaces whatever would otherwise have grown there.

Start with the most measurable thing a screen displaces: sleep. Not because every device use damages rest, but because the evening is the one part of family life where the day's remaining capacity is smallest and the consequences are largest. The show is familiar. A bedroom light is off, but a face is lit. A child says they are winding down, yet their breathing stays quick, their thumb keeps moving, their eyes keep flicking. The concept is sleep encroachment: the slow extension of wakefulness by small, repeatable digital prompts. The explanation is not simply about light or stimulation, though those can matter; it is about the way screens dissolve endings. Bedtime used to be a border. Screens turn borders into gradients. The implication is behavioural and immediate: the next morning begins with a debt. A child who wakes tired does not merely yawn; they argue more easily, forget more easily, and find transitions harder. The household then spends the day paying interest on a debt that was acquired quietly the night before.

The displacement of movement is equally straightforward and just as easy to misread. It is tempting to treat movement as an optional virtue, like extra vegetables, rather than as the body's daily maintenance. The show is the after-school slump: shoes off, bag dropped, body folding into a familiar corner while a device comes alive. The concept is posture capture, a physical analogue of attention capture. The explanation is simple: screens invite stillness because stillness improves viewing and control. A game wants steady hands. A feed wants uninterrupted gaze. A chat wants quick replies from the same spot. The implication is not a moral story about laziness; it is a spatial story about the home. When the default decompression tool is sedentary, movement does not merely reduce; it becomes something that must be deliberately arranged, which makes it rarer in busy weeks.

Boredom is the displacement most adults underestimate, partly because boredom sounds like a problem rather than a capacity. A child says, "I'm bored," and the adult hears complaint. But boredom is also the first draft of creativity, the uncomfortable pause that forces the brain to invent an alternative. The show is a child waiting: in the car, in a queue, between tasks, after finishing dinner early. The concept is boredom suppression. The explanation is not that screens are "fun", which is too vague to be useful, but that they offer immediate structure. A feed supplies content without requiring initiative. A game supplies goals without requiring imagination. The implication is subtle and cumulative: when boredom is consistently extinguished, children get fewer chances to practise moving from discomfort to self-directed activity. That practice matters later, when motivation is required for schoolwork, hobbies, or simply tolerating an ordinary afternoon without constant stimulus.

Chores are displaced in a different way, because chores are not displaced by time alone but by bargaining. A chore is a task with low immediate reward and delayed social benefit. A screen is a task with immediate reward and endless continuation. When both are present, the home becomes a marketplace of incentives. The show is the familiar sentence: "After this." The concept is chore deferral. The explanation is not that children dislike contributing, though they often do, but that deferral is rational when the more rewarding activity has no ending. "After this video" becomes "after this series", "after this level" becomes "after this match", and the task migrates towards bedtime, where fatigue makes it harder and conflict more likely. The implication is practical: the household gradually rewrites its rules without agreeing to. Chores become optional, or they become punishments, and either way they lose their intended function of competence-building and shared responsibility.

Then there is the displacement that families feel most painfully but talk about least precisely: casual family talk. Not the big conversations about values, bullying, or safety, but the loose chatter that stitches a household together. The show is almost invisible: a parent and child in the same room, each occupied, silence thickening not because anyone is angry but because the screen fills the conversational air. The concept is conversational thinning. The explanation is not that screens "reduce communication" in some blanket way; it is that they interrupt the conditions under which casual talk emerges. Casual talk requires shared attention and low stakes. It requires micro-pauses: waiting for pasta to boil, folding laundry side by side, wandering through a shop, sitting in the car without a playlist that demands focus. Screens replace those pauses with content. The implication is not sentimental. It is structural. When casual talk thins, families lose early-warning systems. Worries that might have surfaced sideways do not surface at all. Small misunderstandings linger. Siblings relate through parallel scrolling rather than shared play. When a serious issue arrives, the household may find it harder to start the conversation because it has lost the habit of talking without an agenda.

A second checkable anchor helps place this in a wider context of deliberate design, rather than individual failure. In October 2016, the American Academy of Pediatrics, based in Itasca, Illinois, launched an online Family Media Plan, encouraging families to match media use to sleep, school, and relationships. The show here is not a perfect solution but an institutional acknowledgement: screens are not only about content, they are about allocation. The concept is time budgeting, not in a financial sense but in a behavioural sense. The explanation is that a day has competing goods, and any tool that absorbs time will necessarily crowd out something else unless a family actively defends that "something else". The implication is clarifying: debates about whether a particular app is educational often miss the more decisive question of what it pushes aside. A drawing app used for half an hour may be benign; the same half hour taken from bedtime or from a sibling's chance to talk may not be.

The most revealing displacement tends to occur at transitions, because transitions are where the home's emotional temperature shifts quickly. The show is the post-school doorway moment. A child enters with a body full of held-in stress and a mind still stuck in school social dynamics. The screen offers a smooth ramp into pleasure or connection. The concept is transition avoidance. The explanation is human and unglamorous: switching states is uncomfortable. Going from the demands of school to the demands of home requires re-orienting, and re-orienting requires effort. A feed is effortless. A conversation about homework is not. The implication is that an after-school scroll is not always about entertainment. It can be a refusal of the transition itself, a way of postponing the moment when the child must become, once again, a person who can be asked things. Parents sense this and feel rejected. Children feel pressured and feel misunderstood. The screen sits in the middle, offering relief while quietly postponing adaptation.

This is why families who try to address displacement by arguing about content often get stuck. Content is visible. Replacement is not. A child can easily defend content: "It's just funny videos." A teen can justify content: "It's how we talk." A parent can attack content: "It's rubbish." But none of those positions touches the actual trade. The trade is about time windows and emotional needs. When screen use expands, it tends to expand into the least defended spaces, not the most. The defended spaces are school hours, formal activities, perhaps family meals if they are already protected. The least defended spaces are the margins: mornings before school, that vulnerable after-school stretch, the hour before bed. Those margins are precisely where many of the household's most important functions live: waking gently, reconnecting, winding down. The implication is stark: displacement is rarely random. It is patterned. It clusters where the household is tired, rushed, or unsure of what it wants.

A quiet motif can keep the analysis grounded: the doorway. The doorway is where outside life turns into home life, where expectations shift, where the body takes off shoes and the mind takes off its public face. Screens tend to colonise doorways because doorways are awkward. They are liminal. They hold the discomfort of switching roles. When a child crosses the threshold and immediately reaches for a device, the device becomes a kind of portable doorway, a way of staying half in and half out. The motif matters because it suggests that the fight is rarely about a screen in isolation. It is about the threshold moments when the household needs a shared ritual and instead gets a private retreat.

There is, however, a limitation that must be faced honestly, because without it the argument becomes too neat to be credible. Screens sometimes replace things that were not good in the first place. A child who is isolated, bullied, or simply temperamentally different may find more genuine connection through a digital community than through local peers. A teen with niche interests may finally meet people who share them. A family separated by distance may maintain relationships through video calls and shared messages that would otherwise wither. The show is not fantasy; it is a recognisable modern reality: a grandparent seen weekly on a screen rather than yearly in person, a friend group maintained through a game when geography makes meet-ups rare. The concept is compensatory connection. The explanation is that screens can substitute for missing social infrastructure. The implication is that "replacement" is not always loss. Sometimes it is repair.

Reconciling that limitation requires refusing a simple moral ranking of offline over online. The more accurate approach is to distinguish between replacement that strengthens the household and replacement that quietly degrades it. A weekly video call that increases family closeness is replacement with gain. A nightly scroll that compresses sleep and increases morning conflict is replacement with cost. A creative project built on a tablet that produces pride is replacement with gain. A feed that dissolves chores and provokes arguments is replacement with cost. These are not philosophical categories; they are visible patterns. They show up in bedtime resistance, in morning mood, in how often a child asks for a device, in how quickly they can switch away from it without protest, in whether they can still tolerate the doorway moments of the day without fleeing into a private stream.

For intelligent adults, the temptation is to treat the household as a place where rational policies can simply be declared and obeyed. But displacement reveals a more realistic truth: the home is an attention economy, and like all economies it runs on defaults, scarcity, and incentives. When a screen replaces sleep, the metric is a groggy morning and a shorter fuse. When it replaces movement, the metric is an evening that never leaves the sofa. When it replaces boredom, the metric is the speed with which a child demands stimulation. When it replaces chores, the metric is the number of negotiations per day. When it replaces talk, the metric is the thinning of those small, low-pressure exchanges that make later big conversations possible. These are not abstract "values". They are household outputs.

The doorway returns here, because the most important question is not "How much screen time?" but "Which thresholds does the screen control?" Does it control the threshold between school and home? Between dinner and homework? Between bedtime and sleep? Between sibling proximity and sibling connection? The screen's power grows when it owns thresholds, because thresholds are where behaviour is most malleable and emotions most raw. A family can live with generous screen use if thresholds are protected. A family can also suffer with relatively modest screen use if the device has captured the margins where the household needs coherence.

The forward test is uncomfortable because it resists easy slogans. When a screen enters a given hour, what exactly leaves? Not in theory. In the specific life of a specific home. If a child reaches for a device after school, is it replacing movement, talk, or the simple work of crossing the doorway from one identity to another? If a teen keeps a phone close at night, is it replacing sleep, or is it replacing the quiet that would otherwise force them to feel something they would rather not feel? The friction begins when families argue about the screen as an object rather than about the trade as a pattern. The next step is not a rule. It is a clearer sightline: seeing the true cost in the moments where the household repeatedly trips, and deciding whether those are the moments the family can afford to lose.

## Conflict patterns families repeat

In 1982, in Eugene, Oregon, the psychologist Gerald R. Patterson published *Coercive Family Process*, drawing on work at the Oregon Social Learning Center to describe a grimly ordinary loop: one person demands, the other resists, the first escalates, the second escalates back, and the moment ends not with understanding but with surrender by whoever runs out of stamina first. The "winner" changes from day to day. The pattern stays. Patterson was not writing about phones and tablets. He did not need to. He was writing about how families unintentionally train each other, shaping behaviour through what happens next rather than what anyone believes. The mechanism is older than any app. The countdown always changes things.

A screen conflict often begins with a sentence that sounds reasonable and lands like a spark: "Can you get off now?" The child barely turns their head. "In a minute." The parent feels disrespected. The child feels interrupted. Both interpretations are sincere. Both are incomplete. What follows is a dance learned through repetition: the parent repeats the request, the child repeats the delay, the parent sharpens their tone, the child sharpens theirs, and the device becomes a third party in the room, silently offering the child a more rewarding stream than the conversation beside them. The argument is not merely about time. It is about control, predictability, and whose reality counts.

The most corrosive feature of these fights is their familiarity. Families can feel as if they are arguing about a new problem each day, when they are often re-enacting the same script with different props. The show is the same sequence of moves: a vague boundary appears late, resistance tests whether it is real, escalation makes it real, and the evening is consumed by the enforcement itself. The named concept is the coercive cycle. The explanation is behavioural rather than moral. In a coercive cycle, escalation is reinforced because it works sometimes. The parent learns that raising their voice produces compliance. The child learns that delaying, pleading, or exploding produces extra minutes or a weaker consequence. The implication is uncomfortable but clarifying: the family is not only suffering conflict; it is *teaching* conflict as a tool.

A central reason screens intensify this pattern is that devices make delay easy. Delay is not neutral. It is a strategy. A child who says "In a minute" is not always lying; they may genuinely feel mid-task. Yet delay also performs a test: will the adult return, and if they return, how serious are they? When adults respond inconsistently, children do what scientists and toddlers alike do: they experiment. The show is the parent who sometimes accepts "two more minutes" and sometimes does not, depending on fatigue, social pressure, or whether company is present. The concept is intermittent reinforcement, a term from behavioural science describing rewards delivered unpredictably. The explanation matters because intermittent reinforcement does not simply maintain a behaviour; it makes it resistant to change. A child does not need delay to work every time. They need it to work *often enough* to be worth trying. The implication is that inconsistency is not merely annoying; it is a training schedule that strengthens negotiation.

Screens also encourage a specific form of escalation: the "extinction burst". When a previously rewarded behaviour stops being rewarded, it often spikes before it fades. The show is the child who becomes louder, faster, more emotional at the very moment a parent tries to tighten a boundary. The concept is extinction burst, described in behavioural literature as a temporary intensification when reinforcement is withdrawn. The explanation is stark: the organism is testing whether the old method still works. If the old method has worked before, the test can be vigorous. The implication is that a sudden change in screen limits often produces a short-term surge in protest that feels like failure, even when it is a predictable part of the system's adjustment. People misread the surge as evidence that the boundary is "too harsh" or that the child is "out of control". In many cases it is evidence that the previous pattern was powerful.

The screen conflict script is often written in the language of fairness. Parents believe they are being fair when they give a warning, offer extra minutes, and allow a "proper finish". Children believe they are being treated unfairly when a stop comes mid-stream, when a sibling seems to get more time, or when adults use devices while restricting them. Fairness is not an abstraction here. It becomes a visible metric: who gets a warning, how long the warning lasts, whether the end time is negotiated, and whether consequences follow through. The trouble is that fairness is frequently attempted through improvisation, and improvisation is precisely what children can negotiate. The show is the parent who issues a warning at five minutes, then another at two minutes, then another at "right now", each one diluting the next. The concept is boundary erosion. The explanation is that repeated warnings without an enforced endpoint function as reassurance to the child that the adult is not yet committed. The implication is counterintuitive: what sounds gentle can feel unstable, and unstable systems provoke more testing.

A second named, checkable anchor from outside the screen debate makes the learning process vivid. In 1961, at Stanford University in Palo Alto, California, Albert Bandura conducted what became famous as the Bobo doll experiments, demonstrating that children imitate observed behaviour, especially when it appears effective. The show in those studies was not a family argument over a tablet; it was children modelling aggression they had witnessed. The concept is observational learning. The explanation generalises far beyond aggression. Children copy what works, and they copy what looks normal. The implication for screen conflict is direct and often painful: a child watching an adult respond to stress by doomscrolling is watching a method of emotional regulation; a child watching an adult break their own "no phones at dinner" rule is watching a rule's true status. This does not mean adults must be perfect. It means children learn the real rules from the lived ones.

What makes screen conflicts feel uniquely personal is that they happen at the intersection of authority and attachment. A parent is not only a manager of routines; they are the person a child depends on for safety and belonging. When a parent interrupts a screen, the child can experience it as an interruption of self, especially if the screen is where their friends are, or where they feel competent, or where they have escaped an uncomfortable mood. The show is the teen whose face changes instantly when told to hand over the phone: not the face of someone caught in wrongdoing, but the face of someone suddenly cut off. The concept is threatened autonomy. The explanation is developmental as much as technological. As children mature, they seek more control over their time and social world. Screens provide that control in a concentrated form: a pocket-sized portal that obeys instantly. The implication is that enforcement can accidentally become a proxy fight about growing up, and proxy fights become intense.

Families often get trapped in a particular escalation ladder. It begins with language that is broad enough to invite debate: "Enough now," "Stop soon," "Get off." The child responds with time-smearing: "Soon," "In a bit," "After this." The parent then tries to restore specificity with a threat: "If you don't stop, you'll lose it tomorrow." The child responds with emotional pressure: pleading, anger, tears, sulking. The parent, now in a corner, either backs down to restore peace or escalates to reclaim authority. The behaviour is visible. The underlying mechanism is the same: each side is trying to reduce immediate discomfort. The concept is negative reinforcement, where a behaviour is strengthened because it removes something unpleasant. The explanation is that parents may back down to end the argument, and children may comply to end the shouting; both learn that the fastest route out of discomfort is through escalation. The implication is bleak but hopeful: because the pattern is learned, it can be unlearned, but only if the family stops treating each argument as a fresh moral trial and starts treating it as a repeatable sequence with predictable triggers.

The quiet motif worth keeping in mind is the countdown, not as a tool but as a symbol of how families handle endings. In many homes, the countdown exists in the parent's head, unspoken: dinner needs cooking, bedtime is approaching, the adult is running out of patience. The child does not share that internal clock. The child is inside a different timing system, one shaped by the device's loops and rewards. When the parent finally voices the countdown, it arrives late and loud. The show is the sudden "Right, that's it" after a long period of tolerating the screen. The concept is delayed boundary-setting. The explanation is that delayed boundaries feel arbitrary because they are not tied to a visible rule; they are tied to a private threshold the child cannot see. The implication is that children learn to ignore early cues and wait for the explosion, because the explosion is the only reliable signal that the boundary is real.

A credible limitation must be named, because not every family pattern fits this model neatly. Some children comply quickly with screen limits even when adults are inconsistent, and some households experience little overt conflict despite heavy device use. Temperament matters. Sibling dynamics matter. Some children are naturally less drawn to competitive games or social feeds. Some families have longstanding routines that make transitions smoother even without strict rules. Some children with anxiety may comply outwardly yet suffer inwardly, avoiding conflict at the cost of suppressing needs. The reconciliation is that low conflict is not automatically high health, and high conflict is not automatically moral failure. Conflict patterns are signals. They reveal where the system is unclear, where the child's needs and the household's rhythm are clashing, and where the adult's enforcement tools have become reactive rather than designed.

The most useful shift is to treat arguments as data rather than theatre. Not data in the sterile sense of spreadsheets, but in the behavioural sense of repeatable sequences: what time of day the fights cluster, which activities trigger the strongest resistance, how often "one more minute" is granted, and what behaviours reliably end the confrontation. Trust, in this context, becomes a visible pattern: the child believes the adult's words match outcomes, and the adult believes the child's protests are feelings rather than tactics. Efficiency becomes a visible pattern too: how much evening time is spent enforcing boundaries compared with enjoying the evening. Risk shows up as a pattern of escalation: whether the conflict tends to end in shouting, in withdrawal, in bargaining, or in repair. The screen is only the stage. The script is the real problem.

The forward tension is not whether a child should have a device. It is whether the household is willing to notice the script it is already running. When the next conflict begins, what is the first line spoken, what is the predictable reply, and what does the family's history teach each person about how this ends? If the child's most effective method is delay and the parent's most effective method is escalation, the relationship is being trained towards sharper edges. The unresolved question that hangs over the next page is deceptively simple: when the countdown starts, who is controlling it, and what have both sides learned to do when it reaches zero?

# Chapter 2
# Family Values and Digital Priorities

A parent stands at the sink, washing up with one ear tuned to the living room. The child is quiet, too quiet, the kind of quiet that often means absorption. A request forms in the parent's throat and dissolves again. Not yet. The parent does not want another argument before bedtime. The thought returns a few minutes later, sharper. Still not. Then the child laughs at something unseen, and the laugh lands oddly, like a small door closing. The parent dries a plate, stares at the cupboard, and realises the problem is not only the screen. The problem is that the parent has not decided what they are defending strongly enough to tolerate the discomfort of defending it.

Later, when the request is finally made, the negotiation arrives right on time. The child asks why, asks what harm it is doing, asks what other families allow, asks why the rule changes depending on the day. The parent reaches for a justification and finds only fragments: school, sleep, attitude, "because I said so". None of those fragments is entirely wrong. None of them is steady enough to hold in a storm. The child senses it. The argument grows around the weak point. The parent ends up talking about minutes because minutes are measurable, while the real concern is harder to articulate: the house feels thinner, sleep feels fragile, tempers feel closer to the edge, and no one is sure what the family is meant to be protecting together.

That is the paradox at the heart of screen rules. Families fight most fiercely about the thing that is easiest to count, even when the thing they most want is difficult to count. Time is a number on a clock. Attention is not. Kindness is not. The feeling of being properly with one another, without a device tugging at the edges of the room, cannot be logged neatly. Yet those are the goods parents are often trying to defend. When the defence remains vague, rules become brittle. A child can argue around a vague rule for hours. A child cannot argue as easily around a clear family priority, because a priority is not a preference in disguise; it is a statement about what the household will not trade away, even for convenience.

The central tension here is not between freedom and control. It is between what a family says it values and what its routines actually reward. Many homes sincerely claim to value rest, learning, good humour, and time together. Many homes also reward endless checking, late-night stimulation, and constant negotiation, simply because the path of least resistance becomes the path of habit. A device does not have to be "bad" to become a default that quietly rewrites the household's priorities. The trade-off is uncomfortable: a family can buy short-term peace by allowing more screen use than it truly wants, or it can tolerate short-term protest to defend something it truly cares about. Either way, a cost is paid. The only question is which cost is chosen deliberately.

This matters because children are not only complying with rules; they are learning what rules are for. When rules appear as arbitrary restraints, children learn to treat them as obstacles to outwit. When rules are consistently tied to a protected good, children learn a different lesson: boundaries exist to defend life, not to restrict it. This is a lesson about legitimacy. A child does not need to like a rule to accept its legitimacy, but legitimacy requires coherence. Coherence shows up in small decisions: whether adults keep to their own expectations, whether exceptions are predictable or begged for, whether consequences follow with calm. When coherence is missing, the family ends up relying on force, and force corrodes both authority and closeness.

It also matters because families vary wildly in capacity, and capacity is not a moral achievement. A household with long commutes, irregular shifts, multiple children, or a child whose nervous system runs hotter will have different bandwidth for negotiation and supervision than a household with slower evenings and spare energy. When a family adopts rules that assume more capacity than it has, it sets itself up for a familiar humiliation: ambitious boundaries declared on Sunday, abandoned by Wednesday, and then revived in a burst of guilt when something goes wrong. Children learn this rhythm too. They learn that rules are seasonal, that tiredness dissolves them, that insistence is temporary. A plan that collapses under ordinary stress does not merely fail to help; it trains scepticism.

The emotional stakes are just as real. Screen battles often become the arena where broader tensions play out: resentment about unequal workloads, fear about a child's future, guilt about adult screen habits, exhaustion that turns small irritations into insults. A family can start arguing about a phone and end up arguing about whether anyone listens, whether anyone contributes, whether anyone is respected. When that happens repeatedly, the household begins to associate screens with relational threat. Children become defensive. Adults become reactive. The device is not the only cause, but it becomes the trigger that summons the whole pile of unspoken feelings into the room.

The path forward begins by making the protected goods explicit rather than implied, so the family is not forced to invent a justification mid-argument. From there it turns to the harder, quieter work of aligning boundaries with what the household can actually sustain, not what it wishes it could sustain on a well-rested, well-organised week. The order matters because priorities without realism become sermons, and realism without priorities becomes drift.

The friction to notice now is not the child's pushback, which is often predictable, but the adult's inner hesitation: the moment a rule is softened because explaining it feels awkward, because holding it feels tiring, because the family is hungry and the evening is already brittle. That hesitation is not weakness. It is information. What, exactly, does the household refuse to trade away, even when everyone is tired and the screen is offering an easier version of the next hour?

## Naming what you protect

In October 2016, the American Academy of Pediatrics in Itasca, Illinois, launched its Family Media Plan: a public tool meant to help households align screen use with sleep, school, and relationships. The concrete outcome was not a ban or a warning label, but a framework for decisions that happen in kitchens and hallways. A professional body was, in effect, admitting something many parents already felt in their bones: the arguments are rarely solved by a louder voice or a stricter timer. They are solved, when they are solved at all, by clarity about what the family is trying to defend.

Values beat volume every time.

That line is easy to nod at and hard to live. In a real home, a rule is not a philosophical statement. It is a moment. It arrives when someone is tired, hungry, preoccupied, or socially cornered, and it must still stand. The child who argues is not necessarily arguing about a screen; they are testing whether the adult's "no" has a reason beneath it, or whether it is simply an expression of mood. The adult who hesitates is not necessarily weak; they are measuring the cost of enforcement against the cost of peace. When the adult cannot name what is being protected, enforcement becomes an act of will in a vacuum. Vacuum is where resentment grows.

The most common mistake families make with digital rules is to treat them as traffic laws: neutral, impersonal, equally applicable, requiring only compliance. Screens do not behave like roads. They behave like relationships. A child can feel comforted by a device, ashamed without it, excluded when they cannot reply, triumphant when they win, soothed when they watch, validated when they are noticed. A parent can feel relief when a device keeps a child occupied, guilt when it becomes the default, anger when it breaks the evening, and fear when it seems to swallow the child's attention. The rule sits at the intersection of these feelings. The named concept here is legitimacy: a boundary is more likely to hold when it is experienced as protecting something meaningful rather than exerting control for its own sake. The explanation is behavioural as much as moral. Humans comply more readily with constraints they perceive as fair and purposeful, especially when those constraints are applied consistently. The implication is that "screen time limits" is an impoverished phrase. It speaks in minutes, while family life is shaped by goods that are harder to count.

A family value is only useful if it can be seen. "We value connection" sounds noble until it collides with a Tuesday evening where everyone is irritable and the easiest path is separate screens in separate rooms. When a value remains airy, it becomes a stick children use to beat adults with: "If you cared about connection you'd stop working" or "If you cared about health you wouldn't be on your phone either." The show, in other words, is the hypocrisy argument, often delivered with surgical precision by a teenager. The concept is value drift: the gap between what a family declares and what the household routine rewards. The explanation is that routines are powerful because they happen without discussion. They decide what counts as normal. The implication is that naming what is protected is not about winning debates; it is about preventing drift by giving the household a small number of priorities that survive tiredness.

Consider sleep as an example of a protected good, not because it is the only one that matters, but because it is the one families most often sacrifice accidentally. Sleep is not merely rest; it is the platform that makes emotion regulation, patience, attention, and learning more possible. The show is familiar: a child who was reasonable at breakfast becomes explosive by late afternoon after a poor night. The concept is upstream protection: defending a condition that makes many other conditions easier. The explanation is simple. When sleep is degraded, the whole household spends more time managing moods, enforcing basics, and recovering from avoidable conflict. The implication is that a sleep value does not need to compete with a child's "but everyone else" argument on cultural grounds. It competes on functional grounds. The family is deciding whether it wants tomorrow to be liveable.

Kindness is another protected good that becomes visible quickly when screens are involved. A device amplifies speed and distance. Messages are sent in seconds. Group chats move fast. Social cues are thinned. A child who would never shout an insult across a classroom may type something cruel, half as a joke, half as a release, and then find they cannot retrieve it. The show is a mood turned into a message. The concept is frictionless expression: the reduction of pause between impulse and action. The explanation is not that the child is suddenly "a different person online", but that the medium lowers the cost of acting on passing feelings. The implication is that kindness as a protected good must attach to observable behaviours, not abstract aspirations. Families who cannot name the behavioural line they are defending end up moralising after harm occurs, when the child is defensive and the moment for learning has narrowed.

School focus can also be a protected good, though it often becomes muddled because "school" is used as a blunt weapon rather than a precise priority. A family might claim to protect learning while actually protecting the appearance of productivity: homework done in a rush, attention fractured, work stretched out to accommodate constant checking. The show is the child who is "doing homework" with a screen nearby, frequently switching, constantly resetting focus. The concept is attentional integrity: the ability to sustain attention long enough for deep work to occur. The explanation is that learning is not simply time spent with a book open; it is the quality of cognitive engagement, which depends on minimising interruptions and resisting the lure of immediate rewards. The implication is that "school focus" as a value becomes credible only when it is separated from anxiety about grades and attached instead to the household's observable patterns of work: whether tasks begin without prolonged negotiation, whether distractions are treated as normal temptations rather than moral failings, and whether adults respect the same logic in their own work.

Mental space is a protected good that parents often feel but struggle to articulate because it sounds vague until it is gone. Mental space is the household's capacity to be quiet without being empty, to tolerate a few minutes without stimulation, to have thoughts that are not prompted by feeds or notifications. The show is the child who cannot sit through a meal without checking, the adult who cannot listen to a story without glancing at a screen, the background itch that something else is happening somewhere else. The concept is attentional noise: the low-level cognitive load created by constant prompts and the possibility of constant checking. The explanation is that attention is not only what a person chooses; it is also what the environment asks of them. When the environment keeps asking, the mind keeps paying. The implication is that families who name mental space as a protected good often discover that the battle is not "screen time" but the assumption that every micro-moment must be filled.

Time together is the value most often invoked and most often mishandled. Parents reach for it when they are frightened: "We never talk anymore." Children hear it as confiscation: "You're taking my friends away." The show is a parent attempting to create togetherness by force, and a child experiencing that force as disrespect. The concept is coerced intimacy. The explanation is that connection cannot be commanded, and attempts to command it can make connection less likely. The implication is not that time together is unimportant, but that it needs to be named with specificity: which moments are worth protecting because they are naturally connective, and which moments are better left unforced. Otherwise the value becomes a banner waved in arguments rather than a principle that shapes daily life.

The second named anchor for this conversation can be found in April 2019, when the World Health Organization in Geneva issued guidance on physical activity, sedentary behaviour, and sleep for young children, explicitly locating screens among the daily factors that shape wellbeing. The concrete outcome was a set of recommendations and a public framing: screens were no longer treated purely as entertainment or education, but as part of a system that includes movement, rest, and development. The concept that matters here is systems thinking: seeing screen use not as an isolated choice but as something that displaces or supports other functions in the household. The explanation is that families rarely experience harm from a single session; they experience harm from repeated trade-offs that become routine. The implication is that a family value works best when it clarifies which trade-offs are acceptable and which are not.

A quiet motif helps keep this from becoming too lofty: the fridge note. Not a grand manifesto, just a simple reminder placed where life actually happens. The fridge is where hunger, routines, and time pressures collide. It is where people pass each other without ceremony. A value that cannot survive the fridge is not a value; it is a wish. The show is the household in motion, opening and closing doors, grabbing snacks, checking the time. The concept is environmental reinforcement: the way cues in a space shape behaviour by making some choices easier to remember and easier to repeat. The explanation is that human beings forget principles when tired, and families are tired often enough for forgetting to matter. The implication is that values must be compact enough to be recalled in a tense moment and concrete enough to translate into action without negotiation.

Still, values can become a trap if they are used as moral weapons. A parent may declare "we protect sleep" and then treat any resistance as proof of disrespect rather than as a predictable response to a change. A parent may declare "we protect kindness" and then shame a child for a mistake rather than focusing on repair and learning. A child may respond by rejecting the entire value as hypocrisy, especially if adults make frequent exceptions for themselves. The credible limitation is that values do not automatically create legitimacy; legitimacy also depends on how values are applied. The reconciliation is simple but not easy: a value must remain a protective frame, not a verdict on character. When values are used to label a child as "selfish" or "addicted" or "untrustworthy", the value is no longer protecting the household. It is attacking a person. Households do not become calmer when values become weapons. They become more strategic, more secretive, more brittle.

The most robust values are those that can absorb complexity without collapsing into loopholes. A family may protect sleep and still recognise that a child sometimes needs a late call with a friend in distress. A family may protect mental space and still allow a long, absorbing creative project on a tablet. A family may protect time together and still accept that a teen's private social world is not an optional hobby but part of becoming an adult. The show is a household making distinctions without losing its core. The concept is principled flexibility: the ability to accommodate unusual circumstances without turning every exception into a precedent that empties the rule. The explanation is that families live in real life, not in a policy document. The implication is that "non-negotiable" does not mean rigid; it means anchored. It means the family knows what it is trying to defend, even when the details require judgement.

This is where the "other families" argument reveals its real function. Children invoke it because it is socially powerful and because it shifts the conversation from values to competition.

If a parent can be pulled into comparison, the child gains terrain: the debate becomes about whether the parent is fair relative to an imagined average. The show is the child naming a peer's freedom as evidence. The concept is social benchmarking. The explanation is that children and teens calibrate rules by peer norms because peer norms shape belonging, and belonging matters intensely. The implication is not that peer norms should dictate household rules, but that a family that cannot name its own priorities will be governed by the loudest comparison in the room. The fridge note, in this sense, is not sentimental. It is a refusal to outsource the household's principles to the child's peer group or to the parent's anxiety.

A value earns its keep when it changes what a family notices. If the household says it protects sleep, it begins to notice not only bedtime but the cascade that begins earlier: mood, transitions, the urge to keep checking, the temptation to stretch the evening because the day felt hard. If the household says it protects kindness, it begins to notice how conflict is spoken, how teasing escalates, how online interactions leak into sibling dynamics. If the household says it protects attentional integrity, it begins to notice the difference between tools that support focus and feeds that dissolve it. These are not abstract sentiments. They are attention filters. The family learns what to measure in daily life: not minutes alone, but patterns of mood, the frequency of negotiation, the ease of stopping, the number of times the device interrupts a shared moment.

The fridge note returns one last time as a test of seriousness. When the next argument flares and the parent feels the familiar urge to bargain for peace, what will the parent reach for: a number, a threat, a comparison, or a protected good that can be named without apology? The unresolved tension is not whether the child will agree. The tension is whether the household can tolerate short-term discomfort in order to protect what it claims matters most. When the screen becomes the easiest answer to a hard moment, what does the family refuse to trade away, even then?

## Choosing a realistic baseline

In September 2018, Apple released iOS 12 in Cupertino, California, introducing Screen Time as a set of built-in controls for tracking and limiting device use. The concrete outcome was immediate in many homes: parents who had previously argued in vague impressions could suddenly see patterns, set restrictions, and watch a child discover that the phone itself would say "time's up". The deeper outcome was less tidy. Tools did not remove conflict. They relocated it. A limit that exists only inside a menu still has to be lived in a kitchen where someone is hungry, a sibling is shouting, and an adult is juggling messages from work. The system is only as stable as the household that must carry it.

Perfect plans fail fast.

That sentence is not cynical. It is a description of family life as it actually operates, with its uneven evenings and its sudden emergencies. When parents picture the "right" approach to screens, they often picture a week when everyone sleeps well, meals are calm, homework is straightforward, and the adults have enough emotional surplus to be patient. That week exists. It is simply not the week that repeats reliably. A realistic baseline is the set of boundaries and routines that survives the messier, more common week: the week with the late meeting, the migraine, the broken boiler, the child who melts down after school, the sibling feud that eats the hour you thought you had for calm.

The temptation is to treat a baseline as an abstract moral stance: strict, relaxed, balanced. Yet households do not live inside adjectives. They live inside constraints. The show is the parent who announces a new rule with conviction on a Sunday afternoon and then quietly abandons it by Wednesday because enforcement requires more attention than the adult has left. The concept is capacity mismatch. The explanation is simple and unsentimental: a boundary that demands constant supervision will be enforced only when the supervising adult is calm and available, which is precisely when enforcement is least needed. The implication is that inconsistency is not merely a parenting flaw; it is often a design flaw, created by choosing rules that require resources the household cannot reliably supply.

This is why the most important question in setting a baseline is not "What should children have?" but "What can this household repeatedly sustain?" Sustainability sounds like a soft word until it is given a metric. In a family context the metric is not an idealised sense of harmony. It is whether the rule can be enforced without shouting, bargaining, or frequent exceptions. A baseline that produces daily negotiation is not a baseline; it is a daily referendum. The show is the repeated "just five more minutes" exchange, the moving goalposts, the adult who ends up making the same decision ten times in a single evening. The concept is decision fatigue. The explanation is that each negotiation consumes attention and patience, and those are finite. The implication is brutal in its simplicity: if the boundary requires constant fresh willpower, it will collapse exactly when the household is least able to afford the collapse.

Work patterns are one of the biggest hidden drivers of baseline realism, because they shape supervision without ever announcing themselves as "screen policy". A household with predictable evenings can maintain more nuanced rules: shared viewing, co-play, flexible time windows, device-free rituals that need adult presence. A household with unpredictable shifts, long commutes, or split care arrangements often cannot. The show is the child arriving home to a caregiver who is simultaneously cooking, answering emails, and managing siblings, while the device offers a single-button way to keep the child occupied. The concept is functional dependency: the screen becomes part of the household's logistics. The explanation is not moral weakness but system economics. When the adult must accomplish several tasks at once, the device acts as a temporary childcare substitute, and removing it without replacing the function can destabilise the whole evening. The implication is that a baseline that ignores the household's logistical reality is likely to become performative, producing guilt rather than calm.

Care responsibilities amplify this dynamic because caring labour is relentless, and relentlessness erodes the space needed for principled enforcement. A parent caring for a baby, an ill relative, or a child with additional needs may rely on screens not out of indifference, but because there are moments when the adult must triage: safety first, then nourishment, then everything else. The show is a parent who permits a longer session during a medical appointment or a difficult evening, then feels compelled to "make up for it" by cracking down sharply later. The concept is compensatory strictness. The explanation is that guilt tends to produce overcorrection, and overcorrection tends to provoke rebellion, especially when children sense that the rule is driven by adult emotion rather than household principle. The implication is that a realistic baseline must be able to flex under care pressure without becoming incoherent, otherwise the household lurches between permissiveness and crackdown, and children learn to wait out enforcement.

Neurodiversity introduces a different kind of realism requirement: not lower standards, but different triggers, different benefits, and different costs. A child with ADHD may be drawn powerfully to rapid feedback and novelty; a child with autism may find predictable, solitary digital play regulating in a world that often feels too loud. A child with anxiety may use the screen as a refuge from uncertainty. The show is a child who appears "calm" with a device and dysregulated without it, and an adult who hesitates to remove the one thing that seems to soothe. The concept is regulation substitution. The explanation is that screens can function as emotional prosthetics: not inherently good or bad, but filling a role. The implication is that a baseline framed purely as deprivation misses the lived function of the device for that child. Yet the counter-risk is equally real: when a prosthetic becomes the only tool, it can limit the child's repertoire, leaving them more vulnerable when the screen is unavailable. Realism, here, means admitting complexity without turning complexity into a loophole that empties the plan.

Sibling differences create their own baseline trap. Families often aim for equality because it feels fair, and children are quick to demand symmetry. The show is the younger child pointing to the older sibling's privileges as evidence of injustice. The concept is false equivalence. The explanation is developmental: different ages and maturity levels legitimately require different boundaries, but siblings do not experience fairness as "age-appropriate"; they experience it as "equal treatment". The implication is that a baseline must be simple enough to explain across the family while still allowing differentiation without constant litigation. Otherwise the plan collapses into a courtroom where each child presents evidence and precedent. The household starts spending more time adjudicating than living.

At this point a useful counter-example deserves attention, because the argument for modest, enforceable rules can be misread as an argument for minimal ambition. Some households do sustain highly structured, low-screen routines with little drama. The adults have stable work hours, strong community support, consistent childcare, and an environment where the child's peer norms align with the home's expectations. The show is a family whose routines are not aspirational but embedded: meal times are protected, outdoor time is built into the day, devices have clear places and clear times. The concept is supportive scaffolding. The explanation is not moral superiority but the presence of infrastructure. When a household has more time, more help, and fewer competing demands, it can sustain more complex boundaries without turning them into daily battles. The implication is that "realistic" is not a universal standard; it is household-relative. The reconciliation is straightforward: a realistic baseline is not the lowest common denominator. It is the rule-set that remains coherent under the pressure the household actually experiences.

The most reliable way to think about baseline is to treat it like a thermostat setting rather than a moral badge. A thermostat is not a statement of virtue. It is a practical parameter chosen because it makes the house livable across ordinary variation in weather. Too high and the system runs constantly, wasting energy and still failing to feel comfortable. Too low and everyone is cold, resentful, and tempted to override it. The show is the parent who repeatedly "overrides" their own screen rule in moments of exhaustion, then feels compelled to compensate later. The concept is override frequency. The explanation is that frequent overrides are not merely exceptions; they are signals that the setting does not fit the home. The implication is that a baseline should be judged by how rarely it requires an emotional override. When overrides become routine, the baseline is not realistic. It is aspirational.

This thermostat way of thinking also clarifies why modesty can be powerful. A modest baseline is not "giving in". It is reducing complexity so the household can be consistent. Consistency is not a vague ideal; it is a behavioural pattern children detect instantly. The show is the child who stops arguing once they see that the boundary does not move, because arguing no longer buys them anything but discomfort. The concept is stable contingency: the predictable link between an action and what happens next. The explanation is the same behavioural logic that governs habits everywhere. When the consequence of pushing is inconsistent, pushing continues. When the consequence is consistent and calm, pushing fades because it becomes inefficient. The implication is that a baseline that is slightly less strict but consistently enforced can reduce conflict more effectively than a strict baseline that collapses frequently. Children are exquisitely sensitive to what actually happens.

A second named anchor makes this point without romanticising it. In October 2016, the American Academy of Pediatrics in Itasca, Illinois, released its Family Media Plan tool, emphasising that family media decisions should align with priorities such as sleep, physical activity, and face-to-face time. The concrete outcome was a shift in framing: the question became less about blanket hours and more about fitting media use into a functioning day. The concept is allocation realism. The explanation is that a day has competing needs, and a workable plan recognises trade-offs rather than pretending they do not exist. The implication is that a baseline is a budget of attention and energy, and a budget must be balanced against real income, not imagined income. A parent who is already stretched cannot spend attention like a person who has plenty.

Notice what this does to the "other families" argument. When a child claims that friends have looser rules, the adult is tempted to justify the household's decisions by comparison. Comparison is a trap because it invites a competition of norms. A realistic baseline does not depend on being stricter or more relaxed than a neighbour. It depends on fitting the household's capacity and priorities. The show is a child using peer norms as a bargaining chip and an adult scrambling for a persuasive rebuttal. The concept is normative drift. The explanation is that peer comparisons pull families away from their own constraints and towards an imagined average. The implication is that households that chase the average often end up failing at their own plan, which makes the child's scepticism sharper: "You never stick to it anyway." The thermostat does not care what the neighbour set theirs to. It cares what keeps this house functional.

The hardest part of baseline realism is that it requires adults to confront their own patterns. Not in a confessional way, but in a practical way. Adults often want a plan that will make children easier to manage. A realistic baseline forces a different question: what adult behaviours will quietly sabotage any plan? If adults routinely scroll during family moments, children will perceive restrictions as power, not principle. If adults use screens as the default way to avoid awkwardness, children will follow. The show is the parent asking a child to put away a phone while holding their own phone in the same conversation. The concept is credibility gap. The explanation is that children treat adult behaviour as evidence of what matters, and evidence trumps instruction. The implication is that baseline realism includes adult realism: the plan must fit the adults' ability to model it, not merely enforce it.

The thermostat motif returns as a final test, because it exposes a question families often avoid. When the household is under strain, who reaches for the override button, and why? Is it pressed because the child is genuinely dysregulated and the screen is temporarily stabilising, or because the adult wants quiet at any cost? Is it pressed because the day was unusually hard, or because the baseline is routinely too ambitious? These distinctions are not moral hair-splitting. They are diagnostic. They tell the truth about what the family can sustain and what it merely wishes it could sustain.

The unresolved tension is this: a baseline must be restrictive enough to defend what the family protects and gentle enough to survive ordinary life. Those two demands can feel like they are in conflict. They are not always. The forward test is whether the household can look at its own week, not its ideal week, and name the point at which enforcement repeatedly breaks down. When the next busy week arrives, will the plan hold without the override button being pressed again and again, or will the family discover that its chosen baseline was never a baseline at all, only a brief performance of who it hoped to be?

# Chapter 3
# Age Based Screen Boundaries

A small child is strapped into a pram outside a shop, feet not quite reaching the footrest, the world full of unfamiliar sounds and interruptions. The adult leans in, searching for a dropped mitten, a purse, a moment of calm. The child begins to fuss. The adult hesitates, then produces a phone as if it were a pacifier made of light. The crying stops. The adult exhales. Relief arrives quickly, and relief is persuasive. A few years later, the same child will be taller, sharper, more verbal, and the tool will be the same: a screen offered to smooth a rough moment. The adult will again feel the temptation. It is simple. It works.

Elsewhere, an older child is at the kitchen table with homework spread out like a small battlefield. The tablet is beside the book, face down but present, like a friend waiting for a signal. The child turns a page, sighs, flips the tablet over, checks something, laughs, returns to the book, then checks again. The adult watches and feels torn. The device could genuinely help. The device could also dissolve the task into fragments. The child is not being "naughty". The child is practising attention in the presence of a powerful alternative. Practising is not the same as mastering.

Later still, the teen in the next room is not merely consuming entertainment. They are maintaining a reputation, tracking friendships, responding to group chat momentum, trying on an identity. The phone is both mirror and megaphone. The adult hears nothing but silence and feels unease. Silence is ambiguous. The adult thinks about privacy, risk, trust, and the fear of being left behind by the child's world. The teen thinks about being controlled, misunderstood, humiliated. Both think they are protecting something important. Both are.

The central tension is that screen boundaries must mature at the same pace as the child, and many families try to solve the problem with a single rule that ignores development. A rule that makes sense for a toddler can be absurd for a teenager. A rule that respects a teenager can be dangerous for a toddler. The household wants simplicity. The child's growth demands nuance. When families cling to simplicity, they either infantilise older children or abandon younger ones to tools they cannot yet manage. When they chase nuance without structure, they create loopholes, inconsistency, and endless negotiation. The trade-off is not between strictness and freedom. It is between developmentally appropriate guidance and the convenience of one-size-fits-all.

This matters because children do not experience screens as a neutral hobby. Screens are woven into how they soothe themselves, how they seek stimulation, how they socialise, and how they learn what power feels like. A young child who repeatedly receives a device at moments of distress begins to associate discomfort with immediate digital relief, and that association becomes a habit before anyone has words for it. An older child who has never practised stopping a fun activity cleanly will treat any request to stop as an invasion. A teen who is given unlimited privacy with no shared expectations may not learn the difference between privacy and secrecy, and secrecy tends to flourish precisely where young people feel shame. These are not moral failures. They are developmental outcomes shaped by repeated experiences.

The stakes are also relational. When boundaries are mismatched to age, conflict becomes personalised. A toddler's protest is mistaken for defiance. A nine-year-old's bargaining is mistaken for manipulation. A teen's desire for privacy is mistaken for guilt. Adults respond with either tightening control or withdrawing in defeat, and both responses can damage trust. Trust is not a feeling here; it is a pattern of interactions. It is the child's confidence that adults will be predictable and fair, and the adult's confidence that the child can handle more freedom without hiding. If boundaries are too tight, children learn to deceive. If they are too loose, children learn that adults will not protect them from predictable problems. Either way, the relationship pays.

A practical boundary system must also contend with social pressure, which arrives earlier than many adults expect and changes the emotional charge of rules. A child who uses a tablet for cartoons is negotiating pleasure. A child who uses a device for messages is negotiating belonging. A teen who uses social media is negotiating status, identity, and the fear of missing what everyone will reference tomorrow. Adults often try to respond to that pressure with blanket prohibitions, and children respond with desperation, because the stakes feel existential inside a peer group. A more realistic response requires understanding that "screen time" is not one behaviour but many, and the child's age determines which behaviours are developmentally salient.

The through-line of this chapter is growth: the gradual shift from guided use, to practised skills, to shared responsibility, to independence with safeguards. That order matters because a child cannot be expected to self-manage without first being taught what self-management looks like in the moment of temptation. It also matters because the kind of structure that works must change without collapsing into constant renegotiation, otherwise each new year becomes a lawsuit about what the family promised before.

The everyday motif to keep in view is the handover. A device is handed over to a toddler. A device is handed back by a child. A device is kept close by a teen. Each gesture contains a relationship. Who initiates the handover, under what conditions, with what expectations, and with what emotional tone tells the truth about the family's boundary culture. The device itself is not the only object being exchanged. Responsibility is being exchanged too.

There is a final friction that makes this chapter necessary: parents and carers often try to solve age-based boundary problems retrospectively, after a pattern has already settled. They realise, too late, that the toddler now expects a screen in every queue, that the eight-year-old cannot stop without a meltdown, that the teen uses the phone in bed as if it were a right rather than a choice. The goal is not to induce regret. It is to recognise that development is always happening, whether the household plans for it or not, and that every year of a child's life is a window in which certain skills are easier to teach than they will be later.

The unresolved question is not "What should the rule be?" but "What is the next responsibility this child can realistically carry without the household losing its peace?" If a device were taken away tomorrow, what would the child struggle to do that the device currently does for them, and what does that reveal about the kind of guidance they still need?

## Ages 0 to 5: guided use only

In October 2016, the American Academy of Pediatrics in Itasca, Illinois, updated its guidance on young children and digital media, pushing the public conversation away from panic and towards something more practical: how screens fit into early development, daily routines, and family life. The concrete outcome was not a single rule that could be tattooed on the family fridge. It was a reframing. For the youngest children, screens are not primarily a self-management challenge. They are an environment adults introduce, shape, and interpret. The child is learning what a screen *is* before they can learn how to stop using it.

Small habits become family architecture.

That matters because early childhood is when associations form quickly and settle deep. A toddler does not "choose" a coping strategy in the way an adult chooses one. A toddler repeats what works. If a device repeatedly appears at the precise moment distress rises, the child learns a clean, powerful equation: discomfort equals screen. The screen becomes less like a toy and more like a switch for the nervous system, and switches are hard to give up later. This is not a claim about addiction. It is a claim about learning. Young children are experts in contingency: what happens after what. They do not need language to be trained. They need repetition.

The best way to understand guided use for ages nought to five is to begin with a scene that does not feel dramatic, because drama is not the point. A child is strapped into a pram in a queue. The adult is tired, aware of the eyes behind them, and eager to avoid a meltdown that will be interpreted as bad parenting rather than normal toddler life. A phone appears. The child's face changes. The body stills. The adult feels relief. The named concept is soothing substitution: replacing a difficult moment of regulation with an external regulator that works instantly. The explanation is straightforward. The device provides predictable sensory input and quick novelty with minimal effort from the adult. The implication is that the pram becomes a training ground. Each time the screen appears in the same context, the context itself becomes a cue, and cues are sticky. The queue, the pram straps, the supermarket lights: these begin to predict the screen. Later, when the adult wishes the child could wait or tolerate boredom, the child is not "being difficult"; they are responding to the pattern the environment taught.

Guidance, then, is not about treating screens as inherently harmful or inherently helpful. It is about recognising that under five, the child's relationship to screens is largely borrowed from the adult's choices. A young child has limited ability to forecast consequences, limited tolerance for delay, and limited capacity to self-interrupt when something is engaging. The abstraction is *self-control*, but for this age group it becomes visible as micro-behaviour: whether the child can move from one activity to another without collapse, whether they can cope with waiting without an instant distraction, whether they can accept an adult ending an activity without perceiving it as theft. The named concept here is scaffolding, a term associated with developmental psychology and with Lev Vygotsky's ideas about how children learn through guided support. The explanation is that children develop new skills when an adult structures an experience just beyond the child's current capacity, then gradually reduces help. The implication is that screen habits formed in early childhood are not mere preferences; they are part of the child's emerging capacity to handle transitions, disappointment, and patience.

Co-viewing is often discussed in this age band, and it is worth treating as a behavioural phenomenon rather than a moral badge. The show is a child watching content with an adult nearby, occasionally commenting, occasionally naming what is happening, occasionally turning the moment into a shared exchange rather than a private trance. The concept is shared attention. The explanation is that young children learn language, meaning, and emotional cues through interaction, not through passive exposure alone. A screen can hold their gaze, but it cannot reliably tailor itself to their understanding or respond to their questions in the way a present adult can. The implication is not that every screen moment must become a seminar. It is that the adult's presence changes what the screen does in the child's life. A screen used as a babysitter trains solitude and absorption. A screen used as a shared tool can train language, humour, and turn-taking. The same device. Different learning.

Predictable stopping points matter for the same reason they mattered in the earlier discussion of attention capture, but here the mechanism is even more basic: young children rely on external structure to learn internal structure. A child who is repeatedly stopped mid-stream, without warning and without pattern, does not learn "limits". They learn "loss". The show is a child whose protest spikes when the screen is taken away abruptly, not because the child is uniquely entitled but because the brain has not been taught what an ending feels like. The concept is ending literacy: the ability to recognise and tolerate closure. The explanation is that predictable endings reduce the need for emotional escalation, because the end becomes part of the routine rather than a sudden rupture. The implication is that adults who want calm later often need to design calm earlier, through repetition that makes endings ordinary.

A second checkable anchor helps show how this has been treated beyond individual households. In April 2019, the World Health Organization in Geneva published guidance on physical activity, sedentary behaviour, and sleep for young children, grouping screens with daily rhythms rather than treating them as a separate moral issue. The concrete outcome was not merely a set of recommendations but a public framing: screens sit inside a system of movement, rest, and human interaction. The named concept is displacement. The explanation is that in early childhood, time is not just time; it is the raw material of development. When a screen occupies the pram queue, it displaces a moment of boredom and observation. When it occupies the high chair, it displaces messy self-feeding practice and conversation. When it occupies the pre-bed routine, it displaces wind-down cues and the slow descent into sleep. The implication is that families who argue only about minutes are often missing the more decisive question: what skill or rhythm is being displaced in that particular context.

The most revealing contexts are the ones adults reach for screens most reflexively. Public spaces are one. Meals are another. Bedtime is another. These are not random. They are the moments when adults feel scrutinised, pressed for time, or desperate for peace. The show is the device appearing not because the child asked with persuasive logic, but because the adult needed quiet. The concept is adult-driven reinforcement. The explanation is not accusatory. Adults have legitimate pressures. But the implication is firm: when screens are used as the default tool for adult convenience, children learn to demand them in the same moments, because those moments become associated with reward. The pram, again, becomes a cue. So does the restaurant. So does the car seat. The habit is being installed, not merely indulged.

Language is the overlooked part of guidance because people assume it requires a child who can argue. In fact, language begins earlier, as labels and simple narratives attached to routines. The show is an adult consistently naming what is happening: the start, the middle, the end. The concept is narrative framing. The explanation is that young children cope better with transitions when experiences are organised into predictable stories. Screens can fit into that story as a bounded event rather than an infinite stream. The implication is not poetic. It is practical. When a child has words for what is happening, the child has a handle. Without words, the child has only feeling, and feeling tends to speak through protest.

It is also worth distinguishing between types of digital use, even at these ages, because not all screen experiences train the same attention. Some content is fast, loud, and cut with relentless novelty. Some is slower, more narrative, and easier to leave at a natural pause. Some apps invite tapping and immediate feedback, which can be absorbing in a way that makes stopping harder. Others invite making something: drawing, arranging, building. The abstraction is *quality*, but here it becomes visible as the child's exit behaviour: how readily they shift away, how much protest appears, how quickly they can re-engage with the physical room. The named concept is stop friction. The explanation is that certain designs create more unfinishedness and stronger loops. The implication is that a family can reduce conflict not by demonising screens but by noticing which kinds of screen experiences reliably produce the hardest endings in their particular child.

A credible limitation must be admitted, because a rigid account of "guided use only" can become unrealistic or even unkind to families with heavy demands. Some parents and carers use screens as a necessary support during illness, long travel, or moments when an adult must attend to safety-critical tasks. Some children, including some neurodivergent children, may find certain predictable digital content calming in a way that supports regulation rather than undermining it. The show is the child who becomes less overwhelmed when the environment is too noisy, or the adult who must keep a child safely still during a complex situation. The concept is situational necessity. The explanation is that life sometimes requires compromises, and a screen can be a tool that prevents worse outcomes. The implication is that the point of guidance is not purity. It is pattern. A screen used deliberately as a specific tool in specific circumstances is different from a screen that appears automatically whenever discomfort arises. Reconciling this limitation means refusing shame and focusing instead on the shape of the association being built.

That association is the real battleground for ages nought to five: whether the screen becomes a default soothing tool, or one tool among many. When the screen becomes default, two things tend to happen. The first is that the child's tolerance for ordinary waiting shrinks, because waiting has been repeatedly replaced with input. The second is that the adult's confidence in non-screen soothing shrinks too, because the screen works so quickly that other methods feel slow and uncertain by comparison. The show is the adult reaching for the phone earlier and earlier in a stressful moment, not because the child is worse, but because the adult has learned the shortest route to quiet. The named concept is mutual conditioning. The explanation is that adults and children shape each other's habits through relief. The implication is that screen habits are not a child problem. They are a household system.

The quiet motif of the pram is useful because it captures what is at stake: portability. A television is anchored. A phone travels. It can be deployed anywhere, which means it can colonise any difficult moment. That portability is a marvel. It is also a hazard for habit formation. If the pram becomes a place where screens routinely appear, the child learns to expect the screen specifically in situations where the body is constrained and the environment is dull. Later, when the family wants the child to cope with travel, waiting rooms, restaurants, or shops, the child is not simply resisting; they are noticing the absence of an expected tool. The pram is not just a seat. It is a cue-laden setting where the household teaches the child what to do with discomfort in public.

A realistic approach to guided use keeps returning to the same underlying question: what is the child practising? If the child is practising passive absorption as the main response to boredom, that practice will strengthen. If the child is practising shared attention with an adult, naming feelings, accepting endings, and switching activities with support, that practice will strengthen instead. The abstraction is *development*, but it becomes visible as an accumulation of small competencies: accepting "finished" without panic, coping with a queue without immediate entertainment, tolerating frustration without instant replacement, returning from a screen to the room without seeming to fall through the floor. These competencies do not arrive in a single leap. They are shaped through repetition.

The most important part of "guided use only" is that it treats adult behaviour as part of the intervention. Adults decide where devices live in the home, when they are produced, and whether they become the answer to every small emergency. Adults also decide whether they narrate endings with calm or with sudden confiscation. A child under five is not managing a device. A child under five is learning what boundaries feel like. The way adults handle screens becomes, for the child, an early education in authority: whether authority is predictable or capricious, whether endings are safe, whether protest changes the outcome. Those lessons echo later, when children are older and arguments become more verbal.

The pram returns at the end as a forward test because it is where many families first notice their own reflexes. When the next public fuss arrives, what does the adult's hand reach for before thought catches up: the phone, or the adult's own capacity to stay present through a difficult minute? No household will get this perfect. Perfection is not the point. The unresolved tension is whether the family is building a child who can tolerate small discomforts without immediate digital relief, while still using screens as a tool when they genuinely serve the household. The question that lingers is simple enough to be uncomfortable: in the moments when the child is strapped in and restless, is the screen teaching regulation, or replacing it?

## Ages 6 to 9: structure and practice

In October 2016, the American Academy of Pediatrics in Itasca, Illinois, published updated guidance on children and digital media that emphasised something many parents had already learned the hard way: rules alone do not produce calm, and screens do not sit outside a child's development. The concrete outcome was a shift in public framing towards family routines, content choices, and shared expectations rather than simple bans. For ages six to nine, that framing matters because this is the stretch when children are old enough to bargain fluently but not yet old enough to regulate reliably. They can explain. They can plead. They can promise. They can also melt down with remarkable speed when an ending arrives at the wrong moment.

Endings need practice, not lectures.

The everyday scene is almost always the same: the child comes home, drops a bag, and heads for the screen with the certainty of someone who has rehearsed the route. The adult experiences a small internal argument of their own. The day has been long. Quiet would be helpful. Yet the adult also knows what often follows: the homework postponed, the mood souring at the first request to stop, the evening turning into a sequence of negotiations. The device is not merely entertainment here. It is a competing routine, offering immediate structure in the hour when the household's structure is often weakest.

The central developmental fact of this age band is that children are learning control by borrowing it. They are building the mental skills that will later be called self-regulation: starting a task, staying with it, stopping, switching, accepting disappointment, returning to the real world without resentment. The screen does not only distract from those skills; it can also become the stage on which those skills are either practised or avoided. The named concept is skill transfer. The explanation is that a child who learns to stop a game calmly after a predictable cue is practising the same stopping muscle needed for bedtime routines, homework transitions, and sibling conflicts. The implication is that screen boundaries at this age are not merely protective fences. They are a curriculum in endings.

Families often misread what "structure" means because the word sounds like rigidity. In practice, structure at six to nine is less about strictness and more about predictability. The show is a child who asks for the screen repeatedly across an afternoon, not necessarily because they are obsessed, but because the household has not given them a reliable map of when screens happen and when they do not. The concept is ambiguity hunger. The explanation is behavioural: where a boundary is vague, the child must keep checking whether it has shifted. Each request is a probe. Each probe is rational. The implication is that households without clear time windows inadvertently create more screen talk, more pleading, more argument, because the question remains live all day.

This is why time windows are often calmer than constant case-by-case decisions. A child who knows that screens happen in a particular part of the day is less likely to treat every spare minute as an opening for negotiation. The abstraction is *efficiency*, but it becomes visible as a countable behaviour: how often the child asks. When asking drops, conflict drops with it. The named concept is decision offloading. The explanation is that a routine removes the need for repeated permission-seeking, which reduces both the child's frustration and the adult's decision fatigue. The implication is that the household is not "controlling" the child so much as controlling the number of times the child must face temptation and the number of times the adult must adjudicate it.

At this age, content type matters because it changes stop friction. A video platform built around endless recommendations behaves differently from a short episode with a clear ending. A fast, competitive multiplayer game behaves differently from a creative app where a child makes something and can save it. The show is not theoretical; it is emotional. Some activities produce a mild grumble at stopping. Others produce a spike of outrage. The concept is loop intensity. The explanation is that certain designs keep the child in a state of "nearly finished", with the next reward always one step away, while other designs contain natural closure points. The implication is not that one must label content as "good" or "bad" in the abstract. The implication is that families who treat all screen activities as equal often end up blaming the child for reactions that are, in part, engineered by the activity's structure.

Where devices can be used is equally influential, not because location is morally charged, but because location shapes supervision and switching. A screen in a shared space is a different experience from a screen in a bedroom. The show is the child who remains outwardly connected to the household when the device is in the same room, and the child who disappears into a private world when the device moves behind a door. The concept is social anchoring. The explanation is that shared spaces naturally introduce micro-interruptions: a question about dinner, a sibling passing by, the ordinary noise of family life. Those interruptions, gently handled, can train the child to tolerate switching and re-entry. The implication is that location is not merely about monitoring; it is about training attention to remain flexible rather than tunnelled.

A timer is a humble tool, but it works as a motif for a deeper principle: endings are easier to accept when they are externalised and consistent. When a parent says "time's up" from their own mood, the child hears subjectivity and tries to negotiate it. When an external cue signals the end, the child has less social incentive to treat the end as a personal dispute. The show is the child who protests less at a neutral signal than at a parent's sudden command. The concept is authority displacement. The explanation is that children at this age often experience adult-enforced endings as a contest of wills, especially if the adult sometimes yields. An external cue can reduce the sense that the parent is arbitrarily "taking" something. The implication is that the family's goal is not to win an argument but to lower the temperature of endings so the child can practise stopping without humiliation on either side.

This intersects with a deeper behavioural truth from the earlier discussion of attention capture: the moment of stopping matters as much as the total time. When a child is asked to stop mid-level, mid-match, or mid-clip, the brain registers an open loop, and protest increases. When the child reaches a natural break, protest often decreases. The show is not moral; it is mechanical. The concept is closure timing. The explanation is that closure gives the brain a place to file the experience as complete, reducing the sense of loss. The implication is that a family's boundary can be exactly the same in duration and still feel entirely different in emotional cost depending on where the ending lands.

A second named, checkable example illustrates how settings can reinforce or undermine household routines. In September

2018, Apple released iOS 12 in Cupertino, California, introducing Screen Time as a mainstream feature for tracking use and setting limits. The outcome for many families was a new layer of visibility and a new form of external cueing: the device itself could declare a limit reached. The concept is technological enforcement. The explanation is that when limits are embedded in the device, the parent is not forced to serve as the sole enforcer, which can reduce conflict. The implication, however, is not that tools solve the problem. A child can still plead. A parent can still override. The more important implication is that any system worth keeping must survive the child's protest and the adult's fatigue. The tool is a support beam, not the foundation.

Ages six to nine are also the prime years for the bargaining habit to form. The child is socially aware enough to present arguments and emotionally expressive enough to apply pressure. The parent is busy enough to reward pressure inadvertently. The show is the child who learns that whining extends time, that charm sometimes works, that anger sometimes works, that tears work fastest. The concept is negotiation reinforcement. The explanation is behavioural: if a child's escalating behaviour produces extra minutes even occasionally, escalation becomes worth attempting. The implication is that the household can, without intending to, teach a child that conflict is an effective strategy for managing disappointment. That lesson generalises beyond screens.

This is where "before screens, after screens" routines become psychologically potent, not because they are clever slogans but because they turn access into sequence rather than debate. The child stops asking "Can I?" and starts learning "What comes next?" The abstraction is *order*, but it becomes visible as a behavioural shift: the child moves from permission-seeking to routine-following. The named concept is sequence expectation. The explanation is that children cope better when they can predict the order of events, because prediction reduces anxiety and reduces the need to probe. The implication is that a child who can tolerate the sequence of "snack, homework, play" is practising delayed gratification in a form that feels concrete, not preached.

Yet any account that paints structure as a universal solution would be dishonest. A credible limitation is that some children experience rigid sequences as threatening, particularly if they are prone to anxiety, if they struggle with transitions, or if their school day has already demanded enormous compliance. For such children, an overly tight routine can trigger oppositional behaviour not because the child is wilful, but because the child's sense of agency has been depleted. The show is the child who explodes at what looks like a reasonable request because the request lands on a nervous system already overloaded. The concept is autonomy hunger. The explanation is that children need some domain in which they can choose freely in order to tolerate the many domains in which they must comply. The implication is that structure must be paired with bounded choice, otherwise it becomes a cage rather than a scaffold.

Reconciling this limitation requires noticing the difference between loopholes and legitimate flexibility. Loopholes are the cracks through which all boundaries leak: "just this once" repeated until it is daily. Legitimate flexibility is the capacity to adapt without rewriting the whole plan in the heat of the moment. The show is a household that can accommodate an unusual day without turning the unusual day into a precedent. The concept is rule integrity. The explanation is that children become calmer when they sense that exceptions have a logic, not when they sense that exceptions depend on who shouts loudest. The implication is that the child's trust is built less by softness than by coherence.

Coherence also demands adult credibility. A child in this age band watches adults closely, not in a philosophical way but in an evidentiary way. If adults interrupt conversations to check their phones, the child learns that interruptions are normal. If adults say "no screens at the table" while scrolling at the table, the child learns that rules are about power, not values. The show is the child's quick, devastating observation: "You do it." The concept is legitimacy erosion. The explanation is that children accept constraints more readily when they believe the constraints are principled rather than arbitrary. The implication is not that adults must live like monks. It is that adult exceptions must be intelligible and rare, otherwise the child experiences the entire system as hypocrisy and turns negotiation into a sport.

The timer returns as a quiet symbol of what this age group truly needs: repeated experiences of a calm ending. Not a heroic ending. Not an ending achieved through a shouting match. A calm ending that leaves the child's dignity intact and the adult's authority intact. Each calm ending is a rehearsal. Each rehearsal accumulates into competence. The child begins to internalise a rhythm: start, play, stop, switch. The household begins to internalise a rhythm too: announce, cue, end, move on. When this rhythm is missing, families pay in conflict. When it is present, they pay less.

The unresolved tension at six to nine is that this is the same age when children begin to notice the social meaning of screens. They hear classmates talk about games. They want to join. They want to keep up. They may not yet be in the most intense social arenas of adolescence, but the desire to belong is already there, and it colours every "no" with a hint of exclusion. Structure must therefore do two things at once: reduce bargaining and make room for ordinary social participation. If the household cannot hold both aims, it will swing between indulgence and crackdown, and the child will respond by testing boundaries harder.

A useful forward test is not "Does the child comply?" but "What kind of end does the household repeatedly produce?" When the timer sounds or the adult signals that the session is over, does the child's reaction reveal a skill still being learned or a pattern still being reinforced? If the child escalates and the adult yields, the system is training escalation. If the child escalates and the adult escalates back, the system is training conflict. The difficult, valuable question that pulls towards the next stage is whether the family is building an environment in which a child can practise stopping without drama, or merely enforcing stopping through drama and hoping practice will somehow happen later.

## Ages 10 to 12: growing responsibility

In September 2018, Apple released iOS 12 in Cupertino, California, bringing Screen Time into the mainstream as a built-in way to track and limit device use. The visible outcome for many families was a new kind of argument: less "how long have you been on that?" and more "why does my phone say I am out of time?" The device itself became a referee, which felt both helpful and strangely intimate. A rule was no longer just a parent's voice. It appeared on the lock screen, blunt and unemotional. Children noticed. Adults noticed too.

This age is a hinge.

Between ten and twelve, children step into a new social and cognitive terrain. They can reason, not just react. They can plan, not just plead. They can also be swept away by emotion quickly, particularly when social belonging is involved. The household problem changes shape. Earlier, the work was largely about routines and practice: helping a child tolerate endings and switch tasks. Now the work becomes governance: giving a child a larger share of autonomy while tightening a few non-negotiable protections that keep the week from collapsing. The child's growing competence makes more freedom possible, but that freedom increases exposure to social loops that are less predictable than games or videos.

A typical scene makes the tension concrete. The child is at the kitchen table with homework, and their phone sits nearby, face down but magnetic. A buzz arrives. The child's eyes flick. Their hand moves almost without permission. The adult sees the movement and feels a pulse of irritation. The child is not being "lazy". They are responding to a cue that carries social meaning. The named concept is divided allegiance. The explanation is that, at this age, a child's attention is pulled not only by entertainment design but by peer dynamics, and peers are not passive content. Peers react. They judge. They include or exclude. The implication is that boundaries framed purely as time management often fail, because the child experiences the boundary as a threat to belonging, not as a limit on "screen time".

This is also the age when children start to want privacy with intensity, even if they cannot yet manage the consequences of full privacy. That desire is developmentally normal. It is part of separating from adults and building an identity that is not constantly supervised. The show is the child turning the phone away when a parent walks past, not necessarily because they are hiding wrongdoing, but because they are experimenting with a private social self. The concept is emerging autonomy. The explanation is that autonomy is a psychological nutrient: children need some territory that is theirs in order to grow. The implication is that blunt control can backfire. If every digital interaction feels monitored, children learn secrecy as a skill. Yet if everything is private and unstructured, the child can be left alone with pressures they do not yet know how to handle.

The core design task is to distinguish between agency and control. Agency means the child gets meaningful choices within boundaries. Control means the child sets the boundaries themselves. Adults often confuse the two because both can look like "letting them decide". In practice, they are radically different experiences. The show is the family discussion where a child is offered a choice between two acceptable options, and the child tries to turn the choice into an argument for a third, unlimited option. The named concept is bounded choice. The explanation is that bounded choices protect the child's sense of ownership without handing over the whole system. Children this age are especially sensitive to being treated like "little kids", and bounded choice can reduce that humiliation. The implication is that families who skip this step tend to swing between two unstable poles: dictatorship, which breeds rebellion, and surrender, which breeds chaos.

Sleep remains the first protected boundary precisely because sleep problems do not stay contained. A child whose sleep is squeezed becomes more emotionally volatile, less able to tolerate frustration, and more likely to experience ordinary requests as provocations. Those changes show up in school mornings, sibling dynamics, and after-school meltdowns. The abstraction is *wellbeing*, but at home it becomes visible as patterns: how hard it is to wake up, how often conflict erupts late evening, how much the child's mood changes when tired. The named concept is upstream constraint. The explanation is that protecting sleep is not a moral preference; it is a way of stabilising the system that makes every other boundary easier to hold. The implication is that families who treat bedtime device use as a negotiable detail often end up negotiating everything else too, because fatigue undermines the entire household's capacity.

School focus becomes a sharper issue at ten to twelve because schooling changes. Homework can become heavier, projects more complex, expectations higher. The child is capable of doing more, which means they are also capable of procrastinating more creatively. A screen is an excellent procrastination tool because it offers quick relief and an excuse: "I was checking something for school." The show is the child switching between a task and a feed, telling themselves they are still working. The concept is attentional leakage. The explanation is that the mind pays a cost each time it switches context, and even when the child feels productive, repeated switching can thin the quality of attention. The implication is that "screen use for school" is not a category that automatically protects learning; it depends on how the device is used and what interruptions are allowed to coexist with work.

Respectful behaviour becomes a central boundary for a different reason: this is the age when digital speech begins to carry real social consequences, while judgement is still developing. A child may type something harsh in a group chat, send a meme at the wrong moment, or pile onto a joke that becomes cruelty. They may not fully anticipate the impact. They may also be under pressure to perform humour, toughness, or indifference. The show is a message written quickly, regretted later. The concept is impulsive publishing. The explanation is that a screen lowers the friction between feeling and expression, especially in peer spaces where status is at stake. The implication is that respectful behaviour cannot remain an abstract family value; it must be tied to how communication is handled when emotions are high, because that is when mistakes are most likely.

The first wave of social pressure tends to arrive not as an obvious crisis but as a series of small demands: "Everyone's in the group chat," "They'll think I'm weird," "I'll miss it," "It's how we plan things." These claims are not always manipulative. They are often accurate within a child's social world. The adult's mistake is to treat them as excuses rather than as information about what the child believes is required for belonging. The named concept is peer norm gravity. The explanation is that peer norms shape behaviour through the fear of exclusion, and exclusion can feel physically painful to a child at this age. The implication is that a household that ignores peer norm gravity will mistake the intensity of the child's reaction for irrationality, and the child will mistake the adult's calm for indifference.

A second named, checkable example helps anchor this social layer. In July 2018, France passed a law restricting mobile phone use in primary and lower secondary schools, a move publicly framed as protecting attention and reducing classroom distraction. Whatever one thinks of the policy, the outcome was clear: an institution attempted to protect a shared environment by setting a default, rather than asking each child to self-regulate in a context designed for distraction. The concept is institutional scaffolding. The explanation is that schools, like families, cannot function if every moment becomes a negotiation about personal device access. The implication for the home is not that homes should become schools, but that a child's day is already shaped by multiple regimes of control. If the home offers no coherent regime at all, the child experiences the boundary-setting as arbitrary; if the home offers a regime that is too rigid, the child experiences it as suffocating. The hinge age requires a third path: coherent protections with room for agency.

This is where the lock screen becomes a useful motif. A child sees the lock screen and feels blocked. An adult sees the lock screen and feels relieved. The same surface tells two different stories. For the child, it can feel like the household does not trust them. For the adult, it can feel like the household no longer has to fight. The named concept is proxy authority. The explanation is that families often outsource enforcement to tools because direct enforcement is exhausting. The implication is that proxy authority can reduce conflict but also create a subtle emotional cost: children may feel controlled by a machine, which can increase resentment, and adults may forget that the tool does not teach the child how to choose, only how to comply.

Teaching choice at this age is delicate because children want to be treated as capable even when they are still practising capability. The home can respond by making choice specific and observable. A child may be invited to choose which activity fills a certain time window, or whether social contact happens earlier or later in the day, while the household remains firm about a few protected boundaries. The abstraction is *responsibility*, but the visible behaviour is whether the child can anticipate an ending, save progress, send a closing message, and return to the room without explosive protest. The concept is transition competence. The explanation is that responsibility grows through repeated practice of clean transitions, not through a single speech about maturity. The implication is that when adults treat responsibility as a badge rather than a skill, they either grant too much freedom too quickly or clamp down when the badge is not worn perfectly.

Group chats deserve special attention because they create the most common late-night spiral. A group chat is not simply a conversation; it is a miniature stage. It moves while the child is asleep. It can rewrite social standing by morning. It invites constant monitoring because silence can feel like absence. The show is the child who insists they must check "just in case" something happened, and the adult who suspects manipulation. The named concept is asynchronous anxiety. The explanation is that group chats create a fear of missing what will be referenced later, and they can also produce sudden drama that feels urgent to the child, even if it is trivial by adult standards. The implication is that families who treat group chat as identical to a book or a television programme will be surprised by the intensity of resistance. The resistance is often about social risk.

Here, a credible limitation must be faced: not all social digital spaces are unhealthy, and not all group chats are chaotic. Some are supportive, practical, and benign. Some children use them to coordinate schoolwork, share jokes, maintain friendships across distance, and feel included. The concept is functional connection. The explanation is that screens can genuinely serve social development, particularly for children who find face-to-face interaction draining or for friendships sustained across schools and activities. The implication is that a blanket suspicion of all peer communication can push children into secrecy, not safety. Reconciling this limitation requires seeing the difference between connection that integrates into life and connection that colonises it. The difference shows up in behaviours: whether the child can leave the chat without panic, whether the chat intrudes into sleep, whether conflict spills into the household's mood.

The household's baseline priorities from the previous chapter matter here because they determine what is non-negotiable and what is flexible. A family that has named sleep, respect, and attentional integrity as protected goods has a framework strong enough to withstand "but everyone else". It can treat peer comparison as noise rather than evidence. It can also treat the child's social needs as real rather than manipulative, and still hold boundaries that protect tomorrow's functionality. The abstraction is *trust*, but it becomes visible as a pattern: the adult keeps the same protected boundaries even when tired; the child learns that arguing does not change the boundary, so they stop spending energy on argument and start spending it on adjustment.

The lock screen returns because it raises the forward test for this age group. When a child is blocked, do they respond with negotiation, compliance, or escalation? When an adult is tempted to override, do they do it from a clear exception or from exhaustion? Those are not moral questions. They are diagnostic questions about the household's system. Ten to twelve is the period when a child can begin to internalise the system, but only if the system is coherent enough to be internalised.

The unresolved tension is that growth requires discomfort. A child cannot learn to manage peer pressure without feeling it. They cannot learn to stop checking without sometimes wanting to check. They cannot learn to communicate respectfully without occasionally feeling the urge to be cutting. The home cannot remove those pressures without shrinking the child's life. It can, however, decide where the hardest edges will be: at bedtime, during homework, in moments of disrespect, in late-night social spirals. When the child next pushes against a boundary with a peer comparison or a plea for "just a bit longer", the diagnostic question is sharp: is the household granting agency in the right places while still protecting the places that keep tomorrow intact, or has the lock screen become the family's only source of order?

## Teens: independence with safeguards

On 6 August 1991, at CERN in Geneva, Tim Berners-Lee posted a short message to an internet newsgroup introducing the World Wide Web to the wider technical community. The concrete outcome was not a gadget or an app, but a doorway: ordinary people could publish, connect, and leave traces that outlasted the moment. That doorway has widened and brightened since, but its basic bargain has stayed stubbornly consistent. A young person can build a social self in public. A young person can also make a mistake in public. The home is not outside that bargain. It is where the private costs are paid.

Privacy matters; sleep matters too.

Teen screen boundaries fail when they pretend the teenager is either a child who must be managed or an adult who can be trusted to manage everything. Neither stance fits. Adolescence is a period of accelerated identity work, intensified peer stakes, and uneven self-control that can look like hypocrisy from the outside: impressive judgement in some domains, impulsive risk in others. A phone is not merely a source of entertainment in that period. It is a social instrument, a reputational ledger, a mirror, a map, and sometimes a lifeline. When an adult treats it as a toy, the teen feels insulted. When an adult treats it as sacred, the teen is left alone with a set of pressures that thrive in secrecy.

The usual argument about "freedom" hides a more precise tension: teenagers need independence to grow, yet independence without safeguards can corrode the very goods that make independence usable. A teen who is permanently tired becomes more brittle, less thoughtful, more reactive. A teen who is permanently monitored becomes more strategic, less candid, more motivated to hide. A teen who is left to navigate reputational risk without any shared expectations may discover the rules of the digital public the hard way, when a joke escapes its context or a private message becomes a screenshot. The household is not being asked to choose between control and trust. It is being asked to choose which safeguards are non-negotiable and which freedoms can expand without pushing the teenager into either resentment or secrecy.

A familiar scene shows how quickly this becomes personal. The teen is in bed, door closed, and the light is out. The parent walks past, notices the bluish glow under the door, and feels a surge of irritation that is also fear. The fear is not always articulate. It may be about sleep, about school, about something the teen might see, about someone who might contact them, about the parent's own sense that the house is no longer governable. The teen, meanwhile, feels the phone as a private room they have finally been allowed to build, and the parent's footsteps as an attempt to barge in. The named concept is boundary collision. The explanation is that bedtime is where two legitimate needs overlap: the teen's need for privacy and the household's need to protect the conditions under which tomorrow can function. The implication is that rules about night-time use are rarely "about screens". They are about whether privacy will be respected without becoming a cover for habits that dismantle sleep.

The most durable teen safeguards tend to protect two domains that adolescents care about even when they roll their eyes: health and reputation. Health is not a lecture about wellness. It is the lived experience of waking up able to think, regulate mood, and handle the day. Reputation is not moralism. It is the social reality that a teen's choices can follow them, sometimes in ways they do not anticipate. These are not abstract values floating above the household. They show up as visible behaviours. Health shows up in morning wake-ups, mood volatility, and the ease of staying focused. Reputation shows up in what is posted, what is forwarded, what is said in anger, what is shared carelessly, and what is treated as a joke because the group is laughing.

The social pressure that begins in late primary becomes more complex in adolescence because it is no longer only about inclusion; it is also about performance. Teens learn that digital spaces reward certain tones: relentless humour, quick comebacks, curated attractiveness, performative indifference. They learn that silence can be read as rejection. They learn that "just a message" can be interpreted by several people at once. The show is the teen who keeps one eye on a group chat during dinner, fingers moving under the table, not because they dislike the family but because the chat is live and being absent feels risky. The named concept is ambient obligation. The explanation is that social platforms and messaging systems turn friendship into something that feels always-on, with cues that demand response. The implication is that a household rule framed only as "be present with us" often loses to a teen's fear of social loss. A rule framed as protecting sleep, mental space, and respectful behaviour has a better chance of being experienced as legitimate rather than controlling.

This is where bounded choice becomes more than a technique; it becomes a form of respect. Teens often resist not the boundary itself, but the feeling of being treated as incapable of judgement. Yet a teen's judgement is not complete; it is under construction, and the digital environment is not gentle with learners. The show is a teen who negotiates hard for autonomy and then stumbles when autonomy includes temptations and social traps they did not anticipate. The named concept is graduated responsibility. The explanation is that responsibility grows through repeated exposure to manageable decisions, followed by reflection on outcomes, not through a single grant of freedom or a single crackdown. The implication is that the household's role changes. It becomes less about issuing commands and more about setting the outer parameters within which the teen can learn without taking avoidable damage.

A named, checkable example makes the shift in enforcement culture concrete. In September 2018, Apple released iOS 12 in Cupertino, California, introducing Screen Time as a standard feature. The outcome, for many families, was that enforcement could be partly embedded in the device rather than enacted entirely through parental confrontation. This matters for teens because the emotional texture of enforcement matters. When a parent is the only gatekeeper, every boundary can become personal: "You are doing this to me." When the boundary is partly externalised, the argument can shift from a contest of wills to a discussion of priorities. The named concept is proxy enforcement. The explanation is that a neutral system can reduce the sense of arbitrary parental power. The implication is not that tools solve the problem. Tools can also intensify resentment if they are experienced as surveillance or as humiliation by machine. The deeper implication is that any enforcement mechanism, human or technological, must be nested inside a relationship where the teen feels respected.

Respect, in this domain, does not mean absence of limits. It means clarity about what is being protected and honesty about how privacy will be handled. Teen monitoring is where many families lose trust because they try to avoid conflict through secrecy. Secret checking may produce information, but it also produces a brittle atmosphere in which the teen learns that privacy is a privilege granted by deception rather than a right bounded by responsibility. The show is the teen whose phone is "randomly" searched, whose messages are inspected without prior agreement, who then becomes more careful about what can be seen rather than more thoughtful about what is done. The named concept is surveillance backlash. The explanation is that people who feel monitored adapt by hiding, not by maturing. The implication is that trust becomes measurable: whether expectations are stated upfront, whether boundaries are enforced predictably, whether consequences are connected to behaviour rather than to adult anxiety, and whether the teen believes they can bring a mistake to an adult without being crushed.

School requirements complicate this further because the phone is no longer optional in the way it is for younger children. Schools may require online platforms, messaging for group work, calendar reminders, and quick access to materials. The show is the teen insisting they need the device "for school", and the adult suspecting this is merely an excuse for drift. The named concept is blended necessity. The explanation is that a single device can contain both the tools of productivity and the triggers of distraction, and the boundary problem becomes less about access and more about context. The implication is that families who treat "school use" as a blank cheque often end up with a household where the phone is present in every task, which quietly erodes attentional integrity. Families who treat "school use" as a pretext for confiscation often push teens into evasive behaviours, including hidden accounts and secondary devices.

The sharpest risks for teens are rarely the ones adults imagine in a panic. They are the everyday risks of speed: speed of posting, speed of reacting, speed of escalation. A teen who would have cooled down after a walk may type a cruel message in seconds. A teen who would have shrugged off a rumour may watch it spread through a chat, replayed and amplified. A teen who would have made a foolish joke in a small room may make it in a large one. The show is the screenshot, the forward, the "send" button pressed before the mind catches up. The named concept is irreversible trace. The explanation is that digital communication creates records that can be shared beyond the original audience, changing the social meaning of a moment. The implication is that "respectful behaviour" is not a vague request to be nice. It is a safeguard against reputational harm that can follow a teen into friendships, school life, and future opportunities.

Still, there is a credible limitation that must be handled honestly: strict restrictions can produce harm as well as reduce it. A teen who is barred from normal peer channels may become socially isolated, especially if much of their peer coordination happens digitally. A teen who feels constantly controlled may choose secrecy as an identity. A teen who has no private space at all may stop confiding and start performing compliance. The named concept is autonomy deprivation. The explanation is that adolescence involves separating from parents and building an independent social self; over-control can warp that process, producing rebellion or withdrawal rather than maturity. The implication is that a household cannot optimise purely for risk reduction, because the teen is not merely a risk to manage. The teen is a person becoming an adult, and that process requires some freedom to experiment, make small errors, and recover.

Reconciling this limitation requires a more precise idea of safeguards. Safeguards are not blanket prohibitions. They are targeted constraints that protect the teen's future self from predictable traps while leaving enough space for independence to feel real. Sleep protection is one such constraint because it supports every other skill the teen is trying to develop: attention, patience, emotional control, and judgement. Another is a stance on bed use that is not litigated nightly. The bedside charger becomes a telling motif here, not because the physical object matters, but because it symbolises where the phone "lives" at night. A phone that lives on the bed invites impulse checking. A phone that lives elsewhere changes the friction of that impulse. The teen experiences this as freedom curtailed. The adult experiences it as health protected. The household experiences it as either a predictable routine or a nightly trial, depending on whether the expectation is pre-agreed or improvised.

Social media readiness is the place where parents often drift into fearmongering, which teens can smell instantly. Fearmongering fails because it treats the teen's peer world as foolish, and teenagers respond to contempt with distance. A more credible posture begins with acknowledging what social media offers: social belonging, humour, identity play, creative expression, and a sense of being in the loop. The show is the teen who uses a platform to follow friends, create content, or learn trends that shape peer conversation. The named concept is social currency. The explanation is that participation in a platform can function as a ticket into conversations that happen the next day at school. The implication is that any discussion of readiness that ignores social currency will feel like an adult trying to ban adolescence itself. Yet credibility also requires naming the costs: attention capture, comparison, the speed of drama, the persistence of traces. The family's task is not to predict every hazard but to keep the teen's life wide enough to include joy while narrow enough to avoid predictable injury.

The same logic applies to curfews, understood not as infantilising control but as a boundary around the hours when judgement weakens and consequences intensify. Night-time is where impulsive messaging, doomscrolling, and peer drama tend to expand, because fatigue makes resistance costly and the social world often becomes more active. The show is the teen who insists they are "just chatting" and then stays awake longer than intended because the conversation keeps moving. The named concept is temporal vulnerability. The explanation is that certain hours of the day amplify the pull of screens and reduce the availability of other regulating activities. The implication is that a curfew is less an accusation and more an acknowledgement of human limits, including adult limits. Adults also make worse choices when tired. Teens are simply more exposed.

The bedside charger returns as a practical symbol of the deeper relationship question: can the household agree, in advance, what happens when the phone is used in bed, so that the response is not improvised in anger? Improvisation is where shame thrives. Predictability is where dignity survives. A teen who feels humiliated will not learn; they will harden. A teen who feels protected without being mocked is more likely to return to the conversation after a mistake, because the household has not made mistakes into moral verdicts. Here the abstraction is *trust*, and it becomes visible as a decision: whether the teen discloses problems voluntarily or hides them until discovered.

The hardest part of teen safeguards is that they require adults to tolerate ambiguity. Adults want certainty. They want to know what the teen is doing, who they are talking to, what they are seeing. Total knowledge is not compatible with adolescence. Total ignorance is not responsible either. The household must live in the middle: enough oversight to protect, enough privacy to respect, enough structure to reduce nightly battles, enough flexibility to avoid turning every exception into a courtroom. That middle is not comfortable. It is, however, where independence can grow without becoming a freefall.

The forward test is not whether the teenager complies in the moment. It is whether the safeguards produce the intended outcomes: more sleep, fewer crises, fewer escalations that leave the teen ashamed and the adult furious, fewer situations where the only available response is surveillance or confiscation. When a teen pushes against a boundary, what exactly are they defending: a genuine need for privacy and belonging, or a habit of late-night drift that is quietly dismantling their day? And when an adult holds the line, what exactly are they defending: the teen's health and future self, or the adult's own anxiety dressed up as principle? The next conflict will reveal the answer, and the household will discover whether its safeguards are building an adult, or merely producing a better-trained secret.

# Chapter 4
# Household Rules Kids Accept

A parent stands in the doorway of a bedroom at night, phone in hand, and says the familiar sentence with the familiar fatigue: "Time to hand it over." The child, already under the duvet, tightens their grip as if the device were a passport rather than a rectangle of glass. The parent feels the pull to argue, to explain, to threaten, to bargain for peace. The child feels the pull to delay, to plead, to test whether the rule is real. Somewhere between them is the same uncertainty that has powered a hundred small battles: is this a rule, or is this a request that can be negotiated until someone gives up?

In another home, or perhaps the same home on a better week, the phone is not in the bedroom at all. It is on a charger in the kitchen, where it has been every night for long enough to feel normal. No one makes a speech. No one feels ambushed. The adult does not need to summon authority at the end of the day, and the child does not need to summon defiance. The difference is not virtue. It is design. A boundary that lives in the environment has a different emotional temperature from a boundary that must be re-invented verbally, late, when everyone is tired.

Why do children fight some limits and accept others? The easy answer is to talk about temperament, defiance, or respect. The more useful answer is that children accept limits that are clear enough to predict and fair enough to recognise, and they fight limits that feel arbitrary, improvable, or humiliating. A vague instruction like "less screen time" invites a child to argue about meaning. A sudden instruction like "now" invites a child to argue about timing. A rule delivered in anger invites a child to argue about dignity. The same child who resists in one context can comply in another when the boundary feels like a default rather than a personal contest.

The central tension is that parents and carers want cooperation without surrendering authority, while children want agency without being made responsible for the whole system. When adults try to secure cooperation by giving ground in the moment, children learn that persistence is power. When adults try to secure authority by clamping down without explanation or predictability, children learn that the adult is an adversary rather than a guide. Both approaches produce more conflict than they prevent. The household needs a third way: rules strong enough to hold and humane enough to live with, rules that do not require a nightly performance of strength.

This matters because family screen conflict is rarely just about the screen. It is a rehearsal space for how the household handles disagreement. If the pattern is bargaining, children become professional negotiators. If the pattern is escalation, children become professional resisters or professional liars, depending on temperament. If the pattern is humiliation, children become secretive. None of these outcomes is what the parent thinks they are teaching. Yet children learn from outcomes, not intentions. A household that repeatedly turns screen rules into arguments is quietly teaching that rules are not stable, that feelings are the enforcement mechanism, and that the loudest person in the room controls the agenda.

It also matters because adults pay a hidden cost when rules are not embedded. They spend attention on policing rather than on living. They spend emotional energy on correcting rather than connecting. They begin to anticipate conflict before it arrives, and anticipation changes tone. A parent who expects a battle enters the room differently. A child who expects a battle reads that tone instantly and braces. The result is a kind of low-grade warfare that is exhausting precisely because it is small and constant. The house can look calm and still feel tense. Clarity reduces that tension, not by making children magically agreeable, but by reducing the number of moments that require improvisation under stress.

A good rule is not a slogan. It is an observable behaviour tied to a time, a place, and a purpose, sturdy enough to survive the child's cleverness and the adult's fatigue. The moment a rule requires the adult to argue about what counts, the rule has already begun to fail. Children will always find the seam. That is their job. The adult's job is not to win debates but to remove seams where possible, so compliance becomes easier than contest. This is why defaults matter. A default is simply what happens unless a decision is made to change it. Families that lack defaults end up making the same decisions repeatedly, and repeated decisions are where bargaining breeds.

Fairness enters here not as an abstract ideal but as a practical requirement. Children have a sharp sense for inconsistency, and they interpret inconsistency as either injustice or opportunity. Both interpretations lead to conflict. Yet fairness is not the same as sameness, especially in households with different ages and needs. Fairness, in practice, means that choices exist where choices are safe, and firm lines exist where firm lines protect something the family has already named as important. A child who is offered meaningful choice in the right places is less likely to demand control everywhere. A child who is offered choice in the wrong places learns that everything is negotiable. The stakes are not merely peace in the moment. The stakes are whether the household trains cooperation as a normal mode, or trains contest.

The path forward runs through a simple progression: shifting rules from spoken demands to lived defaults, then making room for choice without turning the household into a marketplace, then placing the shared agreement somewhere visible so the adult does not have to invent language or consequences in the heat of the moment. The order matters because a family cannot negotiate fair choices until it has clear boundaries, and it cannot keep boundaries without a shared reference point that survives tired evenings and changing moods.

The quiet motif to carry into this work is the charger. A charger is ordinary. It is not a moral symbol. Yet it reveals where authority lives in a household. If the charger lives wherever the device happens to die, the household is governed by convenience and impulse. If the charger lives in a chosen place, the household has made a small claim: devices have homes, and their homes are not wherever the child happens to be. That small claim can remove an entire category of nightly argument. It can also expose new arguments, because children push hardest when a system becomes more coherent. Coherence threatens the old bargaining economy.

The unresolved question is not whether children can be made to follow rules. They can, in the short term, by force or fear. The harder question is whether the household can build rules that children follow without the adults becoming referees in every interaction, and without the children learning that power struggles are the way to get what they want. When the next boundary is tested, as it will be, will the house rely on another weary conversation in a doorway, or will it have defaults strong enough that the conversation barely needs to happen at all?

## Turning rules into defaults

In September 2018, Apple released iOS 12 in Cupertino, California, and a quiet domestic shift followed: many families discovered that a phone could now deliver its own boundaries. "Screen Time" appeared as a built-in feature, and the concrete outcome in countless kitchens was oddly specific. A parent no longer had to guess, argue, or plead quite as much about duration; the device could display a limit, refuse access, and absorb some of the heat that usually lands on the adult. The limit did not create harmony. It did create a new kind of clarity. A rule could exist in the environment instead of living only in a tired parent's voice.

Defaults do the heavy lifting.

That sentence sounds like a slogan until one watches how households actually break down. A rule that must be re-stated in every tense moment is not a rule; it is an ongoing negotiation. Negotiation is exhausting. Exhaustion produces inconsistency. Inconsistency trains children to keep trying. The household becomes a small theatre in which every boundary is re-litigated, and the adult becomes both prosecutor and judge while the child becomes a skilled barrister for their own immediate desires. A default, by contrast, is simply what happens unless someone makes an explicit decision to deviate. The power of defaults is not that they eliminate choice, but that they reduce the number of times choice must be defended in combat conditions.

Begin with a concrete scene. It is late. The child is in bed. The parent stands in the doorway and says, "Hand it over." The child says, "Just a minute," because "just a minute" is the most valuable currency in screen conflicts. The parent knows that a minute rarely stays a minute. The parent's tone sharpens. The child's tone sharpens back. The named concept is *rule-at-point-of-use*: a boundary introduced at the very moment it is most likely to be contested. The explanation is that point-of-use rules demand immediate self-control from both parties at precisely the time when both are depleted. The implication is that even a sensible boundary, delivered late and verbally, will be experienced as an ambush, and ambushes invite resistance.

Now take the same household with one small architectural change: the phone's charger lives in a shared space, and the device reliably returns there at a predictable time. The parent does not have to appear in the doorway as a confiscator. The child does not have to stage a defence. The named concept is *environmental enforcement*. The explanation is that the environment carries part of the boundary, which reduces the need for an adult to carry it emotionally. The implication is not that children become magically compliant, but that the household removes a recurring flashpoint: the nightly handover drama. In behavioural terms, the plan reduces opportunities for bargaining, and fewer bargaining opportunities means fewer rehearsals of defiance.

The point is broader than charging stations. A default can be built around time, place, and purpose, because those are the three dimensions children most commonly exploit when rules are vague. "Less screen time" is an invitation to debate: less than what, when, and why? "Not now" is equally porous: now compared with which time, and for how long? A child can always find a seam in vagueness. They are supposed to. The named concept is *arguability*: the degree to which a rule invites dispute. The explanation is simple. A rule becomes arguable when it relies on subjective interpretation in the moment, because children will test subjective interpretations and adults will struggle to apply them consistently. The implication is that the most peace-producing rules are not the most restrictive; they are the least arguable. They specify a behaviour that can be observed without mind-reading, and they tie it to a condition that is visible in the household.

This is where time windows matter, not as a parenting fad, but as a way of closing the permission loop. If the household treats screen access as something that can be requested at any moment, the child must keep asking because the answer might change. If the household ties screens to a particular part of the day, the question is no longer live all day. The show is the reduction in "Can I?" requests. The named concept is *question closure*. The explanation is that a predictable window removes the incentive to probe. Children probe because probing sometimes works. If probing never works outside a window, probing becomes inefficient. The implication is that adults who want fewer conflicts should count the number of permission negotiations per day, not only the minutes on the device. When negotiation frequency drops, the house becomes calmer even if total screen time stays similar.

Place is equally potent because it shapes supervision and social anchoring. A screen used in a shared room behaves differently from a screen used behind a closed door. The show is the child who remains partly in the family's social field when they use a device near others, and the child who disappears, emotionally and verbally, when the device migrates to private space. The named concept is *anchored use*. The explanation is that shared space introduces natural micro-interruptions and makes switching back to the room easier. The implication is not surveillance for its own sake. It is training for flexibility: the ability to remain engaged with the household even while enjoying a digital activity. When a device becomes a private cocoon, switching back often feels like a harsher rupture, and rupture invites protest.

Purpose is the third dimension because it clarifies what the household is permitting the screen to do. "You can use it for homework" is not meaningful unless "homework use" has observable cues: the device is on a specific app, the task is visible, the use occurs in a particular location, the session ends when the task ends. Without observable cues, "for homework" becomes a loophole large enough to drive a feed through. The show is the child switching between a school platform and entertainment, claiming continuity. The named concept is *purpose ambiguity*. The explanation is that modern devices collapse tools and temptations into one object, and purpose is easy to claim and hard to verify if the family has not defined it behaviourally. The implication is that purpose-based rules must be designed to avoid becoming accusations. If a parent must constantly interrogate whether a child is "really" doing homework, the rule produces distrust. Distrust produces secrecy. The household loses both focus and relationship capital.

A second named, checkable example shows how default-setting becomes a deliberate family practice rather than an app feature. In October 2016, the American Academy of Pediatrics in Itasca, Illinois, released its Family Media Plan tool, explicitly encouraging households to align media use with priorities such as sleep, physical activity, and face-to-face time. The concrete outcome was not a universal prescription but a public prompt: treat media as part of a household system, not as a standalone vice. The named concept is *allocation design*. The explanation is that every boundary is a trade, and trades become less painful when they are made in advance, calmly, rather than in the moment under pressure. The implication is that a family plan works best when it creates defaults that defend what the household has named as protected, because protected goods require protection even when nobody feels like enforcing.

Exceptions are where many families lose their defaults. Children are natural exception-seekers because exceptions are where the good stuff lives: special treats, extra time, the thrill of winning a negotiation. Adults are natural exception-makers because exceptions buy short-term peace. The show is the parent who says "just this once" in a moment of fatigue, and the child who remembers the precedent perfectly. The named concept is *precedent creep*. The explanation is that children treat exceptions as evidence about the true flexibility of the rule. If the rule bends when pressure is applied, pressure becomes the tool. The implication is that exceptions, if they are to exist without destroying coherence, must be designed as part of the system rather than extracted through pleading. Planned exceptions preserve legitimacy because they are not rewards for escalation. Begged-for exceptions teach escalation.

This is not about being harsh. It is about making the rule legible. A child can tolerate disappointment when the rule feels stable and impersonal, like a train timetable. A child struggles more when they sense the adult is making it up as they go. The abstraction is *fairness*, and it becomes visible in how the household handles deviations. Does the exception arrive because the calendar is different, because the family has agreed a special occasion, because there is a clear reason that can be repeated next time? Or does it arrive because the child whined long enough? The named concept is *exception logic*.

The explanation is that logic reduces bargaining. The implication is that when families plan exceptions, they reduce both resentment and manipulation, because the child is not being asked to suppress desire forever; they are being asked to wait until the agreed time.

The charger is a useful motif here because it is the physical form of a default. A charger in a shared place is not simply a convenience. It is a boundary with a home. Homes are powerful. What has a home becomes normal. What has no home floats, and floating things get fought over. A device that "lives" anywhere the child happens to be invites constant renegotiation about where it belongs. A device that "lives" in one place invites a different conversation: not "give it to me" but "return it". Return implies a norm. Return implies the device was never fully possessed in the first place. Children often resist confiscation because it feels like theft. They resist return less because return feels like order.

A rule also becomes a default when adults remove their own opportunities to bargain. This is the part families often avoid, because it requires adults to accept that their moods are unreliable governors. If a parent tends to soften when tired, the system must anticipate tiredness. The show is the adult who repeatedly ends up making the same decision at the end of a long day, when their patience is worst. The named concept is *fatigue vulnerability*. The explanation is that boundaries enforced at the point of maximum fatigue become erratic, and erratic boundaries invite testing. The implication is that a good default protects the adult as much as the child. It reduces the number of times the adult must "be strong" in the moment, which reduces the likelihood of shouting, shame, and later regret.

Yet there is a credible limitation to the whole "defaults solve it" story. Some children, especially those who are anxious, highly sensitive, or neurodivergent, can experience defaults as controlling in a way that triggers intense opposition. Some teens, in particular, may interpret environmental enforcement as disrespect: "You don't trust me." Some younger children may respond to new defaults with a burst of protest that feels like the household has created a bigger problem. The named concept is *reactance*: the human tendency to push back when freedom feels threatened. The explanation is that autonomy matters, and when a rule change lands as a sudden loss, reactance rises. The implication is not that defaults are wrong, but that defaults must be introduced with attention to dignity and with enough predictability that the child can adapt without being cornered. A default that arrives as an ambush reproduces the very problem it is meant to solve.

Reconciling this limitation requires noticing what defaults are for. They are not instruments of domination. They are instruments of peace. A good default reduces the number of contested moments and increases the number of ordinary ones. It also makes room for agency elsewhere, because when the household does not have to litigate bedtime or shared spaces, it can afford to offer choice in safer domains without fear that choice will eat the whole system. Defaults and agency are not enemies. They are partners. A household that builds strong defaults can be more generous with flexibility, precisely because it is not terrified of collapse.

Another reconciliation is moral, not technical: defaults must apply to adults too, at least in the zones where family life is meant to be shared. Children watch what is normal. If the adult's phone appears at dinner, then "no devices at dinner" becomes a power play rather than a value. The show is the child's immediate accusation: "You do it." The named concept is *credibility*. The explanation is that rules are accepted when they are perceived as legitimate and fair, and legitimacy collapses when adults exempt themselves casually. The implication is that households that want compliance should aim for coherence. Coherence is not perfection. It is the visible effort to live by the same defaults, with rare, intelligible exceptions rather than casual hypocrisy.

Once rules become defaults, the emotional tone of the house changes. The adult stops issuing constant micro-corrections. The child stops interpreting every correction as an invitation to debate. The attention in the room becomes available for other things: homework, conversation, boredom, rest. That is the real prize. Not victory over a device, but a household that does not spend its best energy on enforcement theatre. The child still wants the screen. Of course they do. The adult still gets tempted to override. Of course they do. But the struggle becomes less frequent and less personal, because the environment carries some of the load.

The charger sits there, quietly, doing its work. The question is whether the household will let it. When the next exception is requested, will it be handled as a planned deviation from a stable norm, or as a reward for pressure? When the next boundary is tested, will the adult find themselves bargaining in a doorway again, or will the default make the argument unnecessary? The forward test is sharp and practical: if a child can predict the household's screen rules without asking, has the family built a system, or merely declared an intention?

## Building fair choices into limits

In 1907, in the San Lorenzo district of Rome, Maria Montessori opened the first Casa dei Bambini and insisted on a principle that still unsettles controlling adults: children behave better when they can choose, so long as the choices sit inside a carefully prepared environment. The concrete outcome was not permissiveness. It was order. Children selected activities, returned materials, moved with purpose, and learned that freedom has shape. Montessori was not designing screen rules, but she was studying the same human fact that makes screens such a flashpoint in families: when autonomy is crushed, resistance grows; when autonomy is indulged without structure, chaos grows. The most stable middle is neither. It is guided choice.

Bounded choice calms many homes.

This is precisely why "fair choices" matter in digital boundaries. Families often assume there are only two stances: the adult dictates, or the child runs the system. Both stances create their own kind of misery. Dictation turns every request into a referendum on respect, especially as children grow older and more socially aware. Total freedom turns every evening into a slow leak of attention, sleep, and household rhythm, until a parent snaps and imposes a sudden crackdown that feels, to the child, like theft. The point of bounded choice is not to create a pleasant tone for its own sake. It is to reduce the incentives for power struggles by giving the child a legitimate form of agency while keeping the household's protected goods intact.

To see how bounded choice works, begin with what happens without it. A parent announces a limit as a blunt "no" or a vague "later". The child hears not only deprivation but disrespect: no reason, no role, no influence. The child responds by bargaining, pleading, delaying, or escalating, because those are the only tools available. The show is the familiar script: "Not now." "Why not?" "Because I said so." "But everyone else." The named concept is *reactance*, the pushback people feel when freedom appears to be threatened. The explanation is not mystical. People, including children, often fight harder to regain agency than to obtain a specific object. The implication is that a family can accidentally turn a modest boundary into a major battle by presenting it as pure control rather than as a structure within which the child still has meaningful choice.

Bounded choice changes the emotional geometry of the moment. It does not ask the child whether they may have the screen in an unlimited sense; that invites a demand for total control. It offers two acceptable options and treats the child's selection as real. The show is a child shifting from "Can I?" to "Which one?" The concept is *agency within constraints*. The explanation is that constraints establish the perimeter and agency supplies dignity within it. The implication is that the child stops needing to fight for a sense of power, because some power is already granted. The adult stops needing to defend every boundary as a personal decree, because the boundary becomes an agreed perimeter rather than an arbitrary mood.

This is often misread as a negotiation tactic, as if the adult were merely manipulating the child into compliance. But the deeper logic is developmental. Children are practising judgement. They do not practise judgement by being told what to do in every situation, and they do not practise judgement by being left alone with high-stakes temptations. They practise judgement when they are offered manageable decisions with visible consequences. The abstraction is *responsibility*, but it becomes visible in what happens next: does the child choose, accept the outcome, and move on, or do they keep litigating? The named concept is *decision rehearsal*. The explanation is that repeated exposure to bounded choices trains the child to tolerate limits without interpreting them as personal attack. The implication is that bounded choice is not indulgence. It is training.

The trick, of course, is that not every boundary should be a choice. Some boundaries exist to protect goods that do not tolerate negotiation, such as sleep protection, school focus, and basic respect in the home. The error families often make is to offer choice where it is dangerous and deny choice where it is safe. A bedtime rule that becomes a nightly negotiation is not only exhausting; it erodes sleep and trains the child to treat fatigue as a bargaining chip. A homework block that becomes "whenever you feel like it" invites procrastination disguised as autonomy. Meanwhile, children are often denied safe choices that would reduce conflict dramatically: which game, which creative app, which order to do chores, whether to have screen time earlier or later within an agreed window. The abstraction is *fairness*, but it becomes visible as a pattern: the child experiences the home as either a rigid dictatorship or a chaotic marketplace. Neither feels fair. Bounded choice creates a third experience: the perimeter is stable, and within it the child has room to steer.

This is where the word "fair" needs precision. Children have an acute sense of unfairness, but they often define fairness as sameness. Adults often define fairness as what is developmentally appropriate. The conflict arises because both definitions feel true to the person holding them. A younger child may insist that an older sibling's privileges must apply to them now. A teenager may insist that adult exceptions prove hypocrisy. The named concept is *perceived fairness*. The explanation is that compliance is not driven only by the content of a rule; it is driven by whether the child experiences the rule as legitimate. Legitimacy is built when the child can predict the rule, see its purpose, and observe that it is applied consistently. The implication is that bounded choice can support legitimacy precisely because it allows differentiation without humiliation. Different children can have different options inside different perimeters, and the household can still feel coherent if the logic is stable.

A second named, checkable example helps anchor this in the modern family context rather than in educational history. In October 2016, the American Academy of Pediatrics in Itasca, Illinois, released an updated Family Media Plan tool, encouraging households to align media use with priorities such as sleep, physical activity, and face-to-face time. The concrete outcome was a public endorsement of a principle many families sense intuitively: rules stick when they defend what the family protects, and they crumble when they are merely about control. The named concept is *values-based constraint*. The explanation is that values define the non-negotiables, and bounded choice defines the negotiables. The implication is that families who skip the values step often offer choices that feel arbitrary ("choose your limit") and then become angry when the child chooses "more". Families who skip the choice step often enforce values through blunt prohibition and then become surprised when the child responds with covert rebellion.

Bounded choice also works because it changes the economics of argument. A child who argues is often seeking a better deal, but they are also seeking attention, recognition, or relief from frustration. When the adult responds with open-ended debate, the child is rewarded with prolonged engagement, and the argument becomes self-reinforcing. When the adult offers bounded choices and then calmly requires a selection, the argument becomes inefficient. The show is the child realising that pleading does not generate new options. The named concept is *argument extinction*. The explanation is that behaviours weaken when they stop producing payoff. The implication is that bounded choice can reduce power struggles not by suppressing emotion but by removing the reward structure that keeps the struggle alive.

There is, however, a crucial distinction between bounded choice and disguised coercion. If the adult offers two options but communicates contempt for one, or frequently overrides the child's selection, the child learns that the "choice" was theatrical. Teens, especially, detect this instantly. The show is the eye roll, the sarcasm, the refusal to engage. The concept is *pseudo-agency*. The explanation is that people respond badly to fake choice because it adds insult to restriction; it says "you are free" while demonstrating "you are not". The implication is that bounded choice must be sincere. The options must be genuinely acceptable to the adult, and the child's selection must be honoured within the boundary. Otherwise the technique corrodes trust rather than building it.

Trust is often spoken of as a feeling, but in families it is a set of observable behaviours. Trust looks like an adult who keeps boundaries stable without humiliating the child. Trust looks like a child who makes choices and accepts outcomes without endless litigation. Trust looks like a household where exceptions are predictable rather than extracted through pressure. The named concept here is *relational predictability*. The explanation is that predictability reduces anxiety and reduces the need to control. The implication is that bounded choice is not merely about compliance; it is about reducing the background stress that makes every small boundary feel like a personal threat.

A quiet motif can carry this: the menu. A menu is not a negotiation about whether the restaurant exists or whether food will be served. It is a set of options inside a perimeter. A good menu makes choices feel real without creating endless confusion. A bad menu offers too many options, or options that are not actually available, and produces frustration. Families can use the same metaphorical structure. When the child asks for screen time, the adult can respond as if the household has a menu: a small set of real options, consistent enough to become familiar. The menu reduces panic. It also reduces improvisation, which is where adults make promises they cannot sustain and children learn to push until something changes.

This is where a credible limitation needs to be faced. Some children respond poorly to choices, not because they are difficult by nature, but because choice can be cognitively demanding. A child who is tired, hungry, anxious, or prone to overwhelm may freeze or escalate when presented with options. Too much agency can feel like abandonment. The show is the child who explodes at "you choose" because they cannot bear the burden of decision in that moment. The named concept is *choice overload*, described in psychological literature as the way excessive options can reduce satisfaction and increase stress. The explanation is that choosing requires effort, and effort is scarce when a child is already dysregulated. The implication is that bounded choice must be calibrated to capacity. Two options are often easier than many. Sometimes, in a high-stress moment, no choice is kinder than a choice, because the child needs containment more than autonomy.

Reconciling this limitation does not mean returning to blunt control. It means recognising that agency is not a constant. It fluctuates with sleep, stress, transitions, and developmental stage. A family that treats bounded choice as a rigid rule will misapply it. A family that treats bounded choice as a principle can adjust without losing legitimacy: choice when the child can carry it, structure when the child cannot. The menu motif helps here too. Restaurants do not offer the entire pantry. They offer a curated set of options that match what the kitchen can reliably deliver. A household does the same. The perimeter protects the family's priorities. The menu protects the child's dignity.

Bounded choice also has an adult-facing benefit that is easy to overlook: it reduces the adult's need to perform dominance. Many parents and carers dislike the way they sound when they issue commands repeatedly. They feel themselves becoming harsher, more threatening, more sarcastic. They dislike the escalation, even when it "works". Bounded choice offers a different posture: firm without theatrical toughness. The show is the adult speaking calmly because they are not improvising. The named concept is *tone stabilisation*. The explanation is that adults speak more kindly when they are not cornered by ongoing negotiation. The implication is that bounded choice supports not only child compliance but adult self-respect, which matters because self-respect is easier to maintain than constant restraint.

The deeper point is that children do not need unlimited choice to feel respected. They need meaningful choice. They need to feel that their preferences matter in domains that are safe, and that the household's non-negotiables exist for reasons bigger than adult mood. When these conditions are met, children often become less combative, not because they suddenly agree with every boundary, but because they no longer need to fight for dignity. They can save their energy for what adolescence and growing up actually require: learning, friendships, and the messy work of becoming themselves.

The menu returns as a final test. When the next conflict arrives, will the household offer a real menu within a stable perimeter, or will it revert to open-ended bargaining and shouted ultimatums? The unresolved tension is that children will still push. They will still test. That is part of growing. The forward question is whether the household's choices are structured in a way that teaches agency without ceding control: when a child asks for more, can the adult preserve the perimeter and still offer a dignified choice, or does the family collapse back into the old economy where the loudest voice wins?

## Writing a simple family agreement

In 1215, at Runnymede near the River Thames, King John sealed Magna Carta, and the concrete outcome was not domestic harmony but a precedent: power could be bound by written terms rather than exercised entirely by mood. It is an odd document to summon into a family discussion about phones, yet its underlying impulse is recognisable in every household that has ever tried to enforce a rule after a long day. When authority lives only in a person's voice, it fluctuates with tiredness, irritation, guilt, and distraction. When authority is partly moved into a shared text, even a small one, the room changes. The argument stops being "you versus me" and becomes "us versus the situation". That shift is not sentimental. It is structural.

Write it down. Breathe easier.

A family agreement is often dismissed as performative, the kind of earnest exercise that ends up ignored on the fridge. That dismissal is understandable because many family "rules" are really aspirations: vague, moralising, and impossible to apply without a debate. A useful agreement is the opposite. It is compact enough to remember, concrete enough to observe, and fair enough to feel legitimate. Most importantly, it is repeatable without escalation. Repeatability matters more than eloquence. A parent who can point to a shared agreement calmly is less likely to shout. A child who knows the agreement exists is less likely to treat every boundary as an improvisation to be tested.

The problem the agreement solves is not that children lack understanding. Children often understand perfectly well what the adult wants. The problem is that, without an agreed structure, every enforcement moment becomes a negotiation about meaning, fairness, and power. The show is the late-evening argument where the adult insists "it's bedtime" and the child responds "but you let me yesterday", and the adult cannot remember whether they did. The named concept is *memory warfare*. The explanation is that families rely on informal memory to govern behaviour, but informal memory is biased by emotion and fatigue. Children remember precedents that favour them. Adults remember precedents that justify their frustration. The implication is that when governance depends on competing memories, the loudest or most persistent person tends to win, and everyone learns that persistence is a valid strategy.

An agreement also reduces the shame that often clings to screen conflict. When parents enforce rules without a shared framework, they are tempted to justify enforcement with accusations: "you're addicted", "you never listen", "you always take it too far". Children respond by defending their character rather than discussing their behaviour. The show is a child who stops hearing the rule and starts hearing an identity verdict. The named concept is *character escalation*. The explanation is that people fight harder when they feel their self-image is attacked. The implication is that even a sensible boundary can provoke an outsized reaction if it is delivered as a judgement on the child's nature. A written agreement, if framed as a household system rather than a child problem, can lower the temptation to moralise, because it keeps the focus on observable actions.

A good agreement begins where earlier chapters have already taken the household: with protected goods and with realistic baselines. It is not a substitute for those decisions. It is the way those decisions become legible in daily life. The show is the family that can answer "why?" without inventing a new explanation each time. The named concept is *legitimacy anchoring*. The explanation is that rules feel fairer when they are linked to a protected good that the household has named, such as sleep, attentional integrity, kindness, or time together. The implication is that the agreement is not merely a list of prohibitions; it is a compact statement of what the household refuses to trade away, even when a screen would make the moment easier.

Specificity is the difference between an agreement that becomes a referee and an agreement that becomes a new battleground. The phrase "be responsible" is not an agreement; it is a demand for mind-reading. The phrase "no phones at the table" is an agreement because it can be observed. The show is the parent who points to an observable rule rather than arguing about whether the child's "attitude" counts as respectful. The named concept is *observable governance*. The explanation is that families reduce conflict when they govern behaviours that can be seen rather than motives that must be inferred. The implication is not coldness. It is mercy. When a child breaks an observable rule, the adult can address the behaviour without speculating about intentions, which reduces defensiveness and makes repair possible.

Consequences are where most agreements fail, not because consequences are inherently harsh, but because families often choose consequences that are either unrelated or impossible to enforce consistently. The show is the adult who threatens to remove all devices for a week and then cannot sustain the chaos this creates, leading to backtracking and loss of credibility. The named concept is *overreach*. The explanation is that consequences that exceed the adult's capacity become empty threats, and empty threats teach children to wait out enforcement. The implication is that an agreement needs consequences that are proportionate and related to the behaviour, not because parents need to be gentle at all costs, but because credibility is the currency of governance. A consequence that cannot be followed through is worse than a smaller consequence that can.

This is the point at which "related and proportionate" stops being a slogan and becomes a design principle. Related means the consequence connects to what happened, so it teaches a logic rather than imposing arbitrary suffering. Proportionate means the consequence matches the scale of the behaviour, so it does not feel like revenge. The show is the difference between a child who used a device in a forbidden place and a child who lied about it; those behaviours are different, and a household that treats them identically teaches that honesty has no benefit. The named concept is *moral calibration*. The explanation is that children learn what matters by observing what triggers which responses. The implication is that a thoughtful consequence structure teaches both responsibility and honesty, because it signals that the household cares about specific behaviours and the trust that holds the system together.

Shared responsibilities are equally important, not for performative fairness but for practical stability. A child will not accept an agreement for long if it is framed as a one-way restriction. A teen will reject it outright if it feels like surveillance without reciprocity. The show is the child pointing out adult phone use during family time, and the adult feeling the sting because the child is right. The named concept is *symmetry of effort*. The explanation is that children accept limits more readily when they see adults making visible effort to live within the same household priorities, even if adult exceptions exist. The implication is that the agreement should include adult commitments that are observable, such as where adults keep phones during meals or how adults handle work messaging in shared time. This does not make adults and children identical. It makes the household coherent.

The fridge is a useful motif because it is where family life intersects with routines and hunger, and hunger makes people less patient. A paper on the fridge is not decorative. It is an interruption to the default drift into argument. It allows an adult to point rather than lecture. It allows a child to remember rather than test. The named concept is *cue-based compliance*. The explanation is that environments shape behaviour by reminding people of what is expected at the moment the expectation is relevant. The implication is that the agreement becomes part of the household's architecture, like the charger in the kitchen. It reduces reliance on adult mood and child memory. It makes the system more automatic.

There is a second named, checkable anchor that underlines why agreements work when they are crafted properly. In October 2016, the American Academy of Pediatrics in Itasca, Illinois, released a Family Media Plan tool that framed digital rules as part of a broader family system, encouraging families to set expectations and revisit them. The concrete outcome was a public validation of something parents often sense: governance is easier when it is explicit. The named concept is *explicit norms*. The explanation is that explicit norms reduce the room for misunderstanding and reduce the child's incentive to probe constantly for loopholes. The implication is that a written agreement is not merely a piece of paper. It is a commitment to stop improvising at the worst times.

A credible limitation must be acknowledged, because written agreements can fail and sometimes fail noisily. They fail when they become legalistic, stuffed with edge cases and punishments, creating a new object to argue about. They fail when adults use them as weapons: "you signed this, therefore you are wrong", without recognising that children sign under adult power and may feel coerced. They fail when the agreement is treated as permanent, even as children mature and circumstances change. The named concept is *contract backlash*. The explanation is that people resist rules more when they feel trapped by them, and teens in particular resent being held to terms that feel outdated. The implication is that a useful agreement must be short, humane, and revisable, otherwise it becomes a symbol of adult dominance rather than a tool of household peace.

Reconciling that limitation depends on tone as much as content. The agreement must speak in a voice that preserves dignity. It should avoid shaming language, because shame produces secrecy. It should avoid courtroom language, because courtroom language invites litigation. It should avoid moral grandstanding, because children respond to grandstanding with cynicism. The show is the adult who can refer to the agreement calmly without reliving the last argument. The named concept is *low-heat enforcement*. The explanation is that calm repetition is possible only when the adult has a stable reference point and the child knows the reference point is real. The implication is that the agreement's greatest value may be the way it protects the adult from themselves, reducing the likelihood of saying something regrettable in the moment.

The agreement also functions as a promise about repair. Families are not machines. People blow up. Children push too hard. Adults snap. A good agreement anticipates this without drama by making room for restoration: how the household returns to normal after a breach, how trust is rebuilt, how the next day is not poisoned by yesterday's fight. The abstraction is *repair*, but it becomes visible as a sequence: pause, consequence, reset. The named concept is *system recovery*. The explanation is that households that treat every breach as a catastrophe train either fear or defiance. Households that treat breaches as information, within clear limits, train resilience. The implication is that the agreement is not only about preventing conflict. It is about preventing conflict from becoming identity.

The fridge motif returns because it captures the humility of the whole approach. A family agreement is not a grand theory. It is a small object in a busy space. Its purpose is not to prove anyone right. Its purpose is to make the expected behaviour easier than the argued behaviour, and to make consequences predictable enough that no one has to improvise punishment in anger. The agreement becomes the referee, but only if the family treats the referee as impartial. That means the adult does not bend the rules based on mood. It also means the child does not treat the rules as a puzzle to solve through pressure.

The unresolved tension that remains, and should remain, is that an agreement cannot guarantee goodwill. A child can still resent a boundary. A teen can still test the edges. An adult can still feel tempted to override for convenience. The forward test is whether the household can turn its screen conflicts from personal battles into system checks. When the next disagreement flares, will the family argue about who is being unreasonable, or will it consult the shared terms on the fridge and notice, quietly and precisely, which part of the system is breaking: the clarity of the rule, the fairness of the choice, the credibility of the consequence, or the adult's ability to enforce without shame?

# Chapter 5
# Device Free Zones That Stick

A family sits down to eat, and the table looks almost ceremonial: plates steaming, cutlery set, a glass sweating slightly on the coaster. The conversation begins, then splinters. A phone vibrates. Someone glances down. Someone else follows. The moment that could have been a shared pause becomes a sequence of micro-departures, each one small enough to deny and large enough to feel. Later, in the car, the same pattern repeats in a different key. A child stares at a screen in the back seat while the road rolls by, and the adult in the front feels both relief and loss: relief at the quiet, loss at the sense that a natural space for talk has been quietly filled. That is how drift happens. Not through a dramatic decision, but through a hundred tiny defaults.

A bedroom tells an even sharper story. It is a place where the day is meant to end, where the body is meant to soften, where the mind is meant to stop responding to external cues. And yet a phone in a bedroom is a portable doorway, constantly capable of opening into noise, novelty, and other people's demands. Adults often discover this not through ideology but through evidence: the teen who is up later than they admit, the younger child whose sleep turns brittle, the morning that begins with exhaustion and argument. The bedroom becomes contested territory, not because parents enjoy control, but because everyone in the house can feel the cost of a night that never truly closes.

The paradox is that the home is full of rooms, but only a few of them matter disproportionately for attention, sleep, and connection. Families often respond to screen stress by attempting blanket bans, and blanket bans collapse under their own ambition. They require constant supervision, invite constant rebellion, and quickly become riddled with exceptions that feel arbitrary. Yet doing nothing leaves the household governed by convenience and impulse. Device free zones offer a third posture: fewer rules, applied in the places where rules matter most, carried by the environment so adults are not forced to police constantly.

The central tension is between convenience and protected space. Screens are convenient in exactly the places where family life can be most fragile: the table, the car, the bedroom. Convenience is not a vice. It is often how parents and carers survive busy days. The difficulty is that convenience, left unchecked, becomes a silent architect. It redesigns the home so that every awkward moment has an escape hatch and every quiet moment has a distraction. Protected space, by contrast, is the deliberate refusal to let certain parts of the home be colonised by devices, not because devices are evil, but because those spaces have jobs to do that screens interfere with: meals that build cohesion, bedrooms that build rest, travel time that can build conversation or at least shared presence.

This matters because the most important family goods are often produced in unremarkable moments. Connection is not only the big talk about values; it is the small talk that happens when hands are busy and minds are half-open. Sleep is not only a biological necessity; it is the foundation that makes patience, judgement, and emotional regulation more available the next day. Attention is not only a school skill; it is the ability to stay with one another long enough to notice feelings before they become explosions. Device free zones protect these goods by reducing the number of times the family must compete with a screen for the same moment. They also reduce the number of daily negotiations, which means less conflict and less need for adults to perform authority in a doorway.

Device free zones also matter because they make rules legible. A child can cope with a boundary they can predict. A teen can respect a boundary that is clear, even if they do not like it, more readily than one that appears as a surprise. When the home has a few zones where devices simply do not belong, the child is no longer asked to infer whether today is a "strict" day or a "tired" day. The household stops relying on adult mood as the enforcement mechanism. That is not just calmer; it is fairer. Fairness, here, is not sameness. It is predictability.

The problem families face is that zones can become porous unless they are designed to be easy. A rule that requires an adult to constantly spot-check and correct will fail during the very moments it is most needed, when the adult is cooking, driving, talking, or tired. Design is what turns a rule into a default. Design is where devices live when not in use, what the child does with their hands at the table, where visitors put phones without being shamed, and how the household handles necessary exceptions without dissolving the whole concept. The house must do some of the work. Humans cannot carry it all.

The path through this chapter moves from selection to architecture. It begins with choosing the few places where a device-free norm has disproportionate value, because clarity beats ambition. It then turns to the mechanics that make those norms self-enforcing: physical cues, landing spots, and routines that reduce the need for supervision and reduce the opportunity for bargaining. The order matters because design without prioritisation becomes clutter, and prioritisation without design becomes a lecture that collapses under pressure.

The quiet motif worth keeping is the basket by the door. Not a grand symbol, just a place where devices go, visible enough to be normal and ordinary enough to be unremarkable. A basket is a way of saying: this house has a default. The phone has a home. The moment you step inside, you step into a different rhythm. When a child sees a parent place their own phone there, it reads as legitimacy. When visitors see it, it reads as culture rather than punishment. The basket makes compliance easy and conversation lighter.

The unresolved friction is that zones trigger status questions. A child may feel embarrassed in front of friends. A teen may interpret a bedroom boundary as mistrust. An adult may worry about safety or emergencies. The next decision is therefore not merely where to ban devices, but where the household is willing to absorb discomfort in order to protect the spaces that keep the family functional. Which room in this home is currently being shaped by convenience rather than by intention, and what would it cost, socially and emotionally, to reclaim it?

## Picking the right places

In July 2018, France passed a law restricting mobile phone use in primary and lower secondary schools, widely reported as an attempt to protect attention and reduce distraction in classrooms. The concrete outcome was not universal compliance or universal praise; it was a clearer institutional default. Phones, in that setting, were treated less as personal property with an automatic right of presence and more as an object whose place must be managed for the environment to function. One can argue about the policy. It still reveals a principle families often miss: a space changes when a device is assumed to belong there.

Choose fewer places. Win more calm.

Homes are not schools, and family life cannot be governed by blanket prohibitions without creating a cold, brittle atmosphere. Yet the underlying logic transfers cleanly. Some rooms are more sensitive than others. Some moments are more fragile. A device free zone is not a moral stance against screens. It is a decision about where the household wants human attention to be the default. A good zone is high-impact, low-argument, and supported by the physics of the home rather than by constant supervision. A bad zone is either too ambitious to maintain or too vague to enforce without nagging.

The temptation for conscientious parents is to attempt a whole-house ban, as if the correct response to a leaky roof were to rebuild the entire house. Whole-house bans create constant boundary-crossings, and constant boundary-crossings train constant conflict. The show is the adult who becomes the roaming police officer, scanning for screens, issuing corrections, and discovering that the child's life is now organised around evasion. The named concept is *enforcement saturation*. The explanation is that humans cannot sustain high-frequency policing without becoming reactive, and children cannot live under high-frequency policing without becoming either resentful or secretive. The implication is that a family should not measure success by how many rules it can declare, but by whether the household can uphold the few rules that matter most without daily warfare.

Picking the right places begins with noticing where screens do the most damage in your specific home, and "damage" must be defined behaviourally rather than emotionally. A family can tolerate plenty of screen use if sleep remains stable, mealtimes remain connective, and transitions do not collapse into bargaining. Another family can struggle even with modest screen use if devices regularly appear in bed, at the table, or during the vulnerable after-school hour. The show is not an abstract worry about "too much". It is a pattern: arguments cluster in certain places, moods shift after certain uses, and the household loses the small moments that used to stitch the day together. The named concept is *friction mapping*. The explanation is that where conflict repeatedly occurs, the environment is making the wrong behaviour easy. The implication is that the right zone is often the one that removes a recurring flashpoint rather than the one that sounds most virtuous.

Bedrooms are the first obvious candidate in many homes, not because bedrooms are sacred, but because sleep is upstream. When a phone enters a bedroom, it brings open loops, social cues, and the possibility of late-night drift. The show is the glow under the door, the "just five more minutes" that expands, the tired morning that follows. The named concept is *night-time vulnerability*. The explanation is that tired brains make worse decisions and are more susceptible to endless content and social pressure. The implication is that a bedroom zone does not merely reduce screen time; it reduces the risk that the day's most fragile resource, sleep, will be quietly eroded by habits that are hard to interrupt once the child is alone.

Yet bedrooms are also where privacy lives, and privacy is not an optional luxury for older children. A teen experiences the bedroom as a territory of identity. A younger child experiences it as a place of safety. A zone that is framed as "we do not trust you" will provoke either defiance or secrecy. The same zone framed as "we protect sleep in this house" is more likely to be experienced as legitimacy rather than surveillance. The abstraction is *trust*, but it becomes visible as a household choice: whether the rule is expressed as a moral verdict on the child or as a protection of a shared good the whole family benefits from. The implication is that the right place is not chosen only by function; it is chosen by what the family can defend without poisoning the relationship.

The table is another high-impact place because it is where casual talk either survives or dies. A device at the table does not always create obvious conflict. It can create something subtler: parallel attention. People are present physically and absent mentally, each micro-check too small to justify confrontation. The show is the conversation that never quite gathers momentum because everyone is half elsewhere. The named concept is *conversational thinning*. The explanation is that shared meals are one of the few reliable daily moments when a household can reconnect without scheduling. Devices break the low-stakes conditions that allow children to talk sideways about their day. The implication is that a table zone is not about etiquette. It is about preserving a space where talk can happen without competing with a feed designed to be more gripping than family chatter.

Car rides are more complicated because they sit at the intersection of safety, boredom, and logistics. For many families, the car is a rare enclosed space where conversation happens naturally, precisely because there is nowhere else to go. For other families, the car is a necessary buffer, especially after school, when children are dysregulated and adults are trying to drive safely. The show is the back-seat device that buys quiet, or the back-seat device that prevents any conversation from ever starting. The named concept is *transitional space*. The explanation is that the car is a bridge between contexts, and bridges are where emotions and attention are unstable. The implication is that a car zone should be chosen only if it supports the family's real priorities: some families will value quiet for safety, others will value talk as a daily touchpoint, and both can be legitimate depending on the household's needs.

This is where "clarity, not perfection" becomes more than a comforting phrase. Device free zones fail when they pretend to be absolute in a world that requires exceptions. Navigation is a clear example. A phone may be needed for directions or traffic. Accessibility needs are another. Some children and adults rely on devices for communication support, sensory regulation, or health-related tools. The show is the parent making an exception and the child immediately arguing that the exception proves the rule is meaningless. The named concept is *exception credibility*. The explanation is that exceptions can either preserve a system or destroy it, depending on whether they are planned and clearly bounded. The implication is that the right zones are the ones where exceptions can be defined without becoming loopholes large enough to swallow the zone.

A useful way to think about this is to distinguish between a device being present and a device being used. A phone used for navigation in the front seat is not the same as a phone used for scrolling at the table. A tablet used for an accessibility function is not the same as a tablet used for endless videos. The abstraction is *purpose*, but it becomes visible as observable behaviour: the screen faces the driver for directions, not the passenger for entertainment; the device is used for a specific task and then put away; the exception has a beginning and an end. The named concept is *bounded exception*. The explanation is that bounding is what prevents exceptions from becoming precedent creep. The implication is that a zone can remain legitimate even with exceptions, if exceptions are treated as structured deviations rather than as rewards for pressure.

A second named, checkable example from the broader culture helps underline why place-based defaults work. In October 2016, the American Academy of Pediatrics in Itasca, Illinois, released a Family Media Plan tool that framed media rules as part of daily rhythms and priorities rather than as isolated prohibitions. The concrete outcome was a public prompt to treat the household as a system: sleep, movement, meals, and media are interlinked. The named concept is *systems governance*. The explanation is that small, high-leverage changes in key contexts can shift the whole pattern of family life more effectively than broad, hard-to-enforce bans. The implication is that choosing zones is not a loss of ambition. It is the correct kind of ambition: targeting the points where the household most often trips.

The quiet motif that keeps this practical is the threshold. A threshold is where a space announces what it is for. The front door threshold, the bedroom threshold, the table threshold, the car door threshold. If devices cross those thresholds without friction, they become assumed occupants. If the threshold carries a cue that says "devices live elsewhere here", then the household is not constantly negotiating; it is simply crossing into a different mode. The threshold cue can be physical, like a basket by the door, or behavioural, like a ritual of putting phones away before sitting down. The named concept is *mode switching*. The explanation is that people behave differently when the environment signals a different mode. The implication is that the right places are those where a mode shift would protect something the family values: rest, connection, or calm transitions.

A credible limitation needs to be faced squarely. Some families will not be able to make certain zones device-free without creating more harm than benefit, at least at first. A single parent juggling siblings may rely on a screen at the table to get food into a picky child. A child with sensory overwhelm may need a device in the car to avoid dysregulation that makes driving unsafe. A teen may need privacy and quiet in their room, and removing a phone entirely might provoke secrecy rather than healthier habits. The named concept is *capacity constraint*. The explanation is that zones must fit the household's logistical and emotional bandwidth, not an imagined ideal. The implication is that the "right places" are not universal. They are the places where the household can be consistent without constant policing, because consistency is what turns a zone into a norm rather than a fight.

Reconciling this limitation brings the focus back to the purpose of zones: reducing daily battles and protecting the household's most fragile goods. If a zone produces constant arguments, it is not yet a zone; it is a battlefield. A better first move is often to choose the place where the rule will reduce conflict rather than increase it, and where the household can support it with design. A bedroom rule supported by a shared charging spot, for example, can reduce nightly arguments. A table rule supported by an obvious phone home can reduce mid-meal checking without lectures. The point is to choose places where the environment can carry the boundary so adults are not forced to enforce it with their voice every single time.

The forward test is not whether a family can declare three device-free zones. It is whether the family can name the one place where screens currently do the most relational or sleep damage and then design a boundary that survives ordinary life, including visitors, tired evenings, and necessary exceptions. When a device crosses a threshold, what is it replacing in that room: talk, rest, or the simple ability to be together without competing claims on attention?

## Making zones easy to follow

In October 2016, the American Academy of Pediatrics in Itasca, Illinois, released its Family Media Plan tool, and the concrete outcome was a public nudge away from heroic self-control and towards household design. The tool did not promise to turn children into monks. It asked families to match media use to routines and priorities, which is another way of saying: stop relying on repeated willpower in the moment and start shaping the environment so the desired behaviour becomes the default. That is the hidden difference between a rule that survives and a rule that collapses at the first busy week.

Design beats discipline.

A device-free zone is a promise the household makes to itself: in this place, attention belongs here. The promise fails when it requires an adult to deliver it repeatedly, with a voice that grows sharper each time. Most families have already discovered this without naming it. The show is the table rule that evaporates whenever someone is tired, the bedroom rule that becomes a nightly confrontation, the car rule that collapses the moment a child whines loudly enough. The named concept is *supervision dependency*. The explanation is that a rule that depends on constant monitoring depends on a scarce resource, and scarcity makes systems unstable. The implication is blunt: if you want zones to stick, you must remove the need for constant supervision by building cues and landing places that carry the boundary when the adult is occupied.

The first design principle is to give devices a home that is more convenient than wherever they would otherwise drift. Drift is the enemy. Drift is what turns "no phones at dinner" into "just this once" and then into "everyone does it anyway". The show is a phone placed on the table "face down" as a compromise, which quickly becomes a phone checked between bites. The named concept is *proximity effect*. The explanation is that objects close at hand are used more, and devices are designed to invite use. The implication is that a zone cannot rely on an object being present but not tempting. If the aim is device-free, the device must have a different home, one that feels normal, not punitive.

This is where the simple physical infrastructure matters: a charging station, a basket, a shelf, a labelled spot. It sounds domestic and trivial. It is, in behavioural terms, a mechanism for changing the path of least resistance. The show is a child entering the house, automatically dropping a device into a known place because there is a ritual and a cue. The named concept is *friction engineering*. The explanation is that small changes in friction can reshape behaviour powerfully: make the unwanted behaviour slightly harder and the wanted behaviour slightly easier, and people follow the easier path. The implication is that a "phone home" by the door is not a cute idea. It is a way of shifting the device from being an ambient presence in every room to being an object that belongs somewhere, like shoes or keys.

The door is a special location because it is a threshold, and thresholds are where habits can be redirected. A person already expects to do something at the door: take off a coat, drop a bag, put keys down. Adding one more behaviour there feels less intrusive than asking for a device handover deep into the evening, when the child is already absorbed. The show is the parent who no longer has to hunt for a phone because the phone has a known resting place. The concept is *search-cost reduction*. The explanation is practical: searching for devices creates conflict because it resembles surveillance, and surveillance invites resistance. The implication is that zones become calmer when the household stops conducting raids and starts relying on location defaults.

The second design principle is to make compliance visible and socially normal, because children are exquisitely sensitive to what "everyone" is doing in the room. A child will comply more readily with a table rule if they see adults comply, and if they see the device being put away as a normal part of sitting down rather than as a punishment. The show is the family member placing a phone in the basket without comment. The named concept is *norm signalling*. The explanation is that humans, especially children and teens, take cues from observed norms more than from spoken ideals. The implication is that the best cue is often an adult's behaviour. Adults who keep their own phones out of zones remove the hypocrisy argument at its source, and hypocrisy is one of the quickest solvents of any rule.

The third design principle is to reduce ambiguity. "No screens in the bedroom" is clearer than "try not to use it too much at night". "No phones at the table" is clearer than "be present". Clarity matters, but clarity alone is not enough. It must be paired with cues that make the rule easy to remember in the moment. The show is the child who forgets, not maliciously, but because the device is habitual. The named concept is *cue scarcity*. The explanation is that without cues, people revert to habit, especially when tired. The implication is that zones should have physical reminders that are hard to miss: a basket on the table, a charger outside the bedroom, a sign by the door if the family can tolerate it without feeling theatrical. These cues are not there to shame anyone. They are there to prevent a rule from relying on memory and goodwill alone.

A design approach also changes how exceptions are handled. Exceptions are inevitable: navigation while driving, a call from school, an accessibility need, a visitor needing to check something. The system collapses when exceptions are treated as proofs that the zone is meaningless. The show is the child arguing that if an adult can use a phone for directions, then the child can use a phone for entertainment in the car. The named concept is *exception hijacking*. The explanation is that children will use any inconsistency as a bargaining tool if the household has not defined the difference between a bounded exception and a loophole. The implication is that zones stick when exceptions are made legible through observable cues: the phone is mounted for navigation rather than held for scrolling, the use is task-bound rather than open-ended, the device returns to its home after the task. The system is preserved not by pretending exceptions do not exist, but by ensuring exceptions do not become precedents for drift.

A second named, checkable example helps anchor the idea that design is not merely a household quirk but a known governance strategy. In September 2018, Apple released iOS 12 in Cupertino, California, and Screen Time made it easier for families to embed limits into devices rather than relying entirely on verbal enforcement. The outcome was a shift in where authority lived: partly in the phone's settings, partly in the household's routines. The concept is *embedded constraints*. The explanation is that constraints embedded in an environment reduce the need for repeated human conflict. The implication is that physical design in the home works in the same way. A basket by the door is an embedded constraint. A charger in the kitchen is an embedded constraint. These are low-tech equivalents of digital limits, and they can be more reliable because they do not depend on menus, passwords, or the child's willingness to admit what they are doing.

Visitors and playdates are where many zone rules collapse, because social pressure is real and parents feel awkward imposing norms on other people's children. The show is the friend who arrives with a phone, the children disappearing into parallel play on separate screens, and the host parent feeling torn between their own rules and the desire to be hospitable. The named concept is *social override*. The explanation is that humans often suspend household rules to avoid social discomfort, and children learn quickly that rules are optional in front of peers. The implication is that zones must be designed to survive guests without turning the host into a scold. This is where a visible "phone home" spot is powerful: it externalises the norm. Instead of a parent issuing a personal demand, the environment gently suggests what happens here. It turns "we are strict" into "this is how this house works".

This does not remove the need for words, but it changes what words do. A parent can refer to a shared norm rather than presenting it as a judgement on the visitor: the phone goes here while you eat, the devices stay here during the play part, the car ride is for music not screens. The abstraction is *hospitality*, but it becomes visible as a decision: whether the host is willing to tolerate short-term awkwardness in order to preserve a household norm that protects connection and calm. The named concept is *norm transfer*. The explanation is that norms travel better when they are presented as simple house culture rather than moral superiority. The implication is that the family's zones will either become stable cultural features or fragile rules that dissolve whenever someone else walks through the door.

A credible limitation deserves a clear, unromantic acknowledgement. Some families cannot make zones fully device-free without losing necessary functions. A child may need a device for communication support. A parent may need to be reachable for caregiving responsibilities. A teen may have school requirements that occasionally intrude into shared spaces. The named concept is *functional dependency*. The explanation is that devices sometimes serve legitimate purposes that a blanket rule would punish unfairly. The implication is not that zones are impossible. It is that zones must be defined by what is being protected and by what kinds of use are exceptions, bounded in ways that remain observable and non-negotiated in the moment. A zone does not have to be pure to be useful. It has to be credible.

Reconciling this limitation returns us to the core idea: zones are not declarations of virtue. They are pieces of household engineering. Engineering begins with constraints and trade-offs. If a parent must keep a phone nearby for emergencies, the design task becomes "how do we keep it present without letting it become a default distraction?" That might mean a specific spot in the zone where the phone rests and stays silent unless needed, rather than living in a hand or on the table. The show is the adult who is reachable without being absorbed. The concept is *bounded presence*. The explanation is that the same object can be present in a way that supports the household or present in a way that undermines it, depending on how it is positioned and used. The implication is that families can preserve zones while meeting real needs, but only if they stop treating the exception as a private judgement call and start treating it as a designed part of the system.

The "phone home" motif is useful because it turns a boundary into a habit. Habits do not require arguments. Habits require cues and repetition. Once the device has a home, the home begins to do the reminding. Children begin to internalise the sequence: enter house, device to basket; sit to eat, device away; bedtime begins, device outside room. The household stops narrating every step. Narration is exhausting. The device home becomes a quiet tutor.

The forward test is whether the family can build zones that survive the moments that normally dissolve rules: tired evenings, hungry children, visitors, and the seductive convenience of "just this once". When a zone is broken, does the household respond with a lecture and a fight, or does it adjust the design so the break becomes less likely next time?

The question that pulls towards the next page is not "Do we have the willpower?" but "What, in the physical and social design of this home, is still making it easier to carry a phone into a protected space than to return it to its home by default?"

# Chapter 6
# Bedtime and Sleep Protection

A parent walks past a child's room and sees the glow under the door, a thin line of light that should not be there. The house is quiet enough to hear the radiator tick. The parent pauses, hand on the handle, and feels the familiar split: intervene and risk a late-night argument that will wake everyone; walk away and risk a tired morning that will poison the next day. The child inside is not necessarily doing anything dramatic. They may be watching something comforting, scrolling without thinking, messaging friends because the chat is still alive. The adult knows one thing with certainty: if the device stays, sleep will be thinner. If the adult goes in, peace will be thinner.

Night makes everything harder.

The same boundary that feels reasonable at four in the afternoon can feel cruel at ten at night, not because parents become tyrants after dark but because the emotional stakes change. Night-time is when willpower is lowest, when the day's grievances and insecurities come out to play, when social life is often more active for older children, and when there are fewer natural stopping cues to help anyone land the plane. A teen can be perfectly capable of ending a session after school and still find the same "just five more minutes" expanding in bed, because the bed is not merely a location. It is a context saturated with fatigue, privacy, and the quiet, intensely persuasive belief that tomorrow can be managed later.

The paradox is sharp. Sleep is the household's most valuable resource and its least defended. People treat sleep as something that happens if there is time, rather than something that must be protected to make time usable. Yet sleep is upstream of almost everything parents are trying to preserve: emotional steadiness, attention for school, tolerance for siblings, patience for chores, basic decency in the morning rush. When sleep is eroded, families often respond by tightening rules elsewhere, which increases conflict, which makes bedtime even harder. Night-time screens then become both the cause and the symptom, the thing everyone argues about and the thing everyone reaches for because the argument itself is exhausting.

The central tension is not between screens and sleep as abstract ideas. It is between two kinds of comfort. A screen offers immediate comfort: distraction, connection, stimulation, the sense of not being alone with one's thoughts. Sleep offers delayed comfort: a body that works, a mind that can cope, a morning that does not begin in debt. Children and teens are not foolish for preferring immediate comfort; adults do it too. The difficulty is that night-time is where immediate comfort is most seductive and delayed comfort is most invisible. A household that tries to solve this with a late-night confrontation ends up treating bedtime like a courtroom, which is the worst possible atmosphere for rest.

This matters because bedtime is where authority and trust meet in their most fragile form. A bedroom is also a private place, and privacy is developmentally important, especially for teens. When adults try to protect sleep by barging into privacy without a shared agreement, the teen experiences it as control and disrespect. When adults avoid the conflict and allow the phone to remain in bed, they often experience it as surrender and anxiety. Children are caught in the middle, because they can sincerely want to sleep and still be pulled into checking by the device's loops and by the social world that does not respect bedtimes. The result is a predictable kind of secrecy: the device hidden, the use denied, the trust thinned.

It also matters because bedtime routines are one of the few areas where families can build stability regardless of school changes, peer drama, or adult work stress. A consistent night pattern reduces the number of decisions that must be made when everyone is depleted. Without that pattern, families rely on negotiation and threats, and both tend to escalate after dark. Even good parents become harsher at night because they are tired and frightened about tomorrow. Even good children become more resistant at night because endings feel sharper and the screen feels like refuge. A household that does not build a calm night structure ends up paying in repeated conflict, which makes sleep harder, which makes conflict more likely. The loop is brutally efficient.

The movement through this chapter follows the night itself. It begins by identifying what makes night uniquely combustible: the combination of stimulation, peer pressure, and the loss of natural stopping points. It then turns to the mechanics of a credible curfew that can survive weekends and special occasions without collapsing into loopholes. It ends by facing the most emotionally charged part of the problem: the pushback, the claims of needing the phone to sleep, the discovery of secret use, and the question of how to hold boundaries without turning bedtime into humiliation.

A quiet motif can carry the whole chapter: the charger outside the bedroom. Not as a moral symbol, but as a practical line in the house that says where the night begins. The charger is a threshold device. It tells the body, and the brain, and the family system, that the day's demands are ending and the night's protections are starting. When the charger sits in a shared space, it reduces nightly negotiation because the handover happens earlier, before everyone is raw. When the charger lives in the bedroom, the negotiation arrives late, at the moment of maximum conflict.

The unresolved question is not whether screens harm sleep in some generic way. The question is whether the household is willing to protect sleep as a non-negotiable good without turning protection into a war. When a child says they need the phone to relax, is the household hearing a genuine need for comfort, or a habit that has fused comfort with endless content? And when the adult feels the urge to storm into the room, are they protecting tomorrow, or merely reacting to fear? The next night will ask the question again, and it will not wait for anyone to be well-rested before it does.

## Why nights are different

In April 2019, the World Health Organization in Geneva published guidance on physical activity, sedentary behaviour, and sleep for young children, placing screens in the same frame as rest rather than treating them as a separate moral category. The concrete outcome was a public shift in emphasis: screen use was discussed as something that can intrude into the rhythms that keep a child functional, especially the rhythm of sleep. That framing matters at night because night is not merely "later in the day". Night is a different psychological climate, one in which small choices acquire sharp consequences.

Night rewrites the rules.

A household can feel this without any policy document. The evening is when patience thins, when voices soften to avoid waking others, when parents and carers want peace more than principle, and when children and teens often want the opposite: one last pocket of autonomy before the day ends. The phone becomes an almost perfect object for this moment. It is quiet. It is private. It is endlessly responsive. A book is quiet too, but a book does not send vibrations, light up with social cues, or deliver novelty on demand. Night-time conflict is not a sign that families are failing. It is a sign that the environment has changed while everyone's defences have dropped.

Begin with a familiar scene. A teen is in bed. The room is dark. A thin line of light sits under the door, just enough to tell an adult what is happening without providing any detail. The adult pauses, weighing options: intervene and trigger an argument; stay silent and risk a morning that begins in debt. The named concept is *low-visibility behaviour*. The explanation is that night-time screen use is often hidden by the very conditions that make sleep possible: darkness, quiet, privacy. The implication is that adults are pulled towards either surveillance or denial, and neither is a stable foundation for trust. Surveillance invites secrecy. Denial invites drift. The line of light becomes a kind of nightly referendum on who controls the boundary.

Night-time screens also behave differently because night removes natural stopping cues. In the daytime, many activities have edges. School ends. A club finishes. Dinner arrives. A friend goes home. A screen at night often has no comparable edge, and the human mind is notoriously bad at stopping an engaging activity without a cue that signals closure. The show is "just five more minutes" expanding into a long stretch of unplanned wakefulness. The named concept is *endless continuation*. The explanation is design: feeds refresh, videos auto-play, chats keep moving, games offer the next reward, and the activity is built to feel unfinished. The implication is not that children lack discipline. It is that night-time offers fewer external brakes, so the activity's internal brake must do all the work, and internal brakes are weakest when the body is tired.

Tiredness does not merely reduce willpower. It changes judgement. It makes the immediate feel heavier than the long-term. It makes the next laugh, the next message, the next clip feel like relief rather than choice. The show is the child or teen who sincerely intends to sleep and sincerely keeps checking anyway. The named concept is *temporal myopia*. The explanation is that fatigue narrows attention to what is immediate, and screens are specialists in immediacy. The implication is that family arguments about night-time use often misfire because they assume the child is making a calm, deliberate decision. Many night-time decisions are made in a state closer to autopilot: the thumb moves, the mind follows, and the cost is paid tomorrow.

Stimulation is the second reason night is different, and stimulation at night is not only about noise or excitement. It is about cognitive and emotional activation. A late-night chat can contain humour, flirtation, exclusion, conflict, and rapid shifts in tone. A video feed can swing from comforting to unsettling in a few swipes. A game can demand fast reactions and keep the body slightly tense. The show is the teen who says they are "relaxing" while their attention remains sharp and reactive. The named concept is *false relaxation*. The explanation is that many screen activities feel restful because they require little physical effort, yet they keep the mind alert by delivering novelty and social signals. The implication is that night-time rules cannot be argued purely on the basis of "relaxation". A household has to distinguish between quiet stimulation and genuine winding down, because both can happen with the lights off.

Social pressure is the third reason, and it is the one adults often underestimate because adult social life rarely feels as compulsory as a teen's does. A teen may believe that not responding is rude, risky, or socially costly. Group chats move while people sleep. Jokes evolve. Plans are made. Subtle hierarchies shift. The show is the teen who insists they must check "just in case" something is happening. The named concept is *ambient obligation*. The explanation is that digital social spaces can create a background sense that one is always needed and always being evaluated. The implication is that a night-time boundary can feel to a teen like a boundary against belonging, not merely against entertainment. When adults dismiss this as manipulation, they make it harder for the teen to talk honestly, and secrecy becomes more attractive.

A checkable example helps show that society has already noticed the role of design in attention and behaviour, even if it has not solved the family-level problem. In September 2018, Apple released iOS 12 in Cupertino, California, introducing Screen Time as a built-in feature. The concrete outcome in many homes was that the device itself could announce a limit and restrict access. The named concept is *externalised stopping*. The explanation is that when the device carries part of the boundary, the family relies less on late-night confrontation and more on a pre-set structure. The implication is not that tools fix night-time use. Tools can be overridden, and teens can find workarounds. The implication is that night-time is precisely where families search for external cues because internal cues are unreliable when exhausted. The desire for a referee is a clue: the problem is not simply a lack of character, but the mismatch between fatigue and an environment designed to continue.

A second checkable anchor, different in tone, underscores that this is also a rhythm issue, not merely a technology issue. The World Health Organization guidance in Geneva framed screens as part of a system that includes sleep and daily activity. The named concept is *rhythm protection*. The explanation is that the cost of night-time screens is rarely confined to the night. It leaks into the morning, then into the day's transitions, then back into the next night. The implication is that sleep protection is not merely about bedtime obedience. It is a stabilising move for the entire household, because a rested child is more able to tolerate limits, switch tasks, and manage emotions without turning every boundary into a personal fight.

Still, a careful reader should resist any tidy story in which "screens at night" are simply harmful and "no screens at night" is simply virtuous. There is a credible limitation. Some children and teens use audio content, calming videos, or messaging to self-soothe, especially when anxious, lonely, or wound up from the day. Some use digital tools for accessibility or communication needs that do not politely end at an adult's preferred time. The show is the child who genuinely feels more settled with a familiar soundtrack or an audiobook, or the teen who calms down by talking to a friend after a difficult social day. The named concept is *coping substitution*. The explanation is that a screen can serve as a coping tool when a child lacks other strategies, and removing it abruptly can intensify distress. The implication is that the question cannot be "screens or sleep" as an absolute. It must be "which digital behaviours support winding down, and which keep the mind in a reactive loop?" Without that distinction, families end up punishing comfort along with compulsion, and the child learns either resentment or secrecy.

Reconciling this limitation requires separating the idea of relaxation from the mechanism of endless content. Relaxation is a physiological and psychological shift into lower arousal. Endless content is a design pattern that feeds the brain novelty and social cues without offering a clean end. The show is the difference between an activity that can be paused and left without a sense of loss and an activity that continually suggests "next". The named concept is *stop friction*. The explanation is that some media formats have natural closure and some are built to keep going. The implication is that a household can treat "winding down" as a category with internal distinctions rather than as a blanket permission that becomes, by night, an all-access pass to the most capturing designs.

Night-time conflict is also different because of status. When a parent enters a bedroom to enforce a rule, the teen may experience it as infantilisation. Even younger children can experience it as intrusion. The show is the snapped "Get out!" or the sulky silence that follows. The named concept is *dignity threat*. The explanation is that bedrooms are symbolically loaded spaces: they represent privacy and control, especially for adolescents. The implication is that bedtime boundaries that rely on repeated intrusions are likely to degrade the relationship even when they reduce screen use. A household can "win" the phone and lose the trust that makes future cooperation possible. That is a poor trade.

The most stable alternative to intrusion is predictability, because predictability reduces the sense of being attacked in the moment. Predictability also reduces bargaining. Earlier chapters established why defaults matter; night is where defaults matter most. The show is the family that does not debate at the edge of sleep because the boundary is enacted earlier, in a shared space, with a routine that is ordinary rather than punitive. The named concept is *pre-commitment*. The explanation is that decisions made earlier, when everyone is more regulated, tend to hold better than decisions improvised when exhausted. The implication is that the emotional temperature of bedtime can be changed by moving the decisive moment away from the bedroom doorway. The line of light under the door is less likely to appear when the system does not wait until midnight to become serious.

Social pressure, however, does not disappear simply because the household has a routine. It changes form. A teen may still feel pulled to respond. They may still worry about being left out. The show is the teen who tries to negotiate an exception late at night with intense urgency because the social moment feels unique. The named concept is *exception urgency*. The explanation is that social life often feels urgent to teens, and urgency is amplified at night when the world is quiet and the screen is the main channel for connection. The implication is that families need to understand that "just tonight" requests are often powered by real feelings, not merely opportunism. Treating the feelings as fake pushes the teen towards secrecy; treating the feelings as real without any boundary pushes the household towards drift. Night makes both errors easier.

A calm routine beats confrontation not because calm is morally superior, but because confrontation is activating. Voices rise, bodies tense, humiliation lingers. Even when the phone is removed, the argument can keep the teen's nervous system alert. The show is the child who stops using the phone but cannot fall asleep because the conflict has become the last event of the day. The named concept is *arousal transfer*. The explanation is that emotional arousal does not end when the stimulus ends; it carries forward. The implication is that the household must consider not only whether the phone is present, but what emotional state bedtime enforcement produces. If enforcement reliably produces anger and shame, it undermines the very goal of sleep.

The motif worth holding is the thin glow under the door. It is not merely a sign of device use. It is a sign of how the night is being governed: by default drift or by deliberate structure. It also symbolises the ethical challenge for parents and carers: the glow is a cue to intervene, yet intervention can itself be disruptive. Families often oscillate between policing and avoidance because both feel wrong. Night asks for a third response: building a system that reduces the need for spying and reduces the need for late-night battles.

A final, uncomfortable observation ties these threads together. Night-time screens are often not about pleasure. They are about avoidance. Avoidance of boredom, avoidance of loneliness, avoidance of anxious thoughts, avoidance of the day's unfinished emotions. The screen fills the space where reflection might occur, and reflection can be painful. The show is the teen who scrolls not because they are delighted but because stopping would mean feeling. The named concept is *affective avoidance*. The explanation is that the mind seeks relief when distressed, and screens provide relief quickly. The implication is that a household that treats night-time use as mere greed will misread the problem and respond with moralism. A household that recognises avoidance can respond with structure that protects sleep while still acknowledging the teen's need for comfort.

The unresolved tension is not whether night-time is different. It is. The tension is where the family chooses to place the decisive moment. If the boundary is enforced at the bedroom doorway, the household is almost guaranteed to pay in confrontation, because that is where dignity and exhaustion collide. If the boundary is enforced earlier through predictable defaults, the household pays in upfront design and in the discomfort of change. The forward test is practical and piercing: when the glow appears under the door, is it a sign that the family has not yet built a routine strong enough to carry the night, or a sign that the teen's social world is pulling harder than the household has learned to acknowledge?

## Setting a workable device curfew

In September 2018, Apple released iOS 12 in Cupertino, California, and Screen Time brought a domestic idea into the operating system: a device could refuse to cooperate after a chosen hour. The concrete outcome in many homes was not immediate peace but a clearer line. A parent could point to a setting. A child could see the boundary on the screen itself. The line was still contested, but it was no longer purely verbal, no longer dependent on a tired adult remembering what they had said yesterday. The curfew became something the environment helped enforce.

Make the line earlier. Keep it calm.

A workable device curfew is not a statement about virtue. It is a piece of household engineering, and engineering begins with constraints. Night is the period when internal brakes fail most often, social cues feel most pressing, and endings feel most insulting. A curfew works when it moves the decisive moment away from the bedroom doorway, where fatigue and dignity collide, and into an earlier, less combustible part of the evening. Families often misunderstand this and treat a curfew as a dramatic confiscation: "hand it over at bedtime". That approach invites the worst possible interaction at the worst possible moment, and then everyone wonders why the rule feels like war.

The first design move is to treat "cut-off time" as a behavioural boundary rather than a moral line. The show is the household trying to choose an hour by asking, "What is reasonable?" which quickly becomes a debate about what other families allow. The named concept is *social benchmarking*. The explanation is that people reach for comparison when they lack a clear internal rationale, and teens in particular weaponise comparison because it is socially powerful. The implication is that a curfew needs to be tied to a protected good the family has already named, such as sleep protection and attentional integrity. When a line is justified by a protected good rather than by parental preference, the argument shifts. It becomes less about whether the parent is strict and more about whether the household is serious about the thing it claims to protect.

A second design move is to recognise that curfews fail when they are treated as a single point in time rather than a sequence. The show is the parent saying "off now" while the child is mid-chat, mid-level, mid-laugh. The named concept is *closure readiness*. The explanation is that ending an activity requires a small process: finishing a loop, sending a closing message, saving progress, preparing emotionally for a switch. At night, closure readiness is lower because fatigue narrows patience and increases reactance. The implication is that a curfew that aims to reduce conflict must include some form of runway, not because children deserve unlimited extensions, but because endings are easier when they are anticipated rather than imposed as a surprise.

This is where gradual introduction earns its keep. A sudden overnight change, even a sensible one, often triggers what families experience as rebellion. The show is the child who becomes louder and more desperate when a previously flexible night becomes strict, because they have not yet learned how to land the plane earlier. The named concept is *habit disruption*. The explanation is simple: when a behaviour has been reinforced repeatedly, the first removal of reinforcement produces a protest spike. That spike is not proof the rule is wrong. It is proof the old pattern was powerful. The implication is that families often abandon a good curfew too early because they confuse the predictable protest spike with permanent incompatibility. A gradual shift can reduce the spike because it changes the routine without snapping it, allowing both child and adult to adapt without turning every evening into a showdown.

The charging location is the physical counterpart to the cut-off time, and it matters because it determines whether the rule is a default or a nightly battle. The show is the phone left in a bedroom "just for the alarm" that quietly becomes "just for one more check". The named concept is *proximity temptation*. The explanation is that devices close to the body invite checking because checking is easy, and at night the cost of checking feels low because the room is quiet and the rest of the household is asleep. The implication is that a curfew that leaves devices within reach is like a diet that leaves biscuits on the pillow. It is not a question of character. It is a question of design. When the device has a home outside the bedroom, the child must take an extra step to violate the curfew, and extra steps matter most when people are tired.

A "workable" curfew also requires an adult backup plan, not because families must be anxious, but because children will test credibility. A teen will ask, sometimes sincerely and sometimes strategically, "What if there's an emergency?" The adult who has no answer will either cave or bluff, and both responses weaken the system. The show is the parent who allows the phone in the bedroom "just in case" and then finds that "just in case" becomes "always". The named concept is *exception creep*. The explanation is that emergencies are emotionally compelling and vague enough to justify almost any relaxation of a rule. The implication is that a curfew remains credible only when the household can specify what "emergency contact" means in practice, where the backup lives, and how it will be used without turning into a loophole. The backup is part of the design, not a last-minute excuse.

Here the earlier chapters' emphasis on defaults becomes unusually important. If the curfew depends on an adult remembering to enforce it every night, it will fail on nights when the adult is tired, busy, or conflict-avoidant. The show is the "we'll be stricter tomorrow" cycle, in which inconsistency becomes routine. The named concept is *fatigue vulnerability*. The explanation is that night is precisely when adult capacity is lowest, so systems that rely on adult vigilance will fail most often at night. The implication is that a curfew must be carried by the environment as much as possible: the charger location, the device's own settings if used, the household's routine, and the shared expectation that devices go to bed before people do.

Weekends and special occasions are where many curfews lose legitimacy, not because families are wrong to relax sometimes, but because unplanned relaxation teaches children that the rule is negotiable by mood. The show is the teen who argues that if Friday is flexible, then any day could be flexible, and the adult who cannot articulate the difference without sounding arbitrary. The named concept is *calendar logic*. The explanation is that rules become more acceptable when exceptions have a predictable logic: a clear difference in schedule, a special event recognised by everyone, a planned variation rather than a begged-for one. The implication is that a curfew survives social life when it has an intelligible relationship to the calendar, because intelligibility reduces the child's incentive to litigate each evening as a special case.

A second named, checkable example helps anchor the idea that curfews are not merely parental whim but an application of broader attention governance. In October 2016, the American Academy of Pediatrics in Itasca, Illinois, promoted its Family Media Plan approach, encouraging families to align media use with sleep and daily routines. The concrete outcome was a public endorsement of rhythm-based rules rather than ad hoc control. The named concept is *rhythm governance*. The explanation is that daily rhythms are easier to protect than moment-to-moment preferences, and sleep is the rhythm most vulnerable to small, repeated intrusions. The implication is that a curfew is less effective when it is framed as "stop because I say so" and more effective when it is framed as "this is how our evenings work", because rhythm reduces argument.

Still, there is a credible limitation to any curfew discussion: some families rely on late-night device use for genuine connection across distance, for caregiving coordination, or for accessibility needs that do not politely end at an adult's chosen hour. Some teens, especially those with anxiety, may experience the loss of night-time messaging as a sharp increase in distress. The named concept is *functional necessity*. The explanation is that devices are not only entertainment; they can be part of a family's practical infrastructure and a child's coping infrastructure. The implication is that a workable curfew must distinguish between purpose-bound uses and open-ended uses, otherwise the curfew becomes either cruel or irrelevant. Reconciling this limitation requires precision: a curfew can protect sleep while still allowing bounded, clearly defined exceptions, but only if the exceptions are designed to be narrow and observable rather than elastic and private.

The quiet motif that helps keep this practical is the charging ledge, the place where the day's devices gather and the night begins. A charging ledge is not magic. It is a visible commitment. It makes the curfew a shared household behaviour rather than a private contest in a bedroom. It also creates a predictable moment when the family can see whether the rule is being followed without sneaking around. Sneaking corrodes trust. Visibility supports it.

The hardest part of a curfew is not technical. It is emotional. A curfew asks a child or teen to tolerate incompletion: the chat left mid-stream, the feed left unwatched, the game left unfinished. It asks an adult to tolerate protest without escalating. It asks both to tolerate a short period of discomfort in exchange for a more stable morning. The forward test is therefore not whether a family can set a time in a settings menu or declare a rule. It is whether the family can make the curfew a default that survives tired evenings, weekend ambiguity, and "just tonight" pleas. When the next bedtime arrives and the screen is still glowing, will the household be forced back into a doorway confrontation, or will the charging ledge and the pre-agreed curfew carry the boundary without turning sleep into a nightly trial?

## Handling sleep-related pushback

In October 2016, the American Academy of Pediatrics in Itasca, Illinois, updated its guidance on children and media, and the concrete outcome was a shift towards family plans that protect sleep and daily functioning rather than relying on vague exhortations. That matters most at night, where the boundary problem becomes emotional. A parent can set a curfew. The real test arrives afterwards, when the child says, with total sincerity, "I can't sleep without it." The household then stands at a fork: treat the statement as manipulation and escalate, or treat it as information and design a response that protects sleep without turning bedtime into a humiliation ritual.

Listen. Then hold the line.

Sleep-related pushback is persuasive because it is partly true. Many children and teens do use sound, story, or contact to settle. They do experience the phone as a comfort object, not in the sentimental sense but in the functional one: it reduces loneliness, distracts from anxious thoughts, fills the quiet that can feel too loud. Adults also know, in their bodies, that sleep comes easier when the mind is soothed. The difficulty is that "soothing" has become tangled with "scrolling", and scrolling is not a bedtime tool; it is a doorway to endless continuation. The task is not to deny the need for comfort. It is to separate comfort from compulsion, and to do it in a way that does not teach secrecy as the price of feeling safe.

A familiar scene makes the stakes concrete. The child is in bed. The lights are low. The adult says the device must leave the room. The child's voice shifts: the protest is no longer about "unfair". It is about "need". "I need music." "I need to talk to my friends." "I need something on in the background." The adult hears bargaining. The child feels vulnerability. The named concept is *need inflation*. The explanation is that when a pleasurable habit is threatened, the mind often reclassifies the habit as a need, partly to defend it and partly because the habit has genuinely become part of the child's settling ritual. The implication is that if the adult responds with mockery or suspicion, the child learns that admitting vulnerability is unsafe. If the adult responds by surrendering the boundary entirely, the child learns that "need" is a powerful key. Both outcomes corrode trust.

The first way to handle pushback is to treat it as a design problem rather than a debate. A child who says "I need music" is not necessarily asking for a phone. They are asking for sound, predictability, and a way to keep intrusive thoughts at bay. A teen who says "I need to chat" may be asking for connection, closure, or relief from social anxiety. The show is the adult who responds to "music" by arguing about phones, and the child who responds by insisting the phone is the only possible vehicle. The named concept is *tool conflation*. The explanation is that a phone bundles many functions: music, alarms, messages, games, feeds. When a child wants one function, they reach for the object that contains all of them. The implication is that boundaries are easier to hold when the family can unbundle functions, allowing the desired function while blocking the undesired ones. Unbundling is not moralising. It is engineering the environment to match the family's priorities.

This is where replacement tools matter, not as a set of clever hacks but as a way of reducing stop friction. A phone provides music and a feed. A phone provides audiobooks and notifications. A phone provides an alarm and an endless stream of "just one more". A separate alarm, an offline playlist, or an audio device that does not carry social cues changes the emotional temperature of the boundary because it meets the child's stated need without opening the door to the capturing designs that make "just five more minutes" expand. The abstraction is *compromise,* but it becomes visible as a household choice: do we meet the need for sound or story without granting access to scrolling? The named concept is *function substitution.* The explanation is that the brain often cares about the effect, not the object; it wants comfort, not necessarily an app icon. The implication is that when families provide substitutes that genuinely deliver comfort, resistance often shifts from desperate to manageable, because the child is not being asked to face the night empty-handed.

A second named, checkable example shows how even mainstream technology companies have acknowledged the need to separate functions and embed boundaries. In September 2018, Apple released iOS 12 in Cupertino, California, introducing Screen Time features that can restrict access to certain apps while allowing others. The concrete outcome for some families was the possibility of allowing a phone to function as an alarm or a music player while reducing access to distracting apps during protected hours. The named concept is *selective access.* The explanation is that selective access reduces the argument that "I need my phone" by making it possible to say "you can have the function without the feed". The implication is not that settings solve everything. A teen can still feel resentful, and a child can still test. But selective access supports the deeper aim: meeting genuine needs without dissolving the curfew into an all-access pass.

Pushback also tends to reveal a second issue: closure. When a teen insists on messaging at night, it is often because the social day feels unfinished. Group chats do not close neatly. Friends escalate drama late at night. A teen may fear waking up to a social landscape that changed while they slept. The show is the teen who cannot leave a conversation without a sense of loss, not because they lack discipline but because the social loop remains open. The named concept is *social incompletion*. The explanation is that adolescents are highly sensitive to belonging and status, and night-time amplifies that sensitivity because the world is quieter and the phone becomes the main channel. The implication is that a boundary that ignores social incompletion will feel cruel and arbitrary to the teen, whereas a boundary that recognises it can still be firm without sounding contemptuous. Recognition is not surrender. It is part of keeping the conversation honest.

Honesty becomes the central issue when secret use appears. A parent finds a phone under a pillow, a second device hidden in a drawer, a browser history that suggests late-night scrolling. The first adult impulse is often fury, partly because the behaviour feels like a betrayal and partly because it confirms the adult's fear: the boundary is being violated when the adult is not present. The show is the late-night discovery followed by a confrontation that escalates into shame. The named concept is *detection drama*. The explanation is that families often respond to secret use as if they have caught a criminal rather than as if they have discovered a predictable outcome of a system under pressure. The implication is not to minimise the seriousness of lying. It is to recognise the cost of humiliation. Humiliation teaches better hiding, not better judgement. If the goal is safer behaviour, the response must reduce the incentive to hide while still holding accountability.

Here, the earlier discussion of coercive cycles returns with force. Secret use often develops in households where the boundary feels either too sudden, too humiliating, or too disconnected from the child's needs. A teen who expects to be mocked for wanting comfort will seek comfort privately. A child who expects punishment for failing will become skilled at evasion. The named concept is *shame-based adaptation*. The explanation is that when mistakes lead to humiliation, people protect themselves through secrecy. The implication is that a sleep boundary can be firm and still be paired with repair.

Repair is not indulgence. It is the mechanism by which accountability stays connected to relationship rather than tearing it.

A credible limitation must be faced, because not all sleep-related pushback is strategic. Some children have genuine difficulty winding down, especially during periods of anxiety, transition, or social stress. Some teens use late-night messaging as a form of emotional support, and in some cases it may be the only place they feel able to speak. Some children rely on predictable audio as a sensory anchor. The named concept is *legitimate distress*. The explanation is that adolescence and childhood contain real emotional turbulence, and a phone can become a coping tool when other coping tools are underdeveloped. The implication is that a household that treats all pushback as manipulation will miss the emotional truth and may push the child away. Reconciling this limitation does not require abandoning sleep protection. It requires offering comfort in forms that do not invite endless continuation, and maintaining a tone that does not punish vulnerability.

This is where language matters as much as infrastructure. When a child says "I can't sleep", the adult's choice of response can either widen the conflict or narrow it. A sarcastic "You'll survive" escalates shame and resistance. An anxious lecture escalates arousal. A flat refusal without acknowledgement escalates the sense of being unseen. The named concept is *tone transmission*. The explanation is that children borrow calm from adults; adults also transmit anxiety and contempt. The implication is that the household's sleep system is not only a set of rules but a nightly emotional climate. A calm routine is effective partly because it reduces the need for emotionally charged conversations at the edge of sleep.

The motif that holds this together is the bedside table. What lives on it matters. A bedside table with a phone invites checking. A bedside table with a book or a simple audio device invites a different kind of settling. The object is not magical. It is a cue. It signals what bedtime is for. If bedtime is for scrolling, the phone belongs there. If bedtime is for sleep, the phone becomes an outsider. The bedside table becomes a small stage on which the household's priorities are enacted nightly, without speeches.

A calm routine beating confrontation does not mean avoiding difficult conversations altogether. It means relocating them. The most useful conversations about night-time use tend to happen in daylight, when neither party is defending their dignity in the dark. At night, the household needs a script that is brief and repeatable, because the goal is sleep, not persuasion. The named concept is *timing of governance*. The explanation is that governance decisions made when people are regulated tend to stick, and governance decisions improvised when people are depleted tend to become fights. The implication is that the family must separate the time for policy from the time for enforcement, otherwise every bedtime becomes a policy meeting.

This brings us back to the core aim: firm boundaries with repair, not humiliation. Firm boundaries mean the household does not outsource its sleep protection to a child's mood or a teen's peer group. Repair means the household remains a place where mistakes can be admitted without losing dignity. The two are not opposites. They are mutually reinforcing. A teen is more likely to disclose a lapse if they believe the response will be proportionate and respectful. A child is more likely to accept a boundary if they believe they are still loved when they struggle.

The forward test is sharp and uncomfortably specific. When a child insists they need the phone to sleep, is the household hearing a need for comfort that can be met without opening the feed, or hearing an argument that has become habitual because it works? And when secret use is discovered, will the response teach the child to hide better, or to speak earlier next time? The bedside table will host the answer, night after night, long after the argument itself has been forgotten.

# Chapter 7
# Apps, Games, and Content Choices

A child sits on the sofa with a tablet and looks peaceful, almost studious. The adult glances over and feels a small wave of relief. Then the adult notices the child's thumb: the same quick, rhythmic flick, again and again, a movement that is not play so much as foraging. A minute later the child laughs, then frowns, then laughs again, emotions skipping like a stone across water. When the adult says it is time to stop, the child protests as if something precious is being taken away. Yet yesterday the same child spent longer drawing on a screen and handed it over without a fuss. The adult is left with a question that feels naïve and urgent at once: why do some screen activities end cleanly and others end like a cliff?

Not all screens are equal.

This is the chapter where "screen time" stops being a useful phrase. Time is a crude measure. A tool used to make something, to learn something, to coordinate a friendship, or to compete intensely does not land in the mind in the same way, even if the clock shows the same duration. Families often sense this intuitively, yet their rules remain blunt because blunt rules are easier to state. The cost of bluntness is predictable: children argue, parents feel arbitrary, and the household ends up fighting about minutes instead of shaping the digital environment so it is easier to live with. The more precise question is not "How much?" but "What kind, in what conditions, with what pull?"

The central tension is between neutrality and discernment. Parents and carers know that screens can be genuinely useful, socially important, and creatively enriching. They also know that some apps and feeds are designed to keep a user checking, reacting, and staying longer than intended. Discernment can tip into paranoia. Neutrality can tip into drift. Drift is where families lose control without noticing, because a device does not need to be evil to become the default. The trade-off is not between being permissive and being strict. It is between governing the digital environment intentionally and letting the loudest designs set the household's mood, sleep, and attention by default.

This matters because content choices shape emotion as well as time. A child can move through an evening in a stable mood and then become irritable, restless, or fixated after an intense competitive session or a scrolling binge. A teen can feel steady and then become anxious or agitated after a run of social comparison or group chat drama. These shifts are often treated as "attitude", and then families argue about character. That misreading is expensive. It wastes energy on blame and leaves the actual causes untouched. When families learn to name what is happening on the screen and what it tends to do to the child afterwards, they gain a lever that is calmer than shouting: they can shape inputs instead of policing outputs.

It also matters because many of the most effective limits are inside the platforms themselves, not in a parent's ultimatum. A home screen full of badges and auto-play is a system designed to summon attention constantly. A home screen that is quiet, with fewer triggers and clearer edges, is a different system entirely. The household often treats this as a technical detail, yet it is governance in disguise. If a child can be pulled back into an app by a red dot, a push notification, or an endless feed, then the family is not only managing "use"; it is managing a landscape of cues. The best plans reduce cue density. They do not rely solely on a child to resist cues hundreds of times a day.

The social layer complicates everything, because screens are not merely content delivery systems. They are social rooms, and social rooms carry obligations. A rule that limits entertainment can be enforced with relative ease. A rule that limits messaging can feel, to a child or teen, like cutting them off from their tribe. When adults ignore that emotional reality, they create pushback that looks irrational from the outside and feels existential from the inside. Yet ignoring the social layer is not an option. Group chats have their own gravity. Social features can create late-night spirals, rapid escalations, and reputational damage that outlasts the moment. A household that does not set expectations around messaging times and digital kindness leaves children to learn those rules from peers, and peers are not hired to be wise.

Then there is the matter adults dread most: the content that should not be there, but sometimes is. Mature or risky content does not require a panicked household to become safer. It requires a predictable response that makes disclosure more likely than secrecy. Panic trains hiding. Humiliation trains lying. A calm, clear boundary with a response plan trains something rarer and more valuable: a child who comes to an adult when something goes wrong. If the family reacts as if the child is guilty for encountering what they did not seek, the child learns not to mention it next time. Silence becomes the risk.

The movement through this chapter follows the logic of a household trying to govern an environment rather than fight it. It begins by sorting digital experiences by purpose, because purpose predicts how an activity affects mood and stopping. It then turns to the internal mechanics that make certain apps more gripping than others, and to the settings that can change the pull without changing the family's values. It then faces the social layer directly, where belonging and conflict live together, and where timing rules can protect sleep and dignity. It ends with the question of red lines and response plans, because the household's reaction to risky content often determines whether children will speak up or go silent.

A quiet motif can anchor the whole chapter: the red dot. That small badge on an icon is an invitation and a claim. It says something is waiting. It says you are behind. It makes a neutral phone feel like a to-do list with social consequences. When the red dot is everywhere, the child learns to scan. When it is reduced or removed, the mind becomes quieter. The dot is not the problem, but it is a symbol of the deeper issue: a digital environment that continually recruits attention, often without the user's deliberate consent.

The unresolved question is not whether a family can ban particular apps. Bans can be declared quickly. The harder question is whether the household can learn to see digital experiences clearly enough to choose them deliberately, shaping the device so it serves the child rather than training the child to serve it. When a child begs for "just one more", what exactly is calling them back: the purpose of the activity, the platform's triggers, the social obligation, or the fear of missing something that feels urgent? The answer determines whether the family is governing content choices with intention, or simply negotiating with a red dot that never sleeps.

## Deciding what is allowed

In September 2018, Apple released iOS 12 in Cupertino, California, and Screen Time turned a private household question into a visible interface: what, exactly, counts as acceptable use? The concrete outcome in many homes was not a simple reduction in screen hours, but a sharper awareness that "screen time" is not one activity. A child can spend an evening making a comic strip and hand the device back cheerfully. The same child can spend far less time in a video feed and react as if the device is being confiscated mid-breath. A parent who treats both as identical will feel constantly baffled.

Not all use is equal.

That bafflement is often mislabelled as inconsistency in the child's character. It is more accurately inconsistency in the activity's purpose and design. A device is a container, and containers hide differences. A tablet contains a drawing tool, a messaging room, a shopping window, a casino of variable rewards, and a stage for social performance, all behind the same glass. If a family's rules remain focused on the container alone, the child learns a single lesson: what matters is whether an adult notices, not what the child is actually doing. That is a poor lesson for adulthood. The more mature lesson is discernment: choosing intentionally among kinds of digital experience, because different kinds produce different after-effects in mood, attention, and willingness to stop.

A useful classification begins with purpose rather than with brand names, partly because brands change and partly because purpose is what the brain responds to. Four purposes capture most everyday use with enough clarity to be governable without becoming legalistic: create, connect, consume, compete. The categories are not moral labels. They are behavioural maps. They help a family move from vague arguments about "too much screen time" to observable patterns about what a child does, how long it holds them, how they emerge afterwards, and how hard it is to end. Purpose becomes the bridge between values and rules: the household knows what it protects, and it can then ask which digital purposes support those protections and which routinely undermine them.

Creation is the easiest purpose to misread because it often looks like "just screen time" from across the room. Yet creation behaves differently from many other forms of use. The show is the child making something: drawing, editing a short video, building a level, composing music, coding, writing a story. The named concept is *productive engagement*. The explanation is that creation typically contains natural stopping points: a saved file, a finished sketch, a completed draft, a satisfying endpoint that feels like closure rather than interruption. The implication is visible in the handover. A child who has made something can often stop with less protest because they are not being pulled away from an endless stream; they are leaving a finished object behind. The emotional aftertaste is often pride or calm rather than agitation. This does not make creation inherently virtuous. It makes it structurally easier to govern.

A checkable example from outside the domestic scene helps illustrate why purpose matters. In April 1984, Apple introduced the Macintosh in Cupertino, California, famously positioning the personal computer as a tool for individuals to make and design rather than merely to receive information. The concrete outcome, culturally, was the strengthening of a narrative: computers as creative instruments, not only as channels. The named concept is *tool framing*. The explanation is that people behave differently when they experience a device as a tool for making rather than as a pipe for content. The implication for family rules is not nostalgia for early computing. It is a reminder that "screen" is not destiny. The same glass can amplify agency when it is used to produce, and it can erode agency when it is used primarily to absorb.

Connection is the category families fear mismanaging most, because it touches belonging. Connection includes messaging, group chats, video calls, shared games, and the ambient social checking that keeps many adolescents tethered to their peer world. The show is the child who wants to reply quickly, who checks repeatedly, who feels slighted when left on read, who becomes anxious when excluded. The named concept is *social obligation*. The explanation is that connection is not only "fun"; it is a form of maintenance work in friendships, and the costs of ignoring it can be real inside a child's social ecology. The implication is that a family that bans connection indiscriminately may not simply reduce screen time; it may reduce a child's social participation, which can increase resentment and secrecy. Yet connection is also the category most likely to intrude into protected household goods, especially sleep, because the social world does not politely stop at bedtime.

Consumption is the category that most often turns "just five more minutes" into a long drift, because it is engineered for continuation. Consumption includes endless feeds, auto-play video, recommendation-driven platforms, rapid scrolling, and the kind of content that requires almost nothing from the user besides attention. The show is the thumb flick, the half-laugh, the quick mood shifts, the glazed resistance when asked to stop. The named concept is *passive absorption*. The explanation is that consumption platforms often remove stopping cues and maximise novelty, which increases stop friction and makes time awareness blur. The implication is not that consumption is always harmful. People relax through stories. People learn through documentaries. The implication is that consumption without clear edges and without deliberate choice is the form most likely to displace sleep, movement, chores, and casual talk, because it asks so little and offers so much.

A second checkable example makes the design of consumption harder to deny. In September 2006, Facebook introduced the News Feed in Menlo Park, California, shifting many users from visiting individual profiles to receiving an endless stream of updates. The concrete outcome included widely reported user backlash at the time and, more importantly, a durable product pattern: the feed as default. The named concept is *stream design*. The explanation is that a stream is never finished, so the user never receives the psychological relief of completion. The implication for families is not about any one platform. It is about the logic of feeds wherever they appear. A child placed in a feed-heavy environment is not merely choosing entertainment; they are entering a system that is structurally resistant to endings.

Competition is the category that creates the most confusion because it can look like either healthy challenge or emotional volatility, sometimes in the same hour. Competition includes multiplayer games, ranked ladders, streak-based systems, and any environment where status is quantified and visible. The show is the child who is intensely engaged, then furious, then euphoric, then unable to stop because "the match is nearly over" or "my team needs me". The named concept is *status activation*. The explanation is that competition recruits social identity and competence, which can be deeply motivating, especially for children who crave a clear sense of progress and recognition. The implication is that competitive use can be developmentally rich and also uniquely disruptive if it bleeds into bedtime, homework, or sibling dynamics. Competition tends to produce stronger protest at stopping because stopping can feel like abandoning a team, losing a streak, or forfeiting status. It is not merely "a game". It is a social commitment layered onto a reward loop.

These categories are deliberately plain. Their value lies in what they allow a family to notice. A parent who observes a child's post-use mood can begin to distinguish purposes without needing to spy. A child who leaves creation calmer and consumption more agitated is giving data. A teen who can stop a creative project cleanly but spirals in group chat drama is giving data. Data does not dictate morality. It makes governance possible. The named concept is *after-effect reading*. The explanation is that the body and mood often reveal what the mind is reluctant to admit: which activities restore, which destabilise, which tempt repeated checking. The implication is that rules can be grounded in observable outcomes rather than in adult taste. A household can say, with credibility, that certain forms are harder to stop and therefore require tighter boundaries, not because the adult dislikes them but because the evidence in the home shows predictable friction.

A quiet motif can help tie the whole exercise together: the red dot. The badge on an icon is small and absurdly powerful. It signals incompletion. It claims urgency. It turns an optional app into a pending task. In the create category, the red dot is often absent; you return when you choose. In connect, it is frequently present; someone is waiting. In consume, it is omnipresent, because the platform's business model depends on return. In compete, it appears as a status marker: your rank, your streak, your reward. The red dot is not evil. It is a cue. The household that can see cues as cues can stop treating children as morally defective for responding to them.

Still, there is a limitation that must be handled honestly: purpose is not always pure. Many apps blend categories by design. A platform can invite creation while also promoting consumption through an endless feed of other people's creations. A game can be a creative sandbox and a competitive ladder at once. A messaging app can be connection and consumption when it becomes a channel for memes and drama. The named concept is *category blending*. The explanation is that modern platforms often increase engagement by moving users between modes, keeping them inside one environment even as their activity shifts. The implication is that a family cannot simply label an app "allowed" or "banned" and be done. It must govern the modes of use. That governance can be achieved through context and settings, but the deeper point is conceptual: the child is not choosing a brand, they are moving between purposes.

Reconciling this limitation is precisely why purpose-based classification is more robust than content-based moralising. If a platform contains both creation and endless consumption, the household can ask which mode dominates in practice and which mode produces the outcomes the family wants. If a game produces both cooperation and rage, the household can notice the conditions under which rage spikes: late nights, long sessions, ranked modes, peer pressure. If a chat supports connection and also triggers anxiety, the household can notice whether the anxiety clusters at certain times, especially at night. The categories become lenses, not cages. They help families see what is happening without pretending digital life is neatly separable.

This approach also reframes a familiar child argument: "But it's educational." Education is not a magical property that makes a screen harmless. Education is a purpose, and it can exist inside create, connect, consume, and compete. A child can learn by creating, by connecting with peers, by consuming high-quality material, and even by competing in ways that build problem-solving. The abstraction is *learning*, but it becomes visible as behaviour: sustained attention, curiosity, retention, the ability to stop without rage, the willingness to return to offline tasks without collapse. The named concept is *learning signal*. The explanation is that educational value is not merely the label on an app but the quality of engagement it produces. The implication is that families who accept "educational" as a blanket permission often find themselves permitting endless consumption in the name of learning, because the word is too broad to govern.

A further implication touches dignity. Children comply more readily when rules feel intelligent rather than arbitrary. A purpose-based system communicates respect: the household is paying attention to what the child is actually doing, not merely to the existence of a screen. That respect matters especially for older children and teens, who experience blunt restrictions as infantilising. The named concept is *adult credibility*. The explanation is that credibility grows when a parent's rule matches reality: some activities are harder to stop because they are built to continue; some are easier because they end. The implication is that credibility reduces bargaining. Children bargain hardest when they believe the adult does not understand the terrain.

The red dot returns because it offers a diagnostic test that is surprisingly revealing. When a child asks for a screen, what are they really asking for: to make, to connect, to consume, or to compete? When they resist stopping, what is resisting: a creative project that wants closure, a social thread that feels urgent, a feed that has no end, a game that has a team waiting? The categories help separate reasonable needs from engineered pulls. They also help families avoid a common trap: blaming the child for what the environment is doing to the child.

The unresolved tension at the end of this subchapter is not whether families can classify apps neatly. They cannot. The tension is whether a household is willing to govern by purpose rather than by panic. When the next conflict begins and a child insists that a screen is "just relaxing", will the family be able to name which purpose is actually in play, what it tends to do to mood and time awareness in this particular child, and whether the red dot is calling them back for a reason the family has chosen or for a reason a platform has chosen?

## Setting limits inside platforms

In September 2018, Apple released iOS 12 in Cupertino, California, and Screen Time made a quiet promise to exhausted households: a device could help enforce the boundary it had spent years encouraging users to cross. The concrete outcome was visible on lock screens everywhere. Time could be tracked. Apps could be limited. Downtime could be scheduled. Many parents felt, briefly, that they had acquired a new kind of authority. Many children felt, briefly, that they were being policed by a machine. Both reactions were reasonable. Both missed the deeper point. A time limit alone does not change the way an app pulls; it only changes when the app is forced to stop.

Limits need architecture.

To govern screens effectively, families must stop treating apps as neutral boxes that simply contain content. Apps are environments with built-in cues, loops, and friction patterns. They are designed to make starting effortless and stopping effortful. A household that sets a daily limit but leaves those patterns intact is like a household that tries to reduce snacking by buying a smaller packet and leaving it open on the counter.

The packet ends sooner, but the urge is still being triggered constantly. The named concept here is *cue exposure*. The explanation is that behaviour is strongly shaped by how often a cue appears and how much action the cue demands. The implication is that the household will still spend its evenings in negotiation, because the child will still be repeatedly prompted to re-enter the app, and repeated prompting is what keeps "just one more" alive.

The most important shift is to think in two directions at once: add *start friction* and add *stop ease*. Start friction means making it slightly harder to begin the most capturing activities, especially those that lead to drift. Stop ease means making it simpler to end an activity cleanly without cliff-edge conflict. These are not moral categories. They are design categories. The show is the child who can open a feed in a single tap and then becomes furious when asked to stop, because the experience has been built as a smooth slide into endless continuation. The named concept is *asymmetrical friction*. The explanation is that many apps minimise the cost of starting and maximise the cost of stopping by removing endings and filling the screen with prompts. The implication is that time limits feel punitive because they arrive as abrupt interruption rather than as a natural close. The family experiences more conflict, not less, because the "stop" event is emotionally sharper.

A clean home screen is a surprisingly powerful intervention because it changes what the child encounters first. The show is the child unlocking a phone and seeing a wall of tempting icons and bright badges, each one signalling something unfinished. The named concept is *attention priming*. The explanation is that the first visual field sets the agenda; it determines which cues get to speak. The implication is that if the home screen is designed by default for maximum engagement, the child will be pulled towards the same apps repeatedly even when they intended something else. A clean home screen reduces accidental drift. It also reduces arguments about "I just opened it without thinking", because the environment is less likely to trigger reflex checking.

Badges are the small red dots of modern life, and they deserve to be treated as behavioural technology rather than decoration. A badge says: you are behind. It creates a sense of incompletion. It invites checking that feels responsible, even when it is merely habitual. The show is the child who cannot tolerate the badge sitting there, whose hand moves before the mind catches up. The named concept is *incompletion cueing*. The explanation is rooted in the same unfinished-task psychology that makes open loops sticky: the mind allocates attention to what feels unresolved. The implication is that a family can reduce compulsive checking by reducing the visibility of unresolved signals, especially in non-essential apps. This is not about making the phone boring. It is about lowering the number of false emergencies the device announces each day.

Notifications are badges that travel. They reach into dinner, homework, car rides, and bedtime. They are the mechanism by which an app refuses to stay in its own lane. The show is the buzz during a family conversation, the flash on a lock screen, the teen's quick glance that breaks the moment. The named concept is *interruptive design*. The explanation is that notifications convert optional engagement into demanded attention by making the user feel they might miss something socially or practically important. The implication is that any plan that ignores notifications is asking a child to resist temptation repeatedly across the day, which is both cognitively expensive and developmentally unfair. Families can reduce conflict not by urging children to be stronger, but by reducing the number of times the environment pokes them.

Auto-play is another design choice with a direct household consequence. A video that ends and then begins another removes the pause where a child might stop voluntarily. The show is the child who says "I didn't mean to keep watching" while the platform keeps rolling. The named concept is *pause removal*. The explanation is that people stop more easily when a system offers a natural break, and auto-play erases those breaks. The implication is that removing auto-play, where possible, is not a technical detail. It is a way of restoring the micro-moments in which choice can occur. Choice is easier when it is invited. It is harder when it is swallowed by continuation.

A named, checkable example illustrates how these ideas entered mainstream device settings. In September 2018, Apple's Screen Time was paired with features like Downtime and App Limits, making it feasible to schedule periods when the device is less inviting. The concept is *scheduled scarcity*. The explanation is that scarcity, when predictable, reduces argument because it is not experienced as a personal judgement in the moment. The implication is that families can move away from constant verbal enforcement by using schedules and settings to create a predictable rhythm. Rhythm matters more than strictness. Rhythm reduces bargaining.

A second named, checkable example comes from the social feed model itself. In September 2006, Facebook introduced the News Feed in Menlo Park, California, establishing the now-familiar pattern of a continuously updating stream. The concept is *feed perpetuity*. The explanation is that a perpetually updating feed offers no completion and therefore no natural stopping point. The implication is that platform-level settings and household-level rules must do some of the work that the app refuses to do: create endings. This is why "stop ease" is as important as "start friction". If a child is trapped in a stream with no edge, the parent becomes the edge, and children resent edges that arrive as confiscation.

There is a mistake families often make at this stage: they try to solve everything with a single global time limit. Time limits are useful, but they are blunt. They do not distinguish between creating a school presentation and binge-watching clips. They do not distinguish between sending a message to coordinate a school project and spiralling in a group chat. When time limits are applied without discernment, children experience them as unfair and therefore feel justified in bypassing them. The named concept is *perceived injustice*. The explanation is that people comply with limits more readily when the limits feel legitimate, and legitimacy depends on proportionality and purpose. The implication is that platform-level settings should be aligned with the purpose-based approach from the previous section: some activities need tighter friction, others need less. Without that alignment, families will spend their energy arguing about exceptions rather than shaping the environment.

A credible limitation must be faced because platform controls are not neutral. They can create their own problems. Teens, especially, can interpret controls as surveillance or infantilisation. Children can become fixated on the countdown, turning the limit into a source of anxiety. Families can become overly dependent on tools and neglect the relational work of explaining values and maintaining trust. The named concept is *tool backlash*. The explanation is that constraints imposed by a device can feel cold and humiliating, particularly if they cut off social connection abruptly. The implication is not to abandon tools. It is to use them as scaffolding rather than as punishment. Scaffolding supports skill-building. Punishment invites rebellion.

Reconciling this limitation requires returning to the design principle rather than the gadget. Start friction and stop ease are concepts that can be applied with or without a particular operating system. They can be implemented through home screen design, notification management, app selection, and routine timing. The show is the family that reduces the number of prompts rather than merely reducing the allowed minutes. The named concept is *temptation reduction*. The explanation is that fewer triggers produce fewer reflexive checks, which reduces both screen use and conflict. The implication is that when the environment is quieter, the child is not being asked to perform constant self-control. They can reserve self-control for harder developmental tasks, such as homework, sibling conflict, and emotional regulation.

The motif that holds this together is the red dot. It is the emblem of low-level urgency, the tiny signal that turns an optional app into a psychological loose end. A phone covered in red dots is a device that demands. A phone with fewer dots is a device that waits. Waiting is a moral good in design terms. It lets the person choose. When the device waits, the child has a chance to practise agency rather than reflex. When the device demands, the child practises compliance to cues, and the household practises conflict about those cues.

Notice how this changes the role of the adult. The adult becomes less of a police officer and more of a curator of the child's digital environment. Curation is not about controlling every experience. It is about shaping the default conditions under which experiences occur. The show is the adult who stops fighting the child at the point of use and instead modifies the environment so the most capturing triggers are less present. The named concept is *upstream governance*. The explanation is that upstream changes reduce downstream conflict. The implication is that the adult's attention is spent once, setting conditions, rather than spent repeatedly, arguing.

A further implication concerns dignity. Children and teens resent being told they cannot manage themselves, and many adults resent feeling they must manage endlessly. Platform-level settings can be framed as support rather than suspicion when they are presented as part of the household's system for protecting sleep, attention, and kindness. The named concept is *shared constraint*. The explanation is that constraints feel less punitive when everyone lives with them, and when their purpose is a protected good rather than adult preference. The implication is that adults who also reduce their own notifications and remove their own badges will often find their children less combative, because the household is no longer arguing about power alone. It is arguing about norms.

The unresolved tension is that every reduction in triggers is also a reduction in immediacy, and immediacy is exactly what many children and teens crave, especially socially. A phone that does not buzz may feel safer for sleep and attention, but it may feel risky for belonging. A feed that does not auto-play may feel calmer, but it may feel less fun. The forward test is therefore not whether the family can find the right settings menu, but whether it can decide where to place friction: at the beginning, to prevent accidental drift, or at the end, through constant conflict. When the red dot appears again and the child reaches reflexively, will the environment invite a pause, or will the household be forced to create a pause through another argument?

## Social features and group chats

In January 2009, WhatsApp was founded in Mountain View, California, and a concrete shift followed for ordinary users: messaging became less like a phone call you deliberately placed and more like a room you could enter, leave, and re-enter at will. A conversation could persist without a meeting. It could also persist without sleep. For families, that persistence is the point of friction. A child can be physically at home and socially elsewhere, because the social room never closes. The phone is not only a screen. It is a door.

Friends do not log off neatly.

That is why messaging limits feel different from limits on games or videos. A parent can say "time's up" to a single-player game and, with enough practice, the child can accept the ending as an ending. A group chat does not end. It moves without you. It jokes, argues, plans, excludes, reconciles, and changes tone while you are brushing your teeth. A child who is told to stop messaging may not hear "stop using a device".

They may hear "leave the room while everyone else stays inside". The rule is interpreted as social risk, not merely as time management. If a family does not understand that emotional meaning, it will misread resistance as manipulation and respond with moral language that invites secrecy.

The social layer is also where many adults underestimate intensity. Children and teens are not only consuming content; they are maintaining a place in a group. That place is fragile, especially in early adolescence, and it can feel as if it must be defended continuously. The show is the child who checks repeatedly during dinner, not because dinner is boring, but because silence in the chat feels risky. The named concept is *ambient obligation*. The explanation is that modern social features create a constant low-level expectation of responsiveness, reinforced by read receipts, typing indicators, streaks, and visible online presence. The implication is that a household limit that ignores ambient obligation will be experienced as arbitrary and may provoke either argument or covert checking, because the child feels they are being asked to absorb social cost for an adult's comfort.

A second show appears at night. A teen is in bed, lights off, phone in hand. They insist they are "just chatting". The parent suspects the chat is a pretext for scrolling. Both may be right. Group chats are not only conversation; they are also distribution systems for memes, links, clips, gossip, and conflict. The named concept is *mode blending*. The explanation is that the same channel carries connection and consumption, and the child's brain slides between them without noticing. The implication is that families who treat messaging as either "good social life" or "bad screen time" will miss the reality: messaging is a social platform with content dynamics, and it can amplify both connection and compulsion.

This is where "messaging times" stop being petty and start being protective. Messaging is emotionally charged because it is relational. Yet sleep is upstream of everything the household wants to preserve, including the teen's ability to handle that relational world with judgement. The show is the morning after a late-night chat spiral: tiredness, irritability, drama that feels larger than it is. The named concept is *temporal vulnerability*. The explanation is that fatigue narrows perspective and lowers impulse control, which makes teens more likely to post quickly, react harshly, and misread tone. The implication is that a family rule like "no messaging after curfew" is not primarily an attempt to control friendships. It is an attempt to protect the conditions under which friendships can be managed without constant crisis.

A named, checkable example from the design history of social platforms illustrates why group dynamics feel so relentless. In September 2006, Facebook introduced the News Feed in Menlo Park, California, shifting social life from something one visited to something that visited you, continuously. The named concept is *continuous social visibility*. The explanation is that a feed converts other people's activity into a steady stream, and a steady stream creates the feeling that one is always behind. The implication for group chats is clear: even without a formal "feed", the chat itself becomes a feed. Messages arrive in a cascade. The child's social mind interprets the cascade as information that must be monitored. The pressure to keep up becomes a habit, and habits do not disappear at bedtime simply because an adult says they should.

If the social layer is the problem, the family's response must also live in the social layer. That does not mean adults must become teens or invade private messages as a hobby. It means the household must govern three observable dimensions: timing, access, and conduct. Timing is about when messaging happens. Access is about who can contact the child and in which contexts. Conduct is about how the child behaves in these spaces and how the family responds when behaviour goes wrong. These dimensions are not moral abstractions. They are visible patterns that affect sleep, mood, and trust.

Timing is the easiest to discuss and the hardest to enforce if the household has not already built credible bedtime protections. A child who can message indefinitely will resist a sudden cut-off because it feels like being thrown out of a room mid-sentence. A child who expects a consistent curfew will still be disappointed, but the disappointment becomes more manageable because the boundary is a known feature of the day rather than a personal rejection. The named concept is *predictable constraint*. The explanation is that predictability reduces bargaining. The implication is that a "no messaging after curfew" norm works best when it is nested in the wider sleep protections established earlier: devices have a home at night, endings are enacted earlier, and the adult is not forced into a late-night confrontation to make the rule real.

Access is more delicate because it touches privacy and trust. The question is not whether children should have friends. The question is whether the device should function as an always-open front door into the child's bedroom. The show is the child receiving messages from many directions, some benign, some intrusive, some intense, and the adult realising they have no clear shared expectation about who can contact the child late or how drama is handled. The named concept is *contact governance*. The explanation is that social platforms and messaging apps make it easy for a group to expand, for new people to appear, and for conflict to spread quickly. The implication is that a household that never discusses contact governance is leaving the child to improvise boundaries under peer pressure, which is rarely where good judgement flourishes.

Conduct is where families often become either moralistic or silent. The moralistic version arrives as lectures about "being kind online" that remain too vague to guide real behaviour. The silent version arrives as avoidance, because adults fear sounding out of touch. Neither helps when the child is about to press send in a moment of anger. The show is the impulsive message typed quickly, then regretted. The named concept is *frictionless publishing*. The explanation is that screens lower the pause between feeling and expression, and group chats amplify this by adding audience and speed. The implication is that families must treat kindness not as a mood but as a set of behaviours that can be practised, especially around tone, timing, and what is shared.

This is where the motif of the screenshot becomes useful, not as a threat but as an accuracy tool. A child can treat a message as "just between friends", yet the technology makes it portable. The screenshot turns a private moment into an artefact. The show is a joke shared beyond its intended context, a snide comment preserved, a moment of anger replayed. The named concept is *trace persistence*. The explanation is that digital speech leaves records that can be copied and moved, changing the social meaning of a moment. The implication is not to frighten children into silence. It is to help the household recognise why certain rules about respect and restraint matter: they protect the child's reputation and relationships from errors that become harder to repair once they are captured.

A common family mistake is to respond to social drama with either blanket bans or total resignation. Blanket bans often backfire because they remove the child from ordinary peer coordination, which can increase isolation and push the child towards secret accounts or secondary devices. Total resignation backfires because it leaves the child alone with group pressure that can be intense and, at times, cruel. The named concept is *false dichotomy*. The explanation is that families imagine only two options because both are emotionally simple: control everything or control nothing. The implication is that a workable approach requires nuance without surveillance: clear timing expectations, clear conduct expectations, and a calm plan for what happens when the chat becomes a problem.

The calm plan matters because social drama tends to arrive suddenly and demand immediate action. A child comes to a parent upset because someone was unkind, or because they were excluded, or because a rumour is spreading. Adults often respond with a burst of panic: "Give me the phone", "We're deleting everything", "I'm calling their parents." Panic can feel protective. It can also teach the child that bringing problems to adults leads to loss of autonomy and public humiliation. The named concept is *disclosure cost*. The explanation is that children weigh the cost of telling an adult against the cost of handling it alone. The implication is that families who want children to come to them need a response style that protects without overreacting, because overreaction trains silence.

A credible limitation deserves attention here. Some group chats are supportive, practical, and emotionally important. They coordinate homework. They maintain friendships across distance. They provide a place to be silly, to belong, to process the day. For some children, particularly those who find face-to-face interaction draining, messaging can be a form of connection that feels manageable. The named concept is *functional connection*. The explanation is that digital social life is not inherently lesser than offline social life; it is different, and sometimes it is the channel through which a child can participate at all. The implication is that a household that treats all messaging as risky will push the child towards secrecy or loneliness, neither of which improves judgement or wellbeing.

Reconciling that limitation requires distinguishing between connection that integrates with life and connection that colonises it. Integration shows up as observable patterns: the child can pause, return to the room, and sleep without panic. Colonisation shows up differently: the child cannot stop checking, becomes volatile when interrupted, and treats bedtime as an assault. The screenshot motif helps here too. In healthier connection, the child is less likely to post in ways they would be ashamed to see captured and shared. In colonising connection, impulsive posting becomes more common because the teen is responding to speed and audience pressure rather than to considered values.

This is also where platform settings and household norms intersect. "No messaging after curfew" is easier to live with when notifications are quiet, badges are reduced, and the phone is not physically present in bed. The show is the difference between a teen who must resist constant pings and a teen who is not being pinged. The named concept is *temptation reduction*. The explanation is that fewer cues reduce compulsive checking, which reduces conflict. The implication is that social boundaries are not sustained by speeches about maturity. They are sustained by environments that do not continually provoke the very behaviour the family is trying to limit.

The household also needs to understand the emotional economy of group chats. Teens often fear that not replying makes them look rude or irrelevant. Children often fear missing a joke that will be referenced tomorrow. The adult who dismisses these fears as trivial loses credibility, because the fears are not trivial within the child's peer system. The named concept is *peer norm gravity*. The explanation is that peer norms shape behaviour through inclusion and exclusion, and those forces are powerful in adolescence. The implication is that adults should not argue that the peer system is unimportant; they should argue, instead, that sleep and dignity are more important than late-night responsiveness, and they should make that argument in a tone that does not belittle the child's world.

The screenshot returns as a final anchor because it provides a simple diagnostic question about conduct without turning into a sermon. Before a message is sent, a child can be helped to consider whether they would be comfortable if the message were captured and shown to someone else. The point is not paranoia. It is foresight. The named concept is *future-self protection*. The explanation is that adolescents are learning to manage reputational risk, and a small pause can prevent a large regret. The implication is that families can protect both kindness and reputation by building norms that slow down impulsive posting, especially late at night when fatigue makes judgement shakier.

The unresolved tension at the end of this subchapter is that social life resists household schedules. Friends message when they feel like it. Group chats flare up at inconvenient hours. Drama does not respect bedtime. A family cannot control the peer system. It can control whether the child must be permanently available to it. The forward test is sharp: when the next late-night message arrives and the child feels pulled, will the household's expectations protect sleep and dignity without shaming the child's need to belong, or will the family be forced back into a nightly argument where the phone is treated as contraband and the screenshot becomes, not a caution, but the symbol of a trust already cracking?

## Handling mature or risky content

In November 2017, The New York Times in New York published reporting on what became widely known as "Elsagate": disturbing, adult-themed videos masquerading as children's content on YouTube, circulated through recommendation loops and innocuous thumbnails. The concrete outcome was not that the internet became safe overnight, but that many parents suddenly grasped a hard truth about modern media: exposure is often accidental, and the boundary between "for children" and "not for children" can be porous when platforms optimise for clicks rather than care. A child does not need to go looking for trouble to find it. Sometimes trouble arrives dressed as a cartoon.

Panic makes children hide.

That is the central discipline of this subchapter. Families cannot control every encounter, and they should not pretend they can. They can control what happens next: whether a child learns that disclosure leads to safety and learning, or that disclosure leads to shame and interrogation. A calm response plan is not softness. It is a way of keeping the line between parent and child intact when the digital world does something abrupt and confusing. If a child expects an adult to explode, the child will stay quiet. Silence is the real hazard.

Mature or risky content takes many forms, and the family must be careful not to reduce everything to a single category of "bad". Some content is obviously inappropriate for a child's age. Some is manipulative, designed to frighten or hook. Some is adult in tone or theme without being overt. Some is predatory in its social layer: messages that pressure, isolate, or coerce. Some is simply too much, too soon. The show, in a home, is rarely a neatly labelled problem. It is a child's face changing; it is sudden secrecy; it is an awkward joke repeated from an older peer; it is a browser tab slammed shut when an adult enters the room; it is the teen who becomes brittle and defensive when asked what they are watching. The named concept here is *unplanned exposure*. The explanation is straightforward. Devices deliver content through feeds, recommendations, and shares, and these systems do not care about a household's values unless the household builds barriers and routines that reduce exposure and increase disclosure. The implication is that a family's real safety advantage is not omniscience. It is a child who comes to the adult quickly.

This is why "red lines" need to be defined, not as a moral sermon but as a household safety policy. Red lines are the non-negotiables that the family agrees will trigger action, not debate. Without red lines, every difficult moment becomes an improvisation, and improvisation is where adults overreact and children learn to hide. The show is the parent discovering something upsetting and responding with a flurry of accusations, threats, and blanket bans that are later softened out of guilt. The named concept is *reactive governance*. The explanation is that when adults respond in the heat of shock, they tend to either moralise ("What's wrong with you?") or catastrophise ("You'll never have a phone again"). The implication is that the child learns the adult is not safe to approach with confusion, curiosity, or mistakes. The parent's reaction becomes part of the risk environment.

A red line should be expressed as behaviour, not as identity. "We do not watch X" is a behavioural boundary. "You are disgusting for watching X" is an identity attack. The difference is not politeness. It is the difference between a child learning a safety norm and a child learning shame. The named concept is *dignity preservation*. The explanation is that dignity is a prerequisite for honest conversation. When a child feels humiliated, they stop cooperating and start managing impressions. The implication is that a family can hold a firm boundary while still communicating, in tone and language, that the child is not "bad" for encountering something unexpected or for being curious about the world. Curiosity is not the enemy. Secrecy is.

The practical question is how a child's disclosure is rewarded. If disclosure reliably leads to screaming, confiscation, and long interrogations, disclosure will disappear. If disclosure reliably leads to calm attention, a predictable next step, and a proportionate response, disclosure becomes more likely next time. The abstraction is *trust*, but it becomes visible in a simple metric: whether the child comes to an adult quickly when something feels wrong. The named concept is *disclosure incentive*. The explanation is behavioural. People repeat actions that lead to safety and reduce pain. The implication is that a predictable response is not merely a parenting style; it is an incentive structure for honesty.

A calm response plan begins by separating three questions that adults often collapse into one: what happened, what is the immediate safety concern, and what will change next time. Collapsing them produces melodrama. Separating them produces clarity. The show is the child who is frightened or embarrassed and the adult who is tempted to demand a full account immediately. The named concept is *sequenced response*. The explanation is that a frightened or ashamed child cannot give a coherent narrative under pressure, and pressure increases the chance of lying. The implication is that families who want the truth should not behave like prosecutors. They should behave like steady adults: secure immediate safety, then return to the meaning-making when everyone is calmer.

This is also where content categories matter. A household might decide that some kinds of content are simply out of bounds, full stop. That is a legitimate red line, provided it is tied to a protected good such as wellbeing, development, or kindness, and provided the household's response does not become punitive theatre. Other kinds of content may be "not for now", which is different from "never", and that difference matters for teenagers, who can sense when adults are pretending that adolescence can be paused. The named concept is *developmental timing*. The explanation is that maturity is not a switch; it is a gradient. The implication is that a calm plan can distinguish between what is categorically prohibited and what is deferred, without becoming vague. Vague rules invite bargaining. Clear timing reduces it.

The social layer is often the most dangerous part, not because every message is predatory, but because social pressure can coerce children into choices they do not fully understand. A child can be pressured to share personal information, to keep secrets, to move a conversation to a private channel, or to accept contact from strangers. A teen can be pulled into escalating drama, risky dares, or cruel group behaviour. The show is not necessarily an obvious "bad person". It is a pattern: secrecy requests, urgency, flattery, isolation, escalation. The named concept is *coercive messaging*. The explanation is that digital contact can bypass the adult's presence and exploit the child's need to belong. The implication is that families need red lines around contact as well as content, and they need to treat contact breaches as safety events, not moral failures.

A second checkable example illustrates why "platform safety" is not a stable guarantee. In September 2019, YouTube announced changes to how it handles children's content in response to a settlement with the U.S. Federal Trade Commission concerning data practices on the platform. The concrete outcome, again, was not a frictionless safe internet. It was a reminder that platforms change policies under pressure, and families experience the downstream effects without being consulted. The named concept is *platform volatility*. The explanation is that the content environment is not a fixed library. It is a shifting marketplace shaped by incentives, moderation choices, and user behaviour. The implication is that household safety cannot depend solely on a platform's promises. It must depend on household norms that remain stable even as platforms mutate.

This is where the notion of "what to say in the moment" becomes decisive. A parent who wants a child to disclose must be able to respond without turning the moment into a courtroom. The response must do two things at once: communicate that the content or contact was not acceptable, and communicate that the child is still safe to talk. The named concept is *dual messaging*. The explanation is that children need both containment and connection; they need to know there are lines, and they need to know the adult's love and respect do not depend on perfect judgement. The implication is that the most effective moment-language is brief and steady, because long speeches at the moment of discovery tend to become either scolding or anxious spirals.

The household also needs to decide how accountability works when the child has deliberately broken a rule versus when the child has stumbled into something accidentally. Treating both the same is convenient, but it teaches the wrong lesson: honesty is punished regardless. The show is the child who admits they clicked something out of curiosity and then regrets telling the truth because the adult reacts as if they committed a crime. The named concept is *honesty calibration*. The explanation is that children learn whether confession reduces consequences or worsens them. The implication is that if a family wants disclosure, it must ensure that disclosure changes the outcome in a way the child can notice. This does not mean "no consequences". It means proportionate consequences that differentiate intent, context, and honesty.

The risk many adults fear is that calmness will be interpreted as permissiveness. This fear drives overreaction. Yet calmness is not permission. Calmness is control. The family's authority is stronger when it can hold a boundary without theatrics, because theatrics invite counter-theatrics. The named concept is *emotional containment*. The explanation is that children look to adults for cues about whether a situation is survivable. If the adult panics, the child feels both frightened and guilty. The implication is that panic produces a double harm: it increases the child's distress and reduces the likelihood of future disclosure. Calm is not softness. Calm is strategy.

A predictable plan also reduces the temptation to spy. Many parents react to risky content by increasing secret monitoring, because knowledge feels like safety. Knowledge can be useful. Secret monitoring, however, is a tax on trust. If children learn that privacy is an illusion, they adapt by hiding better, not by behaving better. The show is the child switching to secret accounts, deleting messages, using private browsing, or borrowing friends' devices. The named concept is *surveillance adaptation*. The explanation is that people under surveillance optimise for not being caught. The implication is that the safest long-term posture is transparent expectations about oversight paired with a family culture in which children disclose problems early. The child who tells you is safer than the child you catch.

Still, there is a credible limitation that must be acknowledged. Not all "mature content" is risky in the same way. Some topics are serious but educational, such as news footage, health education, or discussions about bodies and relationships that children will encounter anyway through peers. Overblocking can create ignorance and shame, which can itself increase vulnerability. The named concept is *information hunger*. The explanation is that adolescents in particular seek understanding about adult realities, and if they cannot ask at home, they will seek answers elsewhere, often in less trustworthy places. The implication is that red lines must be paired with a willingness to have age-appropriate conversations when a child is curious, so the household does not push normal curiosity into secret channels.

Reconciling this limitation requires precision and humility. A family can say "we do not watch content that is cruel, demeaning, or beyond your current maturity" while still recognising that children will have questions and that questions are not crimes. The household can separate harmful exposure from honest inquiry. The named concept is *curiosity channeling*. The explanation is that children need safe ways to ask, and safe ways to ask depend on adults who can tolerate awkwardness. The implication is that a calm response plan is not only about handling problems; it is about creating a household where children ask before they search, where they come to an adult before they get pulled into a peer pressure spiral.

The quiet motif worth threading through this work is the red flag. A red flag is not a catastrophe. It is a signal that something needs attention. The family's aim is to teach a child to notice red flags and to treat them as cues for disclosure rather than as cues for secrecy. When a child sees something unsettling, when someone asks for secrecy, when a conversation suddenly becomes pressurised or personal, the red flag should point towards an adult, not away from one. That is a learned habit. It is learned through how adults respond.

A calm plan also helps families avoid a common mistake: treating the child's device as the enemy. The device is not the moral agent. The child is the learner. The platform is the environment. The adult is the guide. The show is the parent throwing blame at "the internet" and then feeling helpless, because a helpless adult cannot protect effectively. The named concept is *agency placement*. The explanation is that families protect children better when they place agency where it belongs: in household norms, in device settings that reduce exposure, and in the child's developing judgement, supported by adult oversight. The implication is that the household can become proactive without becoming paranoid.

The red flag returns at the end as a forward test, because mature and risky content will not always announce itself clearly. Sometimes it will appear as a joke, a link, a screenshot, a suggested video, a message from someone the child barely knows. The next time your child encounters something that makes their stomach tighten or their curiosity flare, what do they expect will happen if they tell you? Do they expect punishment, interrogation, and humiliation, or do they expect a predictable sequence: safety first, clarity next, proportionate accountability, and a return to dignity? The answer determines whether your family is building a child who comes to you, or a child who learns to handle red flags alone in the dark.

# Chapter 8
# Building Offline Alternatives

A child comes home, drops their bag, and heads straight for the screen with the certainty of someone following a well-worn path. The adult watches it happen and feels a familiar irritation that is also helplessness. The request to wait, to do homework, to talk, to play, to do anything else, lands like a nuisance in the child's body. The screen offers instant decompression. The house offers a list of demands. The child chooses relief. The adult feels rejected. The evening begins with a quiet tug-of-war that nobody formally declared.

Empty minutes get filled fast.

The same dynamic appears in the morning, when the household is rushed and the screen offers quiet compliance, and again before bed, when the day's emotional scraps are still clinging and the phone offers escape. These are not random weak points. They are the hours when human beings are most vulnerable to defaults: when we are tired, transitioning, or bracing for the next task. Families often respond by tightening rules, which is necessary and sometimes effective, but rules without alternatives create a vacuum. The vacuum is not neutral. It becomes a magnet for the very behaviour the family is trying to reduce, because the screen does not simply entertain; it meets needs quickly.

The central tension is that parents and carers want children to spend less time on screens without making offline life feel like punishment. If the message becomes "life is boring unless you are online", children will treat the screen as rescue and the home as deprivation. If offline life is made genuinely appealing and socially meaningful, screens lose some of their grip without needing constant enforcement. This is not romantic. It is competition. Screens compete well because they provide stimulation, structure, and social contact on demand. The household must decide whether it wants to compete intelligently or keep fighting the same battles in the same vulnerable hours.

This matters because the aim is not to create a museum of wholesome activities. The aim is to protect attention, sleep, and connection while allowing children to grow into independence. Children who rely on screens for every transition often struggle to tolerate ordinary discomfort: waiting, boredom, mild loneliness, the awkward pause before homework, the quiet moment before sleep. Those discomforts are not optional parts of life. They are the raw material of resilience. A child who never practises moving through them becomes more dependent on external stimulation, and dependence increases conflict because the screen becomes not a choice but a requirement. That requirement is emotionally expensive for the child and administratively expensive for the adult.

It also matters because a home without appealing offline alternatives becomes a home of constant negotiation. Adults end up policing instead of parenting, because the only tool available is "no", and "no" does not teach a child what to do with themselves next. Children become experts at asking, because asking is the only route to relief. The household's daily tone shifts. A calm room becomes rare. A parent who must constantly refuse becomes harsher. A child who is constantly refused becomes more resentful. The entire family spends more time managing conflict than living.

The work here is not to fill every minute with activities. Over-scheduling produces its own fatigue and its own rebellion. The goal is to remove the vacuum in the vulnerable hours by building small rituals that meet the same needs screens meet, in quieter ways: decompression after school, stimulation when energy sags, connection when loneliness rises, and gentle structure when transitions are hard. A ritual is not a performance. It is a default that makes the next step easier. When the ritual exists, the child is not asked to invent a plan from scratch each day, which reduces bargaining and reduces the lure of the easiest plan available: the screen.

Boredom sits at the centre of this chapter because boredom is both despised and essential. Many families treat boredom as a problem to be solved, yet boredom is a developmental training space. It teaches children to generate ideas, to tolerate mild discomfort, to build internal motivation. The difficulty is that boredom only becomes useful when a child has tools to move through it, and many children have lost those tools because screens have replaced the need to practise them. Adults then either become entertainers or become scolds, and neither role produces independence. The household needs a third role: building an environment where children can choose something offline without turning it into a negotiation.

Friends, movement, and nature are the other pillars because they meet needs screens meet but with different after-effects. Friends provide belonging. Movement changes mood and energy. Nature offers stimulation without the same cognitive demand of constant novelty. These are not moral categories. They are physiological and social realities. When offline options are structured well, they become anchors rather than chores. They can even become identity: the child who is a swimmer, a skater, a baker, a maker, a walker, a friend who meets on Saturdays. Identity competes with screens far more effectively than nagging does, because identity changes what a child wants.

The thread through this chapter moves from time to capacity to appeal. It begins by identifying the vulnerable hours where screens seize control and asking what need the screen is meeting there. It then turns to boredom as a skill that can be rebuilt through scaffolding and choice, so the child is not dependent on constant input. It then expands outwards to the social and physical world, where friends, movement, and small adventures can become reliable alternatives that do not feel like punishments and do not require parents to perform as cruise directors.

A quiet motif can hold this together: the hook by the door. Not a metaphorical hook, an actual one. A place where a bag hangs, where shoes sit, where a coat is dropped, where the day transitions into home. That hook is where routines either begin or dissolve. If the first action after the hook is a screen, the screen becomes the ritual. If the first action after the hook is a small offline default, the house has a chance to reclaim the hour without force. The hook is the hinge between drift and design.

The unresolved question is not whether children should have offline activities. Everyone agrees in theory. The question is whether the household is willing to treat offline life as something worth designing, not something that will happen automatically once screens are restricted. When the next vulnerable hour arrives and the child reaches for the device out of habit, what, exactly, is waiting on the other side of that hook by the door: a vacuum that will be filled by the screen again, or a small, reliable alternative that makes the right choice easier than the default scroll?

## Planning the vulnerable hours

In October 2016, the American Academy of Pediatrics in Itasca, Illinois, released its Family Media Plan tool and pushed a practical idea into the mainstream: screen decisions are less about moral strength than about daily rhythms. The concrete outcome was not a universal rule, but a prompt to look at where media use sits in a child's day alongside sleep, school, and relationships. That prompt matters because most screen conflict does not occur at random. It clusters. It appears in the same pockets of time, like weeds in the same cracks of a pavement.

The cracks have names.

Morning, after school, and the hour before bed are the vulnerable hours not because families are weak then, but because human beings are. These are transition zones. They are moments when the nervous system is either gearing up, coming down, or searching for comfort. A screen thrives in transition zones because it offers immediate structure: a predictable stream of stimulation or connection that asks almost nothing and gives a lot. If a household wants screens to stop colonising the day, it has to stop leaving those cracks empty. Empty time is not neutral. It recruits the most efficient filler available.

Start where the pattern is easiest to see. In the morning, the house is a machine that must run: clothing, breakfast, teeth, bags, time. Adults are focused on logistics. Children are focused on resistance to waking, to effort, to the day's demands. The show is the phone offered as a quieting tool: a child sits still and eats, or at least stops complaining. The named concept is *compliance buying*. The explanation is that screens can purchase short-term cooperation by reducing friction in the moment. The implication is that the purchase has an interest rate. Morning screen use often bleeds into slowness, distraction, and arguments about leaving. The device becomes part of the morning engine, and engines are hard to change once built.

After school is the second crack, and it is the one most families recognise because it is where the child's mood often shifts sharply. The show is the child who enters the house and reaches for a screen before saying hello, or who answers a parent's greeting with a grunt while already scrolling. The named concept is *transition avoidance*. The explanation is that school-to-home is not a small step; it is a change of role, and role changes cost effort. A screen offers instant decompression: no social demand, no homework, no emotional processing. The implication is that a child who scrolls after school is not necessarily lazy; they may be avoiding the discomfort of re-entry. The home is asking them to become a different kind of person again, and the screen allows them to delay that moment.

Pre-bed is the third crack, and it is the most consequential because it sits directly on top of sleep protection. The show is the tired child who claims they need the phone to relax, or the teen who treats late-night messaging as a necessity. The named concept is *fatigue capture*. The explanation is that tired minds seek comfort quickly, and screens offer comfort that feels immediate: distraction, connection, novelty, control. The implication is that late-day screen drift is rarely about fun alone. It is often about emotional regulation, and if the household removes the screen without providing any other path to settling, it invites confrontation at exactly the time everyone is least able to tolerate it.

The point of "planning the vulnerable hours" is not to build an hour-by-hour timetable that turns family life into a programme. Over-scheduling creates backlash and exhaustion. The point is to remove the vacuum. A vacuum is the period when a child's needs are live and the household has not offered a default way to meet them. The show is the child who says "I'm bored" or "Can I have my iPad?" repeatedly, not because they have no imagination, but because the screen has become the household's default answer to unmet needs. The named concept is *default gap*. The explanation is that when a child does not have a reliable, low-friction alternative, they will reach for the highest-reward alternative. The implication is that families who want fewer arguments must build a small number of reliable offline defaults that sit exactly where the gaps are widest.

Rituals are how defaults become real. A ritual is simply a repeated sequence that signals what happens next. It can be short. It should be repeatable. The show is the difference between a child entering the house and immediately seeking a screen, and a child entering the house and following an established micro-sequence: shoes off, snack, a brief check-in, a small decompression activity, then whatever comes next. The named concept is *sequenced decompression*. The explanation is that decompression is not optional; the nervous system needs it. The question is whether decompression is shaped by the family or outsourced to a feed. The implication is that when decompression is structured, screen use becomes a choice later rather than a reflex immediately.

A snack-and-chat routine is a good example not because it is quaint, but because it addresses two needs at once: physiological and relational. Hunger makes children prickly. Lack of connection makes parents anxious. A small ritual that reliably meets both needs can reduce the emotional charge around screens. The abstraction is *connection*, but it becomes visible as a simple behaviour: the child is spoken to before they disappear. The named concept is *contact before content*. The explanation is that humans regulate better when they feel seen, and children often reach for screens faster when they do not feel anchored in the household. The implication is that a few minutes of ordinary talk after school can prevent the screen from becoming the only decompression tool, not through moral pressure but through meeting the child's need for attention in a low-stakes way.

Morning planning requires a different kind of ritual because mornings are not spacious. They are logistical. Here the goal is to reduce decisions and reduce friction. The show is the morning argument that begins with a child checking a device and ends with shouting about shoes. The named concept is *attention bleed*. The explanation is that a screen pulls attention into a stream that does not respect clock time, and mornings depend on clock time. The implication is that a morning default that does not rely on screens will often reduce the number of micro-conflicts that make the entire household late and irritable. The point is not to create a perfect morning. It is to create a morning with fewer triggers for distraction.

Pre-bed planning requires yet another kind of ritual because the nervous system is descending. The show is the child who turns to the screen because the quiet feels uncomfortable, or because the day's emotions have not been processed. The named concept is *quiet intolerance*. The explanation is that many children and teens have trained themselves to fill every quiet moment with input, and the first nights without that input can feel genuinely unsettling. The implication is that pre-bed rituals must be calming without being endless, and they must be designed to end naturally, otherwise the screen is simply replaced by a different kind of drift.

A second named, checkable anchor can help underline why focusing on routines rather than hours is credible beyond parenting culture. The World Health Organization guidance published in Geneva in April 2019 framed screens as part of a daily system that includes sleep and activity, reinforcing the idea that the most important decisions are about rhythm and displacement rather than moral judgement. The named concept is *rhythm integrity*. The explanation is that small disruptions to rhythm compound over days into larger conflicts. The implication is that families who plan vulnerable hours are not being fussy; they are protecting the integrity of the day's architecture.

A credible limitation should be admitted because some families are stretched to the point where rituals feel like an impossible ask. Shift work, multiple children, caring responsibilities, neurodiversity, and limited space can make even a simple routine feel like another task. The named concept is *capacity constraint*. The explanation is that a family cannot plan what it does not have the energy to execute. The implication is that the most effective rituals are often tiny and consistent rather than elaborate and rare. When capacity is low, the household needs a micro-default, not a performance.

Reconciling this limitation brings the focus back to what "planning" really means in this chapter: not filling time, but choosing a few small sequences that reduce bargaining and meet needs. A child who is fed and briefly connected is often easier to govern. A teen who has a predictable pre-bed wind-down is often less likely to drift into late-night scrolling. These are not guarantees. They are probabilities shaped by environment. Planning vulnerable hours is a way of moving probability in your favour.

The motif worth keeping is the hook by the door, the place where the day transitions into home. That hook is where the household can insert a new default. If the first move after the hook is always a screen, the screen becomes the ritual. If the first move after the hook is a small offline sequence, the screen has to wait its turn. Waiting is a skill. Families can either train it or outsource it.

The forward test is not whether a family can ban screens in the vulnerable hours. Bans without alternatives create vacuum, and vacuum invites rebellion or secrecy. The test is whether the household can name the need the screen is meeting in each vulnerable hour and then install a simple ritual that meets that need without the endless pull. When the child reaches for the device at the hook by the door, are they reaching because they are defiant, or because the house has left a crack unfilled again?

## Making boredom useful again

In 1907, in the San Lorenzo district of Rome, Maria Montessori opened the Casa dei Bambini and made a concrete wager against the adult impulse to rescue children from every empty moment. She prepared an environment, offered materials, and trusted that boredom and wandering attention could be the doorway to self-directed work rather than a crisis demanding adult entertainment. The outcome, recorded in her later writings, was not constant cheerfulness. It was concentration. Children learned to choose, persist, and return to tasks without being chased or bribed. Montessori was not fighting

YouTube auto-play. She was studying the same raw material that screens now interrupt: the child's capacity to move from "nothing to do" into "something I chose".

Boredom is a threshold.

Families often treat it as a complaint to fix. A child says, "I'm bored," and adults hear an accusation: you have failed to provide stimulation. Adults then rush to produce options, or they hand over a screen, or they lecture about gratitude. None of these responses builds the skill boredom can teach. The skill is not the ability to tolerate suffering. It is the ability to generate direction. A child who can cross the threshold of boredom learns that discomfort is not a dead end; it is a signal. A child who never crosses the threshold learns that discomfort must be extinguished immediately, and the fastest extinguisher in the home is usually a screen.

The core problem is that screens have turned boredom into an endangered experience. This is not a romantic lament for a pre-digital childhood. It is a behavioural observation. A feed provides structure without requiring initiative. A game provides goals without requiring imagination. Messaging provides contact without requiring the awkward work of asking someone to meet. Screens are efficient. Boredom is inefficient. When a child has been trained by habit to expect instant input, boredom begins to feel like distress, and distress is socially unacceptable in a busy household. Adults then reach for the quickest relief. The named concept is *discomfort intolerance*. The explanation is that repeated immediate relief reduces the child's opportunity to practise self-directed behaviour. The implication is that when families try to reduce screens without rebuilding boredom skills, they often get what looks like defiance but is frequently panic: a child who genuinely does not know what to do next, and who experiences that blankness as unbearable.

Boredom becomes useful only when the environment offers two things: permission to be bored and tools to move through it. Permission matters because children often interpret boredom as shame. They say "I'm bored" and hope the adult will rescue them, because the alternative is sitting with emptiness and looking incompetent. Tools matter because boredom without tools is not skill-building; it is frustration. The show is the child who wanders, complains, and then escalates into mischief or argument, not because they are malicious but because they cannot translate "I need stimulation" into a self-generated plan. The named concept is *initiation failure*. The explanation is that starting an activity requires executive function: choosing, planning, beginning. Those functions develop gradually and are harder when the child is tired or hungry. The implication is that adults who want children to entertain themselves must treat initiation as a skill to scaffold, not a moral quality to demand.

This is where the idea menu earns its place. The phrase sounds twee until one watches what it replaces. Without a menu, a child asked to "go and play" must generate options under pressure, and pressure narrows thinking. With a menu, the child can pick an option without needing to invent it, which reduces bargaining and reduces the temptation to argue for screens as the only idea available. The abstraction is *autonomy*, but it becomes visible as a simple decision: the child chooses an activity without negotiating with an adult. The named concept is *choice scaffolding*. The explanation is that offering pre-selected options supports independence because it lowers the cognitive load of initiation. The implication is that a menu is not a parent becoming an entertainer. It is a parent building an environment that can hold the child's boredom without collapsing into device handovers.

This scaffolding must be age-sensitive, because boredom shows up differently at different stages. A six-year-old may need concrete prompts and accessible materials. A ten-year-old may need permission to do something messy or slightly unscheduled. A teen may need social or physical outlets rather than craft prompts. The point is not to treat childhood as a set of stereotypes. It is to recognise that boredom is not one experience. It is the moment when a child's current coping strategies are insufficient for the gap they are in. The named concept is *fit*. The explanation is that a child will choose an activity when the activity feels achievable and rewarding. The implication is that an idea menu works only if it reflects the child's real interests and the household's real capacity, not the adult's fantasy of wholesome fun.

The second named, checkable anchor for boredom as a capacity comes from contemporary parenting guidance rather than educational history. In October 2016, the American Academy of Pediatrics in Itasca, Illinois, promoted its Family Media Plan approach, encouraging families to align media use with priorities like sleep, physical activity, and family time. The concrete outcome was a public acknowledgement that children need routines and alternatives, not merely restrictions. The named concept is *displacement planning*. The explanation is that if a family removes a default activity, the vacuum will be filled by something, and the fill can be constructive or chaotic depending on what the environment makes available. The implication is that boredom will be experienced more often when screens are reduced, and the household's response to that boredom will determine whether the child becomes more independent or more combative.

One reason boredom is so hard to tolerate, for adults as well as children, is that boredom produces noise before it produces creativity. The first phase often looks like whining, restlessness, and provocation. This is where many families give up. They interpret the noise as evidence that boredom is harmful or that the child is being manipulative. The named concept is *transition turbulence*. The explanation is that when a habitual source of stimulation is removed, the nervous system searches for a replacement. It does not do this politely. The implication is that adults who can tolerate a short phase of turbulence without panicking are more likely to see the second phase emerge: the child starts to tinker, to build, to invent, to call a friend, to move their body. The parent's tolerance is part of the child's learning environment.

Tolerance is not passive. It is active restraint, and it needs structure. Adults can tolerate complaints more easily when they know what they are tolerating and why. If the adult believes the child's whining is a referendum on the adult's competence, the adult will rescue quickly to end the shame. If the adult sees whining as a predictable stage of habit change, the adult can hold the line with less emotional flailing. The abstraction is *patience*, but it becomes visible as a choice: whether to intervene immediately or to wait a little while. The named concept is *delayed rescue*. The explanation is that delaying rescue gives the child time to generate their own solution. The implication is that adults who never delay rescue inadvertently train children to escalate quickly, because escalation works. Adults who delay rescue consistently train children that escalation is not the path to stimulation; choosing is.

This does not mean ignoring a child. Ignoring can become neglect, and neglect does not build skill. The show is the adult who is present but not performing: available for a brief nudge, not available for constant entertainment. The named concept is *supported independence*. The explanation is that children become independent when they experience themselves as capable with light adult support, not when they are abandoned or micromanaged. The implication is that a family can set a tone around boredom that is warm and firm at once: boredom is allowed, ideas exist, and the child is trusted to choose.

A crucial part of making boredom useful is protecting the materials and spaces that allow it to turn into activity. A child who could draw, build, read, invent, or move will still choose a screen if the pencils are missing, the Lego is in a high cupboard, the garden is off-limits, or every non-screen activity requires asking an adult for access. The named concept is *access friction*. The explanation is that when the path to offline activity is full of barriers, children default to the path that is barrier-free. The implication is that a household can increase offline activity without moralising simply by reducing access friction for offline options and increasing access friction for the most capturing digital ones, the same engineering principle used elsewhere in this book.

The credible limitation here is that boredom is not always benign, and it is not always the same for every child. Some children experience boredom as anxiety: the quiet allows worries to surface. Some children with neurodiversity may find unstructured time particularly dysregulating. Some teens may experience boredom as loneliness, especially if their peer group lives largely online or if they are socially excluded. The named concept is *boredom heterogeneity*. The explanation is that boredom is a label for several different internal states, from mild restlessness to genuine distress. The implication is that a family should not romanticise boredom as universally good or use it as a moral test. Boredom becomes useful when it is within tolerable limits and paired with accessible tools and supportive connection. When boredom is actually anxiety or loneliness, the right response may involve strengthening connection and scaffolding rather than simply insisting the child "learn to be bored".

Reconciling this limitation requires sharper observation. What does the child do when bored? Do they become whiny but then settle into play if given options? Do they become agitated and spiral, suggesting the need for more structured support? Do they reach for social contact, suggesting loneliness rather than boredom? The abstraction is *wellbeing*, but it becomes visible as behavioural pattern: restlessness, irritability, withdrawal, or initiative. The named concept is *state reading*. The explanation is that adults can respond more effectively when they identify the underlying state rather than reacting to the complaint. The implication is that the idea menu should not be a one-size-fits-all list. It should be a curated set of options that match the child's likely states in the vulnerable hours: low energy, high energy, lonely, restless, annoyed.

The Montessori origin story returns here not as nostalgia but as a reminder: prepared environments matter because they prevent adult over-involvement. A well-prepared environment reduces the need for adults to entertain and reduces the child's temptation to demand entertainment. It also allows the child to experience agency without negotiating every step. The idea menu is a small version of this. It says: the world is full of options, and you are capable of choosing one.

The unresolved tension at the end of this subchapter is that screens are not only fun; they are the quickest cure for discomfort. A household that removes screens will, for a time, expose discomfort. The question is whether the family will treat that discomfort as failure or as practice. When the child next says "I'm bored," will the adult hear an accusation and rush to rescue, or hear a threshold moment and offer the minimum support needed for the child to cross into self-directed activity? The answer will determine whether the idea menu becomes a living tool on the wall, or a piece of paper that watches the screen win again.

## Using friends, movement, and nature

In October 2016, the American Academy of Pediatrics in Itasca, Illinois, promoted its Family Media Plan tool with a concrete intention: help households align media use with sleep, physical activity, and relationships. That is a quietly radical framing, because it treats screens not as a moral contaminant but as a competitor. The competitor does not win because it is wicked. It wins because it meets needs quickly:

stimulation, connection, identity, relief. If a family wants children to choose offline life more often, offline life must meet those same needs with enough force to feel worth it.

Fun has a job to do.

Many families approach "offline alternatives" as if they were vegetables: unquestionably good, rarely desired, to be consumed for one's own benefit with mild resentment. Children detect this posture instantly. A walk is proposed as penance for too much screen time. A hobby is offered as a virtue lesson. A meet-up is treated as an inconvenience. The result is predictable. Children cling harder to screens because screens are framed as pleasure and offline life is framed as corrective medicine. The aim here is not to shame parents and carers into becoming cruise directors. It is to be honest about the psychology of choice. People choose what feels rewarding, and children are not exempt from that rule.

Begin with friends, because belonging competes with screens far more effectively than lectures do. A child who has a friend expecting them at the park is pulled by a social magnet stronger than a parent's request to "go outside". The show is the child who suddenly finds energy when a friend is involved, even after a lethargic afternoon of scrolling. The named concept is *social anchoring*. The explanation is that humans are wired to orient towards peers; peer attention and peer laughter are powerful rewards. The implication is that families who want fewer screens should treat friendship not as an optional extra after homework, but as a core ingredient of a life that feels full enough to step away from the feed. When friendships are thin, screens become thicker, because they can simulate social presence even when the child is alone.

Friend-based offline time is often harder to arrange than adults admit. It requires logistics, trust, and adult coordination. It also requires safety judgment that changes by age. A younger child's playdate needs more adult scaffolding;

an older child's meet-up needs a different kind of oversight that respects dignity while still being responsible. The abstraction is *safety*, but it becomes visible as decisions: where the meeting happens, who is present, how drop-offs work, what boundaries exist about devices and supervision. The named concept is *structured freedom*. The explanation is that children need space to be with peers without feeling constantly watched, yet they also need adults to manage the conditions that keep social life safe. The implication is that families who do not build structures for offline friendship may find that the only social life available is online, because online requires no lifts, no coordination, no shared public spaces, and no negotiation with other adults.

A checkable example from social science gives this more weight than anecdote. In 1990, the political scientist Robert D. Putnam published "Bowling Alone" as an essay and later expanded the argument in his 2000 book of the same title, describing declines in certain forms of social participation in the United States and the consequences for community life. Whatever one thinks of Putnam's broader thesis, the core idea is useful at the household scale: social infrastructure matters. The named concept is *social capital*. The explanation is that friendships and community ties are not simply personal preferences; they are resources that make life richer and more resilient. The implication for families is that building offline alternatives is not only about keeping children "busy". It is about strengthening the social fabric that makes screens less necessary as substitutes. When social capital is thin, screens are asked to fill roles they were never designed to fill well: companionship, belonging, identity.

Movement is the second pillar because it changes mood quickly and reliably, and that makes it a practical competitor to screens, not a moral one. The show is the child who has been irritable, restless, or flat after a long stretch indoors, and whose mood shifts after moving their body, even if the movement is not "sport" in any organised sense. The named concept is *state change*. The explanation is physiological: movement alters arousal, releases tension, and provides sensory input that can regulate an overstimulated or under-stimulated nervous system. The implication is that movement is not merely an adult-imposed virtue. It is a tool children can learn to use when they feel stuck. When children do not have movement in their repertoire, they often reach for screens as the default mood tool, because screens also change state, though often by numbing rather than by regulating.

To make movement genuinely appealing, it must be tied to identity or companionship, not framed as punishment. A child who is told to "go for a walk because you've been on screens" hears a sentence about deprivation. A child who is invited into a routine that feels like theirs hears something else: a ritual, a habit that belongs to the family's culture. The named concept is *identity bonding*. The explanation is that children commit more readily to activities that signal who they are: the child who is a climber, a skater, a dancer, a walker who knows the best route to the café. The implication is that the most effective movement habits are those that carry a story, not those that carry a lecture. Stories survive. Lectures invite rebellion.

Nature is the third pillar because it offers stimulation without the same cognitive demands and without the same engineered pull. Nature is not a mystical cure. It is a setting with different cues: wind, light, uneven ground, distant sounds, small discoveries. The show is the child who begins a walk sulking and ends it talking, or at least less braced. The named concept is *soft fascination*, a term associated with environmental psychology and, in particular, with Rachel and Stephen Kaplan's attention restoration theory, articulated in work from the late twentieth century. The explanation is that certain environments draw attention gently rather than aggressively, allowing directed attention to recover. The implication is that nature-based time can feel surprisingly restorative even for children who claim to hate it, not because nature is magical but because it does not behave like a feed. It does not demand constant reaction. It allows the mind to wander without being hijacked.

A second checkable anchor can help ground the claim that outdoor rituals can become cultural infrastructure, not just occasional outings. The National Trust in the United Kingdom, founded in 1895, is a recognisable institution built on the premise that access to natural and historic spaces has public value. The named concept is *place stewardship*. The explanation is that when people have access to meaningful places, those places become part of family rhythm. The implication for households is that nature does not have to be a grand expedition. It can be a local park, a familiar path, a small "micro-adventure" that feels like a real event because it is repeated and owned. The place becomes an anchor, and anchors compete with screens because anchors create anticipation.

This is where the Saturday walk-and-hot-chocolate tradition becomes more than a charming idea. It meets multiple needs at once: movement, companionship, novelty, reward, and a sense of family identity. It is also predictable, which reduces bargaining. The child does not have to be persuaded every week; the ritual becomes part of the weekend's shape. The named concept is *ritualised reward*. The explanation is that rituals work because they remove repeated decision-making and attach a positive expectation to an offline activity. The implication is that families can build offline alternatives that are not framed as "less screen time" but as "this is what we do". Children are more likely to accept "what we do" than "what you are not allowed to do".

Still, a credible limitation must be faced honestly. Not every child has easy access to friends, safe outdoor spaces, or affordable activities. Some children are socially anxious. Some families live far from parks or in environments where independent movement is not safe. Some parents and carers work weekends. Some households are stretched by care responsibilities and cannot coordinate frequent meet-ups. The named concept is *constraint reality*. The explanation is that families cannot build offline alternatives that their context does not support. The implication is not resignation. It is realism. The most effective alternatives are those that fit the household's actual constraints. A short, repeatable outing to a nearby place can outperform an ambitious plan that happens twice and then dies. A small meet-up with one trusted friend can outperform a complicated social calendar that collapses under logistics.

Reconciling this limitation returns us to the core principle: compete on needs, not on virtue. If friends are hard to coordinate, the household can still build micro-social moments: a predictable call with a relative, a neighbour's child meeting in a shared space, a scheduled club that provides peer contact without parents doing all the organising. If movement is hard, the household can still design movement that feels like play rather than exercise, and that can happen close to home. If nature is scarce, the household can still seek outdoor light and open space in whatever form is locally available. The named concept is *minimum viable alternative*. The explanation is that a small alternative that reliably meets a need will weaken the screen's monopoly over that need. The implication is that families should measure success by whether the child has a few non-screen ways to decompress, connect, and stimulate themselves, not by whether the family can replicate an idealised childhood.

Safety and supervision, handled well, are part of making these alternatives appealing rather than frightening. If a parent's anxiety dominates every outing, the child will associate offline life with tension and screens with relief. The show is the adult who cannot stop checking the phone while insisting the child be present, turning the whole plan into hypocrisy. The named concept is *anxiety transmission*. The explanation is that children borrow emotional cues from adults, and adult worry can make even pleasant activities feel stressful. The implication is that adults who want offline life to compete must find a way to make it feel safe without making it feel surveilled. This often means choosing settings that reduce genuine risk so the adult can relax, rather than trying to relax in settings that feel unsafe.

The motif that ties these pillars together is the thermos. A thermos of hot chocolate, a flask of tea, a shared snack carried to the park. It is an ordinary object, but it signals something important: offline life is not deprivation. It contains comfort. It contains reward. It contains care. The thermos also makes repetition easier. The ritual becomes portable. Children remember the taste. They anticipate it. Anticipation is a rival to the feed's promise of novelty.

The forward test for this subchapter is not whether a child can be forced outdoors or signed up to a club. Force produces compliance at best, resentment at worst. The test is whether the family can build a small number of offline anchors that the child begins to choose because they meet real needs with real pleasure: belonging, movement, stimulation, identity. When the next vulnerable hour arrives and the child reaches for a screen, what is the stronger pull: the infinite convenience of the feed, or the tangible, social, embodied life the family has made available enough to feel worth choosing?

# Chapter 9
# Teaching Self Regulation With Screens

A parent hears the familiar words, spoken with earnest confidence: "I'll stop in a minute." The child is not sneering. They mean it. The parent waits, because waiting feels kinder than confrontation. The minute stretches. The parent returns, voice tighter, and the child reacts as if something important is being torn away. Both sides feel misunderstood. The child feels interrupted mid-flight. The adult feels played. Neither experience is the whole truth. The real truth is that the child has not yet learned how to land, and the adult has been forced into the role of air-traffic control.

Stopping is a skill.

So is starting well. So is noticing the pull before the pull becomes a spiral. Families often treat these as moral qualities: disciplined children stop, undisciplined children protest. Yet screen design does not ask for small amounts of discipline; it asks for repeated micro-decisions against powerful cues, often when a child is tired, hungry, lonely, or stressed. Self regulation in this context is not an abstract virtue. It is a set of learnable behaviours: planning a session, choosing a stopping point, saving progress, saying goodbye in a chat, leaving the app, turning attention back to the room. These behaviours can be taught and practised. When they are not, the household ends up enforcing boundaries through conflict, and conflict teaches children to associate limits with humiliation rather than with competence.

The central tension of this chapter is between external control and internal capability. External control is tempting because it is immediate: timers, locks, confiscation, firm rules. Internal capability is slower because it requires practice: children learning to notice urges, tolerate incompletion, and end cleanly without drama. Families often get trapped in a false choice. They either rely on external control and create a child who behaves only when controlled, or they hand over responsibility too quickly and then conclude the child is "not ready". Both paths miss the developmental middle: guided independence. The child becomes capable by borrowing regulation from adults and systems, then gradually internalising it. The goal is not to remove adult involvement overnight. The goal is to change what adult involvement is doing: from policing to coaching.

This matters because self regulation with screens is not only about screens. It generalises. A child who can stop a game without melting down is practising frustration tolerance. A teen who can end a chat and sleep is practising prioritisation and social boundary-setting. A child who can plan a session and stick to it is practising time awareness and follow-through. These capacities will later be used for revision, work, relationships, and health. A household that focuses only on restriction can keep screens in check for a while. A household that teaches self regulation is teaching a life skill in a context where the skill will be repeatedly needed.

It also matters because constant external enforcement has side effects. It increases secrecy in older children and teens, because autonomy is a developmental need and humans respond to control by seeking escape. It increases bargaining in younger children, because inconsistency rewards negotiation. It increases adult fatigue, because acting as a constant enforcer is exhausting and often shame-inducing. The household becomes organised around screens, which is the opposite of what it wants. When capability grows, the household changes shape. Boundaries remain, but they can be held with less heat because the child has more tools to comply without feeling robbed.

The challenge is that capability does not grow evenly. Children can be impressively responsible in one domain and impulsive in another. They can stop well on Tuesday and melt down on Thursday. They can manage screens well in the afternoon and poorly at night. Adults misread this variability as manipulation or as failure. It is often neither. It is the reality of developing self-control in a system designed to keep pulling. A child's "not yet finished" feeling is real. It is the internal experience of an open loop. Naming it does not excuse it. Naming it makes it coachable. When a child can recognise the sensation and anticipate it, they are less likely to treat the boundary as a sudden ambush.

This is also where the idea of gradual independence becomes essential, because responsibility cannot be transferred in a single grand gesture. A one-time graduation produces either overconfidence or disappointment. Overconfidence leads to drift and conflict. Disappointment leads to clampdown. Both teach the child that independence is fragile and conditional, which can make them either defensive or indifferent. A more stable approach treats independence as incremental and testable. The child is given small areas of responsibility, supported by reviews that focus on what happened rather than on moral judgement. A child who experiences responsibility as a series of learnable experiments is more likely to take it seriously than a child who experiences responsibility as a trap: one mistake and freedom is revoked for months.

The movement through this chapter follows that developmental logic. It begins with the micro-skills of starting and stopping, because the household cannot hand over responsibility for something the child has never practised. It then turns to the question of which responsibilities shift by age and temperament, and how to shift them without creating loopholes or power struggles. The emphasis is on growth that survives the inevitable bad week, because real independence is not demonstrated on a good day; it is demonstrated under ordinary stress.

A quiet motif can anchor this work: the landing. A plane does not prove it can fly by taking off; it proves it by landing well. Screens are similar. Starting is easy. Ending is the test. Families often focus on take-off rules, such as "only after homework". The more decisive moment is the landing: the child closes the loop, saves, signs off, and returns to the room without leaving a crater behind. When landing becomes teachable, the household stops treating screens as contraband and starts treating them as a context for learning self-control.

The unresolved question is not whether children can regulate themselves perfectly. They cannot. Adults cannot either. The question is whether the household is willing to invest in teaching the skills that make regulation more likely, rather than relying indefinitely on external control and hoping maturity will arrive on its own. When the next "just a minute" appears, will the family treat it as defiance that must be crushed, or as the moment when a child can learn to land cleanly, and thereby earn the next small step towards real independence?

## Coaching the start and stop skills

In 1999, at Stanford University in California, psychologist Walter Mischel published *The Marshmallow Test*, popularising a line of research about delay of gratification and self-control that had begun decades earlier. The concrete outcome was a cultural shorthand: children who can wait for a better reward are often better prepared for later challenges. The story has been debated and nuanced over time, but its core relevance for screens is not the marshmallow. It is the moment of waiting itself, the moment when a child feels an urge and must decide what to do with it. Screens create that moment repeatedly, often without warning, often when the child is tired, and often in environments designed to make waiting feel unbearable.

Stopping is learned behaviour.

So is starting well. Families often focus on the stop because the stop is where conflict becomes visible. Yet start and stop are a pair. A child who begins a session with no plan, no endpoint, and no awareness of the pull is far more likely to end in protest, because the session has been allowed to expand until the screen feels like a place the child lives rather than a thing the child uses. Coaching is the work of turning screen use from a drift into a sequence: decide, begin, stay aware, close, return. This is not about turning childhood into a productivity seminar. It is about building the internal skills that make external rules less necessary over time.

Start with what a child experiences at the moment you ask them to stop. They often feel the same thing, regardless of age: *not yet finished.* This is not only a thought. It is a sensation: unfinishedness, incompletion, the itch of an open loop. The show is the child who protests more when stopped mid-level, mid-message, mid-clip, not because they are unusually entitled but because the brain resists being pulled away from a loop that feels unresolved. The named concept is *incompletion discomfort.* The explanation is that humans allocate attention to unfinished tasks; the mind treats them as pending. The implication is that if families want fewer meltdowns, they must stop treating "not yet finished" as a cheeky excuse and start treating it as a predictable internal experience that can be named, anticipated, and managed.

Naming matters because it shifts the child from pure feeling into language. Language is not a magic spell, but it is a handle. A child who can say "I feel not-finished" is already doing something important: observing their state. The named concept is *metacognition*, the ability to think about one's own thinking. The explanation is that metacognition reduces impulsivity because it inserts a pause. The implication is that the household's vocabulary around screens is part of the coaching. When adults only say "stop" and children only say "no", the family has two blunt tools and endless arguments.

When the family has words for urge, loop, ending, and return, it can work with the experience rather than simply battling it.

A practical coaching stance is to treat screen use as a series of small rehearsals rather than as a single compliance test. Rehearsals are how skills are built. The show is the child who practises ending a session at a natural break, saving progress, and leaving without losing dignity. The named concept is *closure practice*. The explanation is that closure can be trained just as tidying can be trained or toothbrushing can be trained: through repetition in predictable contexts. The implication is that adults who wait until the child is fully absorbed and then demand an immediate stop are choosing the hardest possible training environment. Skill training works better when the task is within reach. That does not mean adults avoid difficulty forever. It means they choose the moment difficulty is most teachable.

This connects to the earlier idea of start friction and stop ease, but now the focus is internal rather than technical. A child who starts a session without considering what comes after is more likely to be shocked by the ending. A child who starts with a small plan is more likely to accept the ending as part of the plan. The abstraction is *agency*, but it becomes visible as a decision made before the first tap: what is the purpose, what is the end point, what will happen when the end arrives? The named concept is *pre-commitment*. The explanation is that pre-commitment reduces mid-session bargaining because the child has already agreed, at least internally, to an end. The implication is that coaching should focus on the beginning of sessions as much as on the end. Many screen battles are lost at the start because the start was allowed to be casual and limitless.

A named, checkable example shows that mainstream device design has acknowledged the need for pre-commitment and external cues, even if it cannot supply the human skill. In September 2018, Apple released iOS 12 in Cupertino,

California, introducing Screen Time features that allow app limits and scheduled downtime. The concrete outcome for many families was an external stopping cue that could reduce arguments. The named concept is *external scaffolding*. The explanation is that when the environment provides a cue, the child does not have to generate the cue internally every time. The implication is that external scaffolding can support coaching, but it cannot replace it. A child can comply with a lock and still fail to develop the ability to stop voluntarily. Coaching aims for voluntary stopping because voluntary stopping is the skill that will matter when the child is older, away from home, and faced with temptations no parent can see.

Voluntary stopping depends on recognising urges early. An urge often arrives as a subtle sensation: the desire to check a notification, the thought "I wonder what's next", the feeling that boredom might be relieved by a quick scroll. The show is the hand reaching for the device before the mind has fully decided. The named concept is *urge surfing*, a term used in some psychological and addiction contexts to describe noticing an urge without acting immediately. The explanation, broadly, is that urges rise and fall; they are not commands. The implication is not a clinical intervention but a behavioural insight: children can learn that the urge is a wave rather than a law. This is especially important for screens because cues are frequent. If a child treats every cue as a command, the day becomes a chain of micro-obligations. If a child can notice and pause, even briefly, they begin to reclaim agency.

Notice how the coaching goal differs from mere restriction. Restriction says "do not". Coaching says "notice, plan, end, return". Return matters. Many children can stop if the stop is followed by something they want. Many children melt down when the stop is followed by emptiness or by a demand they dread. The show is the child who hands over a device and then hovers, lost, because they do not know what to do with themselves next. The named concept is *transition support*. The explanation is that stopping is a transition, and transitions are difficult when the next step is unclear. The implication is that coaching includes helping a child plan the "after", not as entertainment, but as a predictable next move. A child who knows what comes next is less likely to fight the end, because the end does not feel like falling off a cliff.

This is where routines for saving progress and saying goodbye become unexpectedly powerful. A child who is mid-game often protests because they fear losing progress or losing their place socially. A teen who is mid-chat protests because they fear missing something or seeming rude. The show is the child sending a closing message or saving at a natural checkpoint. The named concept is *social closure*. The explanation is that leaving a social space abruptly can feel like breaking a rule of belonging. The implication is that coaching should treat social endings as a skill: how to sign off politely, how to tell friends "I'm off now", how to leave without leaving anxiety behind. This is not about controlling friendships. It is about teaching boundaries that protect sleep and reduce late-night spirals.

A second named, checkable example helps anchor the idea that humans learn by observing and rehearsing. In 1961, at Stanford University in Palo Alto, California, Albert Bandura's Bobo doll experiments demonstrated observational learning: children imitate behaviours they observe, especially when those behaviours appear effective. The named concept is *modelled regulation*. The explanation is that children learn what calm stopping looks like by seeing it, not by being told. The implication is that adult behaviour around their own screens matters for coaching. If adults frequently say "just a second" and then drift, children learn that drifting is normal. If adults demonstrate closing a loop, putting the phone away, and returning attention to the room, children receive a model they can copy.

A credible limitation must be faced: some children respond to coaching language as if it were patronising, especially older children and teens. They can also experience "naming feelings" as intrusive if it is delivered in a therapist voice. The named concept is *tone mismatch*. The explanation is that adolescents are sensitive to dignity threats, and some children dislike being psychoanalysed. The implication is that coaching must match the child's age and temperament. With some children the simplest language works best. With teens, coaching may need to be framed as competence-building rather than emotional processing: a practical skill for managing time, reputation, and sleep. The principle remains the same. The delivery changes.

Another limitation is that coaching does not work in the middle of an escalating conflict. A child in full meltdown is not available for skill learning. A teen in a state of rage or humiliation is not available for reflection. The named concept is *learning window*. The explanation is that skill learning requires a minimally regulated nervous system. The implication is that coaching should occur when the child is calm enough to practise, not when the adult is desperate to end an argument. Families who try to teach skills in the peak of conflict often conclude the child is unteachable. Often the timing was wrong.

Reconcile these limitations by returning to what coaching actually is: repeated low-heat practice in ordinary moments. The show is the family treating stopping as a routine that can be rehearsed, not as a moral showdown. The named concept is *habit rehearsal*. The explanation is that habits change through repetition, and repetition works best when it is predictable and not drenched in shame. The implication is that a family can build competence by choosing moments to practise clean starts and clean stops when the stakes are low, so the child has a template to draw on later when the stakes are high.

The quiet motif that unifies this work is the landing. Screens invite take-off easily. Landing is where skill shows. A child who can land a session cleanly has done something that matters far beyond screens: they have practised ending on purpose. They have practised leaving a rewarding activity without needing it to be forcibly removed. They have practised returning attention to the room, which is the raw material of family connection and of later adult life.

The unresolved tension is that the digital world is built to keep the loop open, and the child's developing brain is not yet built to close loops consistently. Coaching does not eliminate that mismatch. It helps the child notice it. The forward test is whether the household is willing to treat the next "not yet finished" protest as an opportunity to build a skill rather than as evidence of defiance. When the next session begins, will the family allow a casual drift into an endless loop again, or will it insist, calmly and consistently, that every take-off includes a planned landing?

## Gradual independence by age

In 1762, Jean-Jacques Rousseau published *Emile, or On Education* in Paris, arguing that children do not become capable through lectures alone but through carefully staged experiences that match their development. The concrete outcome was not a tidy curriculum but a durable educational idea: independence is cultivated, not declared. Rousseau was not thinking about group chats or auto-play, yet his central premise lands cleanly in modern family life. A parent cannot hand a child a powerful tool and say "be responsible now" any more than they can hand a child a violin and say "play". Responsibility is built through graduated practice in conditions where failure teaches rather than ruins.

Independence is not a switch.

Families often treat it as one, because a switch is emotionally satisfying. A child turns a certain age, gets a phone, receives a speech about trust, and is expected to self-manage. Or a child breaks a rule, loses privileges, receives a speech about consequences, and is expected to improve. These switch-like events create drama but rarely create skill. The show is the household that oscillates between full control and full freedom, with each swing justified by the last crisis. The named concept is *lurching governance*. The explanation is that adults respond to anxiety by tightening and respond to exhaustion by loosening, and children learn to ride the waves rather than to manage themselves. The implication is that the child does not internalise boundaries. They learn to wait for boundaries to change.

The task in gradual independence is to decide what responsibilities shift, when, and how, without demanding perfection and without leaving the child alone with a system designed to pull. This is where age matters, but not in the simplistic sense of "young children cannot, teens can". Capability is uneven and context-dependent. A child may be able to stop a creative app reliably and still melt down in a competitive game. A teen may manage homework time well and still struggle to disengage from late-night group chat. The named concept is *domain-specific competence*. The explanation is that self-regulation develops in patches, and patches fill in through practice. The implication is that independence should be granted in patches too, not as a blanket status.

This approach changes what "trust" means. Trust is often discussed as a feeling: "I trust you." Children hear this as either a compliment or a threat, because it can be revoked. A more useful definition is behavioural: trust is the set of responsibilities the child has demonstrated they can handle in predictable conditions. The show is the child who can keep a device out of bed for a week, end sessions cleanly, and stick to agreed windows without constant reminders. The named concept is *earned latitude*. The explanation is that latitude expands when behaviour shows capability, and contracts when behaviour shows strain, without turning every mistake into a moral verdict. The implication is that trust becomes measurable. That measurability reduces both adult anxiety and child resentment, because the rules of the system are legible rather than mysterious.

Small experiments are the natural unit of this system because experiments create feedback without humiliation. A family can treat a new level of independence as a trial with a review. The show is the household agreeing on a limited change, watching what happens, and then adjusting without drama. The named concept is *pilot testing*. The explanation is that pilots reduce risk. They prevent the common disaster of granting too much freedom too quickly and then responding with a punitive crackdown that damages relationship and teaches secrecy. The implication is that children can learn from setbacks without being branded untrustworthy, and adults can adjust without feeling they have failed.

A named, checkable example from technology history helps make the logic of pilot testing feel normal rather than weak. In September 2018, Apple released iOS 12 in Cupertino, California, introducing Screen Time features that allow families to set limits and review use patterns. The concrete outcome for many households was the ability to observe rather than guess. The named concept is *feedback loops*. The explanation is that feedback allows adjustment. Without feedback, adults rely on impressions and children rely on persuasion. The implication is that gradual independence works best when the family can review what actually happened rather than arguing about what someone believes happened. Review does not require surveillance. It requires agreed markers of success: sleep remained stable, homework began on time, sessions ended cleanly, conflicts reduced.

The "review" part matters as much as the "experiment" part because experiments without review become performative. A child learns to behave for a short time to get what they want, then drifts. An adult becomes suspicious. Suspicion invites control. The system collapses back into lurching governance. The named concept is *accountability without theatre*. The explanation is that accountability works when it is predictable and proportionate, not when it is dramatic. The implication is that the household should treat reviews as ordinary maintenance rather than as court hearings. The emotional tone of review determines whether the child sees it as a chance to learn or a chance to be judged.

Age-based differences appear most clearly in what kind of supervision is appropriate. Younger children benefit from visible structure, external cues, and adult proximity. Older children benefit from bounded choice and the beginnings of self-management with check-ins. Teens need privacy respected as a developmental necessity, but they still need safeguards around sleep, reputation, and respectful behaviour. The named concept is *scaffold transfer*. The explanation is that scaffolding should move from external to internal gradually. The implication is that a teen who has never practised self-management in small ways will not suddenly self-manage well because they are older. Age alone is not training.

What happens when independence goes badly is the moment families most often get wrong, because it triggers adult fear. A teen misses sleep. Homework slips. Mood deteriorates. The adult feels vindicated: "See, you can't handle it." The teen feels humiliated: "You wanted me to fail." Both interpretations poison the relationship. The named concept is *failure framing*. The explanation is that framing determines whether a setback becomes a learning event or a shame event. The implication is practical. If the family treats a setback as data about what conditions were too loose or what supports were missing, it can tighten one variable without collapsing the whole project of independence. If the family treats a setback as proof of character failure, it will likely overcorrect, and overcorrection tends to provoke secrecy and rebellion.

There is a credible limitation to gradual independence that must be acknowledged: some children, due to temperament, anxiety, neurodiversity, or external stress, may need longer periods of external structure, and some families may have less capacity for fine-grained experimentation because life is chaotic. The named concept is *capacity mismatch*. The explanation is that a household cannot run a delicate system if it lacks time and emotional bandwidth. The implication is that gradual independence should be scaled to the household's capacity. A simpler experiment that is consistently reviewed can outperform a sophisticated plan that no one has the energy to maintain. The goal is not elegance. It is stability.

Reconciling this limitation requires returning to the principle that independence is a trajectory, not a target. A child can move forward in one domain while remaining supported in another. A teen can be granted freedom around content choice while still being held firmly on bedtime device location. A younger child can be asked to practise clean stopping with adult help while adults keep the broader structure stable. The named concept is *partial autonomy*. The explanation is that autonomy is not all-or-nothing. The implication is that families can avoid the trap of either controlling everything or letting everything go, and instead build capability in the areas that most reduce conflict and protect wellbeing.

A quiet motif can hold the chapter's logic: the training wheels. Training wheels are not an insult. They are a design that allows a child to practise balance without the full consequence of falling. They are also temporary, and they come off in stages. The phone's settings, the household's defaults, the agreed zones, and the coached start-stop routines are all forms of training wheels. Some will be removed earlier. Some will stay longer. The dignity of the child depends on how the family talks about them: as supports for learning, not as chains for control.

The unresolved tension is that modern digital life is not something children will "graduate" from. It will intensify as they grow. They will carry devices into new schools, new friendships, new freedoms, and eventually into adult life where no one is counting minutes for them. The forward test is therefore not whether a child can comply while supervised. It is whether the household can build a progression in which the child repeatedly practises self-management under slightly looser conditions, learns from setbacks without humiliation, and gradually internalises the ability to plan a session, land it cleanly, and return to the world without being dragged. When the next request for more independence arrives, will the family treat it as a switch to flip, or as a training plan to design?

# Chapter 10
# Handling Pushback and Meltdowns

A parent stands in the hallway with a phone in their hand, the device warm from someone else's use, and says, as evenly as they can, that it is time to stop. The child reacts fast. The protest is not elegant. It arrives as pleading, as rage, as tears, as a sudden collapse onto the floor, as a storm of words that aim to wound because the child has no better weapon. The parent feels their own heat rising. The parent knows that if they argue, the argument will feed itself. The parent also knows that if they retreat, the boundary will dissolve. The house becomes a pressure cooker in a matter of seconds.

This is the hard part.

No family plan is real until it survives the moment a child refuses. All the design in the world cannot prevent every explosion, because children are not machines and neither are adults. Screens add intensity because they are bound up with reward, identity, and social life, but the deeper issue is not screens. It is what the family does when the boundary is tested by strong emotion. A household can have sensible rules and still end up with daily battles if it has no method for handling pushback without humiliation, bargaining, or threats that cannot be sustained.

The paradox is that the more parents care about a boundary, the more likely they are to enforce it badly. Caring raises the stakes. A bedtime rule is not only about bedtime; it is about tomorrow. A group chat rule is not only about messages; it is about reputation and kindness. An after-school limit is not only about minutes; it is about homework and mood. When the child pushes back, the adult feels the future wobble, and fear tends to speak in two voices: anger and control. The child, meanwhile, is often feeling a more immediate fear: loss, exclusion, unfinishedness, humiliation. Both parties are trying to protect themselves. The clash produces escalation.

The central tension of this chapter is between firmness and relationship. Many adults believe they must choose: either hold the boundary and damage the relationship, or preserve the relationship and give up the boundary. That is a false choice. It becomes true only when the adult uses humiliation, sarcasm, and power plays to enforce a rule, or when the adult bargains so much that the boundary becomes meaningless. A family can be firm and relational at the same time, but it requires skill. It requires language that lowers the temperature rather than raises it, consequences that teach rather than retaliate, and repair that restores dignity without rewriting the rule.

This matters because meltdowns are information. They are not good information, not pleasant information, but they are information about what the child cannot yet tolerate and what the household has trained. If a child melts down every time a game ends, the household is seeing stop friction and unfinishedness. If a teen melts down around messaging limits, the household is seeing social pressure and fear of exclusion. If a child's pushback becomes cruel, the household is seeing a deficit in respectful conflict skills, not merely "bad attitude". When adults treat meltdowns only as misbehaviour to crush, they miss the chance to teach regulation. When adults treat meltdowns only as suffering to soothe, they miss the chance to build resilience. The household needs a third posture: calm containment with learning later.

It also matters because consequences are inevitable, whether families choose them or not. The consequence of bargaining is that bargaining increases. The consequence of shouting is that shouting becomes normal. The consequence of humiliation is secrecy. The consequence of inconsistent enforcement is constant testing. These are all consequences. The question is whether the family will choose consequences that are related, respectful, and consistent, or whether it will allow the heat of the moment to choose consequences that feel satisfying and then backfire over days and weeks. A consequence that restores trust may be temporarily unpopular, but it has a chance of reducing future conflict. Punishment that aims to hurt tends to produce smarter resistance.

Repair is the second half of firmness that most households forget. Repair does not mean reversing the boundary. It means restoring relationship after conflict so that rules do not become scars. A parent can regret shouting and still keep the rule. A child can regret rude words and still accept that the device is put away. Without repair, each conflict deposits a little resentment, and resentment accumulates until even small limits trigger outsized reactions. With repair, the family teaches a powerful lesson: conflict can happen without breaking us. That lesson matters far beyond screens.

There is also a point at which pushback signals something larger than a boundary problem. Some screen conflict is the surface expression of anxiety, friendship stress, learning struggles, sensory overload, or chronic sleep debt. Families can often feel this in the texture of the conflict: it is not only frequent, it is disproportionate; it is not only loud, it is despairing. Treating those moments as pure discipline problems can increase shame and reduce honesty. Recognising them as possible signals allows the family to seek support without framing the child as defective. The household can keep clarity while widening compassion.

The path through this chapter follows the arc of a real conflict. It begins with language that stops the debate without crushing the child, because the way adults speak in the first ten seconds often determines whether the conflict escalates. It then turns to consequences that aim to teach and restore trust, rather than to retaliate in anger. It then turns to repair, because even the best systems fail sometimes and families need a way back. It ends by widening the lens, because some conflicts persist not due to weak rules but due to deeper pressures that deserve attention and support.

A quiet motif can hold this work: the thermostat. In a heated moment, the household is tempted to act like a kettle, rushing to boiling. A thermostat does something else. It notices heat and regulates it. It does not argue with heat. It does not shame heat. It prevents the whole system from blowing. Families need thermostat skills: phrases, routines, and consequences that keep the emotional temperature within a range where learning remains possible and dignity remains intact.

The unresolved question that pulls into the first section is simple enough to be uncomfortable. When your child pushes back, what do they reliably get: a debate, a bargain, a threat, or a calm boundary? And when you push back as the adult, what do you reliably lose: your tone, your consistency, your confidence, or the relationship itself? The next meltdown will answer, unless the household learns to regulate the temperature before it reaches boiling.

## Scripts that lower the temperature

In 1962, at the University of Kansas in Lawrence, Thomas Gordon published *Parent Effectiveness Training*, turning a set of communication ideas into a widely adopted programme. The concrete outcome was not instant family harmony but a practical shift: parents were encouraged to separate feelings from control, to listen without capitulating, and to speak in ways that reduced escalation. Whatever one thinks of the programme's later popularisations, the underlying insight is sturdy. When adults are under stress, they improvise. Improvisation in conflict tends to produce either lectures or threats. Children respond with either defiance or collapse. A script is an antidote to improvisation, not because families should speak like robots, but because a calm, repeatable line can keep everyone out of the ditch.

Words can change the room.

That is not sentimental. It is behavioural. A child's escalation is often an attempt to change the adult's behaviour, and the adult's escalation is often an attempt to change the child's behaviour. Both are trying to control the situation through tone. If you change tone, you change reinforcement. The family learns, over time, what kinds of words lead to bargaining, what kinds lead to shouting, and what kinds lead to a clean ending. A useful script is not a slogan. It is a small piece of language that does three jobs quickly: it acknowledges the feeling, it states the boundary, and it closes the debate without humiliation.

Consider a typical screen conflict. The adult says "time to stop." The child says "no," or "in a minute," or "it's not fair." The adult hears challenge and tries to persuade: "You've had enough," "You were on it all day," "If you don't stop now you'll lose it tomorrow." Persuasion becomes argument because the child responds with counter-arguments, and counter-arguments are rewarded by attention and by the possibility of a better deal. The named concept is *argument reinforcement*. The explanation is that every time a child's protest prolongs the interaction, the protest gains value. The implication is that parents who want fewer arguments must stop paying the child in debate time. That does not mean becoming cold. It means closing the bargaining channel while keeping empathy open.

Empathy is often misunderstood here. Many adults assume empathy means agreeing or giving in. Children often assume the same. A script that acknowledges feelings without shifting the boundary teaches a more useful lesson: feelings are real, and rules are real. The show is the adult who says, calmly, "I can hear you're upset," and then does not negotiate the stop time. The named concept is *validation without concession*. The explanation is that people calm faster when they feel heard, yet boundaries hold only when they are not reopened under pressure. The implication is that the most effective scripts often sound almost boring. Boring is good. Boring does not escalate.

A common adult error is to treat the child's protest as disrespect rather than as distress. Distress can look rude. Children often lack the language to express incompletion, disappointment, or social fear, so they express power: "You're mean," "I hate you," "You can't make me." If the adult responds by defending their own moral character, the conflict becomes personal and expands. The named concept is *identity entanglement*. The explanation is that when a parent hears "you're mean" as an accusation about their goodness, they respond with anger or self-justification. The implication is that scripts should avoid turning the moment into a debate about who is right. Rightness is irrelevant at the point of enforcement. The family needs calm execution, not courtroom arguments.

The key to lowering temperature is to keep the focus on process rather than on motive. Process is observable. Motive invites speculation. "You're addicted" is a motive claim and it provokes shame. "The rule is no screens now" is a process statement and it can be enforced without humiliation. The named concept is *behavioural framing*. The explanation is that children can comply with a behavioural frame even when they disagree, while motive framing invites them to defend their identity. The implication is that scripts should describe what is happening and what happens next, not why the child is "like this". Families do not reduce conflict by diagnosing in the moment.

A named, checkable example from behavioural science helps clarify why steady scripts work. In 1982, Gerald R. Patterson published *Coercive Family Process* based on work associated with the Oregon Social Learning Center, describing how families can accidentally train escalation: one person escalates, the other yields, and the escalation behaviour is reinforced. The named concept is *coercive cycles*. The explanation is that when escalation changes outcomes, escalation becomes rational. The implication is direct. If a child learns that whining extends screen time, whining will continue. If a child learns that shouting triggers a lecture and then a delay and then sometimes a concession, shouting will continue. Scripts that lower the temperature are not merely polite. They are a way of changing reinforcement: protest no longer buys a better deal or a longer debate.

The most dangerous moment in screen conflict is the micro-bargain that adults offer without noticing. "Just five more minutes" seems compassionate. It can be. It can also become the currency that trains negotiation, especially if the minutes are granted in response to protest rather than as part of an agreed plan. The show is the parent who offers an extension to quiet the child and then feels resentful, and the child who learns that protest works. The named concept is *accidental bargaining*. The explanation is that adults bargain when they are tired because bargaining buys short-term peace. The implication is that scripts should protect adults from their own impulse to bargain in the heat. A script that points to review time, rather than reopening the deal, is not rigid. It is strategic. It delays negotiation to a calmer context, where negotiation can be fair rather than emotional.

This is where "review time" becomes a powerful phrase. Review time is the opposite of "never". It signals that the child's perspective will be heard, but not under duress and not as a price for shouting. The named concept is *deferred negotiation*. The explanation is that children often escalate because they fear there is no other channel for their preferences to matter. The implication is that a family that genuinely holds reviews, even brief ones, gains credibility when it says "not now". The child believes the door is not locked forever. The adult protects the boundary in the moment. Both sides retain dignity.

A second named, checkable anchor is useful because it shows this is not only a parenting tactic but a common principle in conflict management. Thomas Gordon's work in 1962 emphasised listening skills and I-messages, and while the language can feel dated, the core mechanics still apply: acknowledge feeling, state boundary, avoid blame. The named concept is *low-heat communication*. The explanation is that blame triggers defence; defence triggers escalation. The implication is that families can reduce screen conflicts by using language that does not corner the child into defending their worth. Children cornered into defence often attack back.

Scripts also matter because they regulate the adult's nervous system. In conflict, adults tend to speed up: faster speech, longer explanations, sharper tone. Speed communicates threat. Children react to threat with either fight or flight. A slow, simple script can keep the adult from spiralling, which keeps the child from spiralling. The named concept is *co-regulation*. The explanation is that children borrow regulation from adults, and adults can also borrow steadiness from their own prepared language. The implication is that scripts are not only for children. They are a tool for adults to remain the kind of authority they want to be: firm without cruelty, calm without collapse.

The challenge is that scripts can become patronising if delivered like a performance. Teens, especially, can smell the therapy voice. They can interpret scripted empathy as manipulation. A credible limitation, then, is that a script must sound like the adult who is speaking it. The named concept is *authentic phrasing*. The explanation is that children accept boundaries more readily when they believe the adult is sincere. The implication is that each household should find versions of these lines that match its tone, while keeping the underlying structure intact: acknowledgement, boundary, closure, review. The structure does the work. The exact words can vary.

Another limitation is that scripts alone cannot override a badly designed system. If the household's rules are inconsistent, if exceptions are extracted through pleading, if adults often give in when tired, scripts will be experienced as empty. Children listen to outcomes, not sentences. The named concept is *credibility dependence*. The explanation is that language works when it is backed by predictable follow-through. The implication is that scripts should be paired with the earlier work of defaults and agreements. A calm line that points to a shared rule has far more power than a calm line that floats in a vacuum.

A quiet motif can hold this subchapter: the pause. A pause in speech. A pause before responding. A pause before bargaining. The pause is the moment the family chooses not to escalate. Screens are built to remove pauses: auto-play, feeds, pings. Families can reintroduce pauses through language. A good script is a verbal pause button. It stops the debate from becoming a chase.

The forward test is deceptively simple. When the next protest arrives and your child raises their voice or demands an exception, what happens next in your home: a debate that rewards escalation, a bargain that teaches pressure, or a calm line that acknowledges feeling and closes the deal? If you can predict your own next sentence under stress, you can predict the child's next behaviour. The work begins when you decide which sentence you want to be predictable.

## Consequences that teach

In 1982, Gerald R. Patterson published *Coercive Family Process*, drawing on work associated with the Oregon Social Learning Center, and put a concrete name on what many households experience without understanding: families can accidentally train the very behaviours they most want to stop. When escalation leads to adult surrender, escalation is reinforced. When adult shouting leads to child compliance, shouting is reinforced. The "consequence" in these cycles is not the one the parent intends; it is the one the behaviour reliably produces. That is the uncomfortable value of Patterson's work for screen conflict. It reminds us that consequences are always happening. The only question is whether they are teaching what the family wants taught.

Punishment feels satisfying briefly.

Teaching feels slower. It also lasts.

Screen battles tempt parents into punishments that are large, theatrical, and hard to sustain: the kind of punishment that promises to fix the problem through force. "No devices for a week" is the classic example, often declared in anger because anger wants a big lever. The lever seems sensible in the moment, yet it contains three design flaws. It is usually unrelated to the specific behaviour. It is often impossible to enforce consistently, especially if devices are needed for homework or family logistics. And it teaches the child to focus on the parent's power rather than on their own choices. A teaching consequence does something different. It is related to what happened, it is proportionate, and it is consistent enough to be believable. The goal is not to hurt. The goal is to restore trust and build skill.

The first step is to define what a consequence is meant to teach, because without a teaching target, the consequence becomes emotional discharge. A child uses a device in bed after curfew. A teen posts something unkind. A younger child refuses to stop and becomes rude. These are different problems. They require different lessons. The show is the parent who responds to all of them with the same punishment: total device confiscation. The named concept is *consequence mismatch*. The explanation is that mismatched consequences feel arbitrary, and arbitrary consequences invite resentment and rebellion. The implication is that the family loses legitimacy, which makes future compliance harder. Children do not become more responsible because adults become more severe; they become more responsible when the link between behaviour and outcome is clear.

A related consequence means the consequence connects to the behaviour in an intelligible way. This is not a fashionable idea. It is basic learning theory. If a behaviour produces an outcome that is logically linked, the child can infer what to change. If the outcome is random, the child learns only that the adult is powerful. The show is the difference between pausing a specific app after the child repeatedly broke the agreement about it, and taking every device away regardless of which behaviour caused the breach. The named concept is *contingency clarity*. The explanation is that clear contingencies teach cause and effect. The implication is that a temporary pause on a specific app can teach more than a sweeping ban because it says, precisely, "this behaviour with this tool broke trust; we are adjusting this tool until trust is rebuilt". It targets the problem rather than staging punishment.

Respectful consequences are not gentle. They are dignified. Respect means no humiliation, no sarcasm, no public shaming, no character assassination. It also means the adult's response does not create fear as a primary motivator, because fear teaches hiding. The show is the parent who discovers a breach and announces it at dinner in front of siblings, turning the child's mistake into family entertainment. The named concept is *shame escalation*. The explanation is that shame triggers defence, defence triggers lying, and lying triggers further control. The implication is that humiliating consequences produce short-term compliance and long-term secrecy. A respectful consequence can still be firm. It simply avoids turning the child into "the kind of person who does this". It focuses on the behaviour and on repairing trust.

Consistency is the third ingredient, and it is where many well-meaning families stumble. A consequence that is applied sometimes is not merely inconsistent; it is intermittent reinforcement, which is particularly good at maintaining behaviour. If a child learns that pleading occasionally eliminates a consequence, pleading will continue. If a teen learns that anger occasionally leads to adult backing down, anger will continue. The show is the household where consequences depend on adult fatigue or on whether guests are present. The named concept is *variable enforcement*. The explanation is that variable enforcement teaches children to test more often, because the boundary is not stable. The implication is that the family ends up spending more time in conflict even if the rules are sensible, because the enforcement schedule is teaching negotiation as a skill.

A named, checkable example from mainstream technology helps show why specificity matters. In September 2018, Apple released iOS 12 in Cupertino, California, introducing Screen Time as a built-in way to restrict specific apps and schedule downtime. The concrete outcome was that families could, if they chose, impose a targeted restriction rather than an all-or-nothing confiscation. The named concept is *granular limits*. The explanation is that granular limits allow proportionality: the response can match the behaviour. The implication is that proportionality supports legitimacy. A child is more likely to accept a boundary when they can see its logic, even if they dislike it. Granularity also supports learning. If the child loses access to the specific app that caused trouble, they learn to connect action with consequence rather than learning only that "screens make parents angry".

This does not mean every family must use device settings or become technical. The principle stands with or without settings. Target the behaviour. Preserve dignity. Follow through. These principles are also why consequences should be decided in advance, when possible. In the heat of a meltdown, adults are tempted to overreach. Overreach produces threats that cannot be sustained, and threats that cannot be sustained teach children to wait out adult intensity. The show is the parent who declares a long ban and then quietly shortens it, hoping the child will not notice. The child notices. The named concept is *credibility loss*. The explanation is that children treat adult backtracking as evidence that boundaries are negotiable. The implication is that even a smaller, enforceable consequence is often more effective than a grand one that collapses.

Consequences that teach also attend to the social and relational damage that can occur during a screen conflict. Many families focus on the screen rule breach and ignore the way the conflict was handled: the rudeness, the shouting, the insults. Yet those behaviours are part of what must be taught. A child can learn that they are allowed to be angry and still required to be respectful. A teen can learn that they are allowed to disagree and still required to repair if they lash out. The abstraction is *respect*, but it becomes visible as an action: making amends after rude behaviour. The named concept is *relationship repair obligation*. The explanation is that families are small social systems, and harm within the system requires repair for trust to remain. The implication is that a consequence can include a repair step not as humiliation, but as restoration. It signals that the household cares not only about rules but about how people treat each other when rules are enforced.

A second named, checkable anchor reinforces why restorative approaches are not merely soft modern sentiment. In 1971, the psychologist Albert Bandura published *Social Learning Theory*, emphasising how people learn through observing models and consequences. The named concept is *observational learning*. The explanation is that children learn how conflict works by watching adult responses. The implication is that a parent who enforces consequences with contempt models contempt as a legitimate tool. A parent who enforces consequences with steadiness models steadiness. Children copy what works and what feels normal. A consequence that teaches is also a lesson in how power can be used without cruelty.

A credible limitation must be acknowledged. Some children, particularly those who are highly reactive, anxious, or dealing with neurodiversity, may not respond to consequences in the same way as others. A consequence that feels proportionate to an adult can feel catastrophic to a child with a sensitive nervous system. A teen may respond to a consequence with withdrawal rather than argument, and adults may misread withdrawal as compliance when it is actually shame. The named concept is *differential impact*. The explanation is that the same consequence can land differently depending on temperament, stress, and developmental stage. The implication is not to abandon consequences. It is to calibrate them and to pair them with repair and clarity, so that the consequence remains a learning tool rather than a relational wound.

Reconciling this limitation returns us to the teaching target. If the target is "sleep is protected", the consequence should reinforce sleep protection without creating a battle that destroys sleep. If the target is "respectful behaviour", the consequence should reinforce respectful communication and include a path back into dignity. If the target is "honesty", the consequence should make honesty safer than lying, otherwise the family will train secrecy. The abstraction is *accountability*, but it becomes visible as a predictable sequence: breach, consequence, repair, reset. The named concept is *system recovery*. The explanation is that families need a way back to normal after enforcement; otherwise each conflict lingers and poisons the next day. The implication is that a consequence that teaches always includes a reset path, because the aim is not to keep the child in trouble. The aim is to return the household to stability with a clearer trust boundary.

A final problem deserves attention because it is where well-meaning families often sabotage their own teaching consequences: they attach consequences to adult emotion rather than to behaviour. "You made me angry, so you lose it." Children then learn that the adult's mood is the rule. That creates anxiety and testing, because mood is unpredictable. The named concept is *mood-based governance*. The explanation is that mood-based governance turns the household into a lottery. The implication is that children respond to lotteries by gambling, and gambling looks like constant probing: "Can I have it now?" Teaching consequences reduce gambling by making outcomes predictable and tied to behaviour, not tied to the adult's internal weather.

The motif that holds this subchapter together is the bridge. A consequence is not merely a wall that blocks access. It is a bridge back to trust. A wall produces standoffs. A bridge communicates: you can get back to normal by doing specific things, and those things are within your control. Children need bridges because they are learners. Teens need bridges because they are practising adult responsibility and need to know the system is not designed to trap them in shame.

The forward test is uncomfortable because it asks adults to examine their own impulses. When your child breaks a screen rule or becomes rude in the conflict, do you reach for the largest punishment because it feels satisfying, or for the most related consequence because it teaches? When you imagine the consequence, can you describe the lesson it is meant to produce in the child's behaviour, and can you enforce it consistently without escalating the household's emotional temperature? If the consequence cannot be explained as a bridge back to trust, it is probably a wall, and walls are where resentment learns to live.

## Repairing after a blow-up

In 1994, John M. Gottman published *Why Marriages Succeed or Fail* in New York, bringing a concrete idea into the popular understanding of relationships: conflict is not the main predictor of relational health; repair is. The outcome was a shift in emphasis. The question stopped being "Do you argue?" and became "What happens after you argue?" Families are not marriages, and parent-child power is not symmetrical, yet the principle translates with unnerving accuracy to screen conflict. A household will have blow-ups. The difference between a blow-up that strengthens a family and a blow-up that scars it is whether repair is possible, predictable, and dignified.

Repair is how rules survive.

Without repair, boundaries become a slow grind of resentment. Children remember not only what was enforced, but how it felt to be enforced. Adults remember not only the child's defiance, but how it felt to lose control of themselves. Each conflict deposits a residue: a child's shame, an adult's guilt, a sibling's fear, a household's tension. Residue accumulates. Then the next small boundary triggers an outsized reaction, not because the boundary is new, but because the old residue is still in the room. Repair is the method for removing residue. It is not a sentimental gesture. It is maintenance.

A blow-up has a recognisable arc. A boundary is stated. The child protests. The adult repeats. The child escalates. The adult escalates back. Words become sharper than necessary. Someone slams a door or throws a cushion. A sibling watches and learns something, often silently. Later, the house becomes quiet again, but the quiet is brittle. The named concept is *post-conflict fragility*. The explanation is that the nervous system does not instantly reset when the shouting stops; people carry adrenaline and humiliation forward. The implication is that families who treat the end of the argument as the end of the event are mistaken. The event continues until repair occurs, because the meaning of the argument is still being written in everyone's head.

Repair begins with a refusal to confuse two different things: the boundary and the adult's behaviour while enforcing it. A parent can hold a boundary and still admit that their tone was too harsh. A child can accept a boundary and still admit that they were rude. This separation is essential. When a parent refuses to apologise because they fear it will weaken authority, they create a false link: authority equals infallibility. Children then learn that power never admits error, and they either imitate that posture or resent it. When a parent apologises by surrendering the boundary, they create the opposite false link: apology equals collapse. Children then learn that emotional intensity can force rule reversal. The named concept is *boundary-apology confusion*. The explanation is that families often think they must choose between being right and being kind. The implication is that repair must teach a third lesson: we can be firm and still be accountable for how we speak.

This is why repair is a skill, not a mood. Many families wait for everyone to "calm down" and then hope the awkwardness fades. Sometimes it does. Often it turns into avoidance, and avoidance teaches that conflict is too dangerous to revisit. The named concept is *avoidance settling*. The explanation is that people prefer the relief of silence to the discomfort of a repair conversation, especially after anger. The implication is that unresolved conflict becomes a background tension that leaks into the next day. Children may become prickly. Parents may become colder. Siblings may become more likely to antagonise each other because the household mood is already charged. Repair is the deliberate choice not to let avoidance write the ending.

A useful repair sequence is short, specific, and focused on behaviour and impact rather than on grand moral judgement. It starts by naming what happened without litigating it again. It includes an apology that is concrete: "I spoke too sharply," not "I'm sorry you feel that way." It states the boundary again briefly so the apology is not misread as surrender. It then offers a path back to normal: what the family will do next time, how the child can recover dignity, how everyone returns to the shared rhythm. The named concept is *repair script*. The explanation is that repair is easier when it is practised and predictable. The implication is that families who develop a repair script recover faster and argue less over time, because each blow-up does not become a permanent stain.

A named, checkable example of repair as a measurable skill can be found in Gottman's research and writing from the 1990s, which emphasised "repair attempts" as small behaviours that de-escalate conflict. The named concept is *repair attempts*. The explanation is that repairs do not need to be dramatic; they need to be effective. The implication for families is that repair can be taught and modelled. A parent who says "I'm getting too angry; I need a pause" is making a repair attempt. A child who says "I was rude; I'm sorry" is making a repair attempt. These are not mere manners. They are conflict management behaviours that protect relationships.

Repair also matters because it supports the very values the household is trying to teach. A family that enforces kindness online but cannot repair after shouting at home is teaching a contradiction. A family that demands respect from children while adults refuse to acknowledge their own missteps is teaching hierarchy, not respect. The named concept is *value integrity*. The explanation is that children learn values through lived behaviour, not through stated ideals. The implication is that repair is a form of modelling. It shows that strength includes accountability, and that dignity can be restored without denying what happened.

Siblings add complexity because screen conflict rarely affects only the child who is using the device. Siblings are audience members, and audiences learn. A sibling may feel envy if one child gets more freedom. They may feel relief if the "problem child" is being punished. They may feel fear if shouting becomes loud. They may also learn tactics: if the older child can derail the evening through a meltdown, the younger child may imitate the strategy. The named concept is *social contagion*. The explanation is that behaviour spreads within families, especially when it appears to change outcomes. The implication is that repair must include siblings, at least indirectly. The household should restore safety in the room, make clear that aggression is not a tool, and avoid turning one child into a scapegoat in front of the others. Scapegoating creates long-term sibling resentment and teaches cruelty.

This is also where dignity becomes essential. After a blow-up, a child often feels ashamed, even if they are not ready to admit it. Shame can become sulking, sarcasm, or a refusal to rejoin the family. Adults sometimes respond by demanding a full apology immediately, as if the apology is a toll the child must pay to regain belonging. The named concept is *apology coercion*. The explanation is that coerced apologies rarely teach empathy; they teach performance. The implication is that repair should aim to restore dignity so the child can take responsibility without being cornered. Dignity is not indulgence. It is the precondition for genuine accountability.

A credible limitation must be faced: some children, especially those who are highly reactive, anxious, or neurodivergent, may find repair conversations difficult in the immediate aftermath. Some teens may interpret repair attempts as manipulation, particularly if the adult's apology is vague or if the adult often apologises and then repeats the same behaviour. The named concept is *repair distrust*. The explanation is that repair loses power when it becomes performative. The implication is that repair must be paired with behaviour change, however small. A parent who apologises for shouting and then shouts again the next night without any adjustment teaches the child that apologies are meaningless. A child who apologises and then repeats the same rudeness without any learning also drains the repair process. Repair must carry a forward-looking commitment that is observable, otherwise it becomes ritualised without effect.

Reconciling this limitation means treating repair as part of the household's system, not as a one-off emotional event. Repair is strengthened by predictability: the family knows when repair happens, what it sounds like, and what it leads to. Repair is strengthened by specificity: naming the behaviour and the impact. Repair is strengthened by proportionate consequences that remain in place, because accountability and repair are partners. The named concept is *system recovery*. The explanation is that healthy systems recover from perturbations without collapsing. The implication is that a family plan becomes robust when it includes not only rules and consequences but also recovery mechanisms. Bad days are not proof the plan is wrong. They are proof the family is human.

The motif worth holding here is the reset button. Screens have reset buttons. You close an app and it stops, at least for a moment. Families need reset buttons too: short, repeatable actions that mark the end of a conflict episode and the return to normal. Without resets, conflict episodes bleed into the next hour and the next day. With resets, the family can enforce boundaries without leaving emotional wreckage. The reset is not amnesia. It is closure.

The unresolved question that pulls this forward is sharp. After the next blow-up, what will be left in your home: a boundary held at the cost of shame, or a boundary held with dignity restored? When you replay the argument later, will you remember only the defiance and the shouting, or will you be able to point to the moment the family repaired and returned, teaching everyone, quietly, that rules are not the only thing that must be protected? The answer is not written during the conflict. It is written after it.

## When you need extra support

In 1948, the World Health Organization was established in Geneva, and a concrete shift in public language followed over the decades: health was framed not merely as the absence of disease but as a broader state that includes mental and social wellbeing. That framing matters in family screen conflict because screens are rarely the whole story. They are often the most visible story, the object in the child's hand, the argument that hijacks dinner. Visibility is seductive. It makes the screen feel like the cause. Sometimes it is. Sometimes it is a symptom with a bright display.

Look under the argument.

Most families can reduce screen battles with clearer rules, better defaults, and calmer enforcement. Yet some households do all of that and still find themselves stuck in a cycle that feels disproportionate: meltdowns that seem too intense for the trigger, secrecy that persists despite calm responses, sleep that stays fragile despite curfews, a child whose mood or functioning does not improve even when the screen is reduced. In those cases, the most helpful move is not to tighten rules again. It is to ask what the screen is doing in the child's life that the household has not yet addressed directly.

The central idea here is diagnostic, not accusatory. When screen conflict is unusually intense or unusually persistent, it can be masking a larger issue such as anxiety, friendship stress, learning struggles, or chronic sleep problems. Masking does not mean the child is faking. It means the child is using the screen as a coping tool or an avoidance tool because the underlying stress is harder to face and harder to name. The show is the child who explodes at the moment of stopping, not because the device is sacred, but because the device is the only place they feel competent or safe. The named concept is *coping substitution*. The explanation is that children, like adults, seek relief. When they lack other strategies, they use what works quickly. The implication is that a family can win the phone and still lose the child's wellbeing if the underlying need remains unaddressed.

Anxiety is a common driver because screens are excellent anxiety management tools. They distract. They fill quiet. They provide predictable stimulation. They offer social reassurance through checking. They can also worsen anxiety through comparison and drama, but the point is not simple causality.

The show is the child who reaches for the device at the first sign of discomfort: waiting, homework, bedtime, social uncertainty. The named concept is *avoidance reinforcement*. The explanation is that avoidance reduces anxiety in the moment, which makes avoidance more likely next time. The implication is that screen limits alone can feel like removing a child's main coping tool without replacing it, which often increases conflict. In such cases, support should focus on building alternative coping skills and reducing the underlying anxiety, not merely on enforcing a stricter boundary.

Friendship stress is another driver that parents can miss because children often hide it. Social pain is hard to discuss, and screens can both amplify and conceal it. A child may cling to group chats because they fear exclusion. They may scroll because it numbs rejection. They may play online because it provides a clear status system when school social life feels messy. The show is the child who becomes intensely distressed about messaging access or who seems preoccupied with the phone even when not using it. The named concept is *social vigilance*. The explanation is that when belonging feels uncertain, children monitor for cues. Screens make monitoring easy and endless. The implication is that conflict about messaging is sometimes conflict about social safety. A household that treats it as mere defiance may inadvertently teach the child to handle social distress alone, which is rarely the safer option.

Learning struggles can also sit beneath screen conflict in plain sight. A child who finds homework genuinely hard will seek escape at the moment homework is expected. A screen offers escape without requiring the child to admit they feel stuck or ashamed. The show is the child who "forgets" homework, who melts down when asked to begin, who becomes oppositional when the screen is removed. The named concept is *competence avoidance*. The explanation is that avoiding a task protects the child from feeling incompetent in the moment, even if it creates bigger problems later. The implication is that a screen plan may need to be paired with support for learning, executive function, or attention strategies, otherwise the screen becomes the lightning rod for a deeper struggle with school demands. In such cases, the family's most helpful shift is often to treat "screen resistance" as a clue about workload, comprehension, or stress rather than as a pure discipline problem.

Sleep problems can be both cause and amplifier. A child who is chronically tired is more emotionally reactive, less tolerant of frustration, and more likely to use screens for comfort because tired minds crave easy rewards. A child who uses screens late at night can become more tired, which increases emotional volatility, which increases screen reliance. The show is the household stuck in a loop: sleep deteriorates, conflict increases, screens feel more necessary, and bedtime becomes a battleground. The named concept is *fatigue spiral*. The explanation is that sleep is upstream; when it fails, everything downstream becomes harder. The implication is that families may need additional support to stabilise sleep routines, address underlying sleep difficulties, or manage the day's stressors that feed into night-time coping. Again, the point is not diagnosis. It is system awareness.

A named, checkable example helps ground the broader point that children's wellbeing involves social and emotional dimensions, not only behaviour management. The World Health Organization, founded in 1948 in Geneva, has consistently framed health in terms that include mental and social wellbeing. The named concept is *whole-child framing*. The explanation is that children's behaviour is often a signal of internal state and environmental fit. The implication is that a family that seeks extra support is not "failing". It is recognising that the child's needs may exceed what household rules alone can meet.

The question then becomes how to seek support without turning the child into a problem to be fixed. Shame is a barrier.

It prevents parents from asking for help and prevents children from accepting help. The show is the parent who delays seeking support because they fear judgement, or the child who refuses to talk because they fear being labelled. The named concept is *shame avoidance*. The explanation is that shame thrives in secrecy and isolation. The implication is that the family's first task is to maintain a stance of clarity without accusation: something is hard, we can see it, and we will find support that respects you. That stance makes it more likely the child will cooperate rather than resist.

Support is also most effective when it is approached as a set of conversations across systems, not as a single dramatic intervention. Schools, health services, and community organisations exist in most places precisely because children develop in contexts that extend beyond the home. A child can be struggling socially at school and coping through screens at home. A child can be struggling with attention in the classroom and melting down at homework time. A child can be overwhelmed by transitions and using screens as regulation. The named concept is *context integration*. The explanation is that a child's behaviour is shaped by multiple environments, and changing one environment may not be enough. The implication is that families often benefit from coordinating support rather than trying to solve everything privately.

There is a credible limitation that must be admitted: seeking support can be hard. Access varies. Waiting times exist. Schools and services differ. Families may have financial constraints or previous negative experiences. The named concept is *support friction*. The explanation is that systems designed to help are not always easy to navigate. The implication is not to give up. It is to keep the aim modest and specific: reduce conflict, increase sleep stability, increase the child's coping repertoire, reduce secrecy, improve school functioning. A family does not need a perfect service landscape to take a first step towards support.

Another limitation is that some children interpret "getting help" as confirmation that they are broken. This is where the household's language matters. If support is framed as punishment or as evidence of failure, the child will resist. If support is framed as skill-building and stress-reduction, the child is more likely to engage. The named concept is *meaning framing*. The explanation is that people cooperate more readily when they believe the process protects their dignity. The implication is that families should keep the focus on practical outcomes: fewer fights, better mornings, calmer bedtimes, less stress, more freedom earned through competence. Dignity is not soft. It is functional.

A quiet motif can hold this: the smoke alarm. A smoke alarm is noisy and irritating. It is also an early warning system, not the fire itself. Screen conflict can function similarly. It is loud. It is disruptive. It can also be telling you something important about what is burning underneath: anxiety, loneliness, shame, exhaustion, learning frustration. A family that only silences the alarm may miss the fire. A family that checks for fire without panicking uses the alarm correctly. The goal is not to pathologise every argument. The goal is to recognise when the frequency, intensity, or persistence of conflict suggests the need to look deeper.

Notice what this does to the family plan. It does not abandon boundaries. It strengthens them by removing false blame. When a child is struggling, the household can remain firm about the boundary while becoming more curious about the struggle. It can hold the line on bedtime screens while acknowledging that the child's anxiety is real and deserves support. It can hold the line on homework-time devices while recognising that the child may need learning support. It can hold the line on group chats after curfew while recognising the child's fear of exclusion. Firmness and support are not opposites. They are a partnership.

The unresolved question is not "Do we need help?" in some global sense. The question is whether the family's current tools are producing the outcomes it wants. If conflict remains high, secrecy remains high, sleep remains unstable, or the child's mood and functioning remain strained despite sensible rules and calm enforcement, the smoke alarm is doing its job. Something else is going on. Will the family interpret that noise as evidence that the child is difficult, or as evidence that the household needs extra support to help the child build skills and stability?

# Chapter 11
# Monitoring Without Spying

A parent picks up a child's phone from the kitchen counter to move it out of the way and notices a message preview flash across the screen. The parent's thumb pauses, hovering, as if the device has suddenly become heavier. Curiosity rises. Worry rises faster. The parent can justify a quick look: safety, responsibility, just checking. The child walks in, sees the phone in the parent's hand, and their face changes in an instant. The child does not ask what was seen. They ask, with a tight voice, why the parent is "going through my stuff". The argument has not yet begun, but the trust has already moved.

Secrets grow in shadows.

Families often treat monitoring as a binary: either you trust your child and never look, or you suspect your child and you check everything. Both stances produce avoidable harm. Never looking can be a form of abandonment dressed up as respect. Checking everything can become surveillance dressed up as love. The household needs a more intelligent middle: transparent oversight that is proportional to age and risk, paired with enough privacy for a child to develop an independent self without learning secrecy as a survival skill. That middle is harder than either extreme because it requires the adult to tolerate not knowing everything while still being responsible.

The central tension is between safety and dignity. Adults are right to worry about what children can encounter: social pressure, risky content, impulsive posting, strangers, drama that feels trivial to adults and catastrophic to kids. Children are also right to care about privacy. Privacy is not an indulgence. It is a developmental need, especially in adolescence, when identity is being built and tested. Monitoring that disregards dignity creates a child who becomes strategic, not necessarily safer. Privacy without boundaries creates a child who may be left alone with situations they are not equipped to handle. The trade-off is not "trust versus control". It is "transparent boundaries versus secret surveillance".

This matters because the emotional meaning of monitoring often matters more than the technical details. A child who knows what adults might check, when, and why is less likely to feel ambushed and more likely to accept oversight as part of household safety. A child who discovers checking after the fact learns a darker lesson: adults will violate privacy when anxious and then deny it. That lesson trains two behaviours that undermine safety: hiding and lying. Once a child believes privacy is fragile, they build thicker walls. The adult then responds with more monitoring. The cycle escalates. A family can end up with more knowledge and less trust, which is a poor bargain.

It also matters because children will make digital mistakes, and the household's response to those mistakes determines whether future mistakes are disclosed. A child will misjudge tone. A teen will overshare. Someone will post too quickly, forward something thoughtless, or click the wrong thing. These are not edge cases. They are normal learning events in a medium designed for speed. The question is whether the child learns that mistakes are handled with fear and punishment, or with accountability and learning. Fear produces secrecy. Learning produces growth. Monitoring without spying supports the learning path because it keeps the adult-child relationship intact enough for honest conversations to happen.

Adults are not outside this system. If a parent demands restraint and privacy from a child while practising compulsive checking themselves, the plan collapses under hypocrisy. Children do not follow speeches. They follow norms. Norms are visible. The phone on the dinner table, the constant work notifications, the scrolling while saying "listen to me" are all lessons. When adults model boundary-respectful behaviour, they reduce the hypocrisy argument instantly and strengthen the legitimacy of the household's monitoring expectations. When adults hide their own exceptions or deny their own habits, they train children to do the same. The household becomes a culture of secrecy.

The path through this chapter moves from transparency to response to modelling. It begins with the simple but difficult act of stating monitoring expectations upfront in a way that sounds like safety rather than suspicion. It then turns to how families talk about mistakes so that accountability does not become fear and repair does not become humiliation. It then turns the lens back on adults, because monitoring without spying is not credible if adults insist on standards they do not live by. The order matters. Without transparency, monitoring feels like betrayal. Without a learning-first response, transparency feels like a threat. Without adult modelling, the whole system becomes a power play.

A quiet motif can hold the chapter's logic: the kitchen counter. The counter is a shared surface. It is where devices often land, where family life passes by, where adults can see without sneaking, where oversight can happen in daylight. A phone checked in a shared space feels like a household norm. A phone checked secretly in a bedroom feels like spying, even if the adult had good intentions. The physical setting is not a technical detail; it changes the moral meaning of the act. A family that wants to avoid secrecy should choose shared spaces for oversight and shared language for expectations.

The unresolved question is not whether children deserve privacy. They do. The question is what kind of privacy the household is cultivating: privacy that is bounded, understood, and partnered with adult responsibility, or privacy that is defended through secrecy because the child expects ambush. When you next feel the urge to check, what exactly are you protecting: your child's safety, or your own anxiety? And when you explain your expectations, will your child hear a safety plan spoken in daylight, or a warning that their life will be searched whenever you feel uneasy?

## Transparency and trust by age

In October 2016, the American Academy of Pediatrics in Itasca, Illinois, released its Family Media Plan tool, and the concrete outcome was a public endorsement of an idea many parents had been stumbling towards: digital boundaries work better when expectations are explicit, shared, and revisited, rather than improvised in panic. That principle applies as much to monitoring as it does to screen time. A child who discovers monitoring after the fact feels ambushed. A child who is told, plainly, what adults may check and why is far more likely to accept oversight as part of household safety, even if they do not love it.

Surprises breed secrecy.

The most common failure mode in monitoring is not that parents check. It is that parents check secretly, then deny it, then act on what they found as if the child should have known they were being watched. This sequence teaches an elegant lesson in distrust: adults do not say what they mean, and privacy is an illusion. Children respond to that lesson with predictable adaptations: hiding, deleting, secondary accounts, private browsing, silence. The adult then feels justified in more surveillance. The cycle tightens. Transparency breaks the cycle by refusing the initial lie. It turns monitoring from a trap into a policy.

Transparency is not a confession of suspicion. It is an agreement about how responsibility works in a household that contains powerful devices. A child does not have to be "untrustworthy" for adults to have oversight. Adults are responsible for safety and for shaping the environment in which children learn. The named concept here is *guardianship*. The explanation is that guardianship is a role with duties, not a feeling. The implication is that adults can say, without accusation, that some oversight is part of responsible care. The child's dignity is protected not by the absence of oversight but by the honesty of it and the proportionality of it.

Proportionality is where age matters. Young children do not need privacy in the same way teens do, and teens do not need oversight in the same way young children do. Yet families often swing to extremes: either total control for too long, which breeds rebellion and secrecy, or abrupt withdrawal of oversight, which leaves children alone with pressures they cannot yet manage. The named concept is *scaffold transfer*. The explanation is that as children mature, oversight should shift from direct supervision to shared expectations and periodic check-ins, with safety protections remaining firm. The implication is that a child's sense of trust grows not when adults disappear, but when adults gradually hand over responsibility while staying available and clear.

A useful way to make this concrete is to distinguish between privacy and secrecy. Privacy is a bounded space in which a child can think, explore, and develop an identity without constant adult presence. Secrecy is a strategy for avoiding accountability and hiding behaviour that the child expects adults would not accept. The show is the teen who wants a private conversation with a friend and the teen who deletes messages because they assume discovery will lead to humiliation. The named concept is *dignity-preserving privacy*. The explanation is that healthy privacy depends on clear boundaries about safety and respect. The implication is that a family can offer privacy while still stating, openly, that certain contexts remain subject to adult oversight, especially where risk is higher.

This is why the location and manner of checking matters as much as the fact of checking. A clear statement such as "I may check this device in shared spaces" does several things at once. It sets a boundary. It reduces the feeling of spying. It signals that the adult is not rummaging through a child's world in secret. The named concept is *daylight governance*. The explanation is that rules applied in daylight feel more legitimate than rules enforced through ambush. The implication is that a parent who checks a device at the kitchen counter, occasionally and predictably, is building a different culture from a parent who checks late at night in a bedroom while the child sleeps. The first can be framed as household safety. The second feels like intrusion, even if the parent's worry is sincere.

A named, checkable example from the wider world helps show that transparency is a foundational concept in trust systems, not a quirky parenting preference. In 1998, the UK passed the Data Protection Act, embedding a principle that has been echoed across many privacy frameworks: people should know what data is collected and how it is used. The household is not a court or a regulator, and parents are not bound to behave like institutions, yet the human psychology is similar. The named concept is *informed expectations*. The explanation is that people tolerate oversight better when it is disclosed and bounded. The implication is that children, too, tolerate oversight better when they are not shocked by it. Shock turns oversight into betrayal.

Transparency must also include what adults will not do. Children need to know where the line is, not only where it is absent. If the household says "we may check in shared spaces" but then conducts secret searches, the child learns that adult promises are flexible. If the household says "we will not read every message unless there is a safety concern" and then respects that promise, the child learns that boundaries apply to adults too. The named concept is *adult credibility*. The explanation is that credibility is built when adult behaviour matches stated expectations. The implication is that transparency is not merely a speech at the start of device ownership. It is a practice adults must keep, because children measure the difference between talk and reality with brutal accuracy.

An honest account must include a limitation: transparency does not guarantee cooperation. A teen may still feel angry about oversight even when it is explained calmly. A child may still test boundaries. A parent may still feel tempted to check secretly when anxious. The named concept is *anxiety override*. The explanation is that fear can make adults abandon their own policies, especially after a scare or a rumour. The implication is that transparency must be designed to survive adult fear. That is why rules about when and how checking happens should be explicit, not vague. Vague policies are the ones adults break when stressed.

Reconciling this limitation requires seeing transparency as a stabiliser for both sides. For the child, it reduces the sense of ambush and increases the chance of disclosure. For the adult, it reduces the temptation to do covert monitoring because a legitimate channel exists. The show is the parent who can say, calmly, "We will look at this together," rather than secretly searching. The named concept is *shared review*. The explanation is that shared review preserves dignity and allows learning. The implication is that shared review can become a routine, like any other, and routines reduce conflict because they remove improvisation.

Another limitation is that some children interpret any monitoring as proof of mistrust, regardless of how it is framed. This is where families must hold a firm conceptual line: monitoring is not accusation; it is guardianship. The adult can acknowledge the child's feelings without yielding the responsibility. The named concept is *role clarity*. The explanation is that children often want adult protection and adult freedom at the same time, and they experience the tension as unfairness. The implication is that adults should not argue about whether the child "deserves" oversight. They should state the oversight as part of the household's safety design, while offering privacy in ways that are meaningful and appropriate for age.

The motif that holds this practical is the kitchen counter. It is a shared place. It is also where family life happens: charging, meals, conversation, routine. A device that lives in shared space invites shared norms. A device that lives in private space invites private behaviour. Privacy is not wrong. Secrecy thrives in private spaces when oversight policies are unclear or coercive. The kitchen counter, in this sense, is not just furniture. It is a symbol of daylight governance: oversight without sneaking.

The forward test is not whether you can state a monitoring rule once. It is whether the rule stays credible under stress. When you feel anxious and tempted to check secretly, will you follow the policy you have set, or will you teach your child that the real rule is "privacy exists until my fear overrides it"? And when your child makes a mistake, will they come to you because they expect a fair, predictable response, or will they hide because they expect surveillance and shame? The answer is shaped, quietly, by whether your monitoring lives in daylight or in the dark.

## Talking about digital mistakes

In 1971, Albert Bandura published *Social Learning Theory*, setting out a concrete account of how people learn: not only through direct instruction, but through observing consequences, modelling, and feedback. The outcome was a framework that has aged well, because it captures something parents see daily. Children do not become wise because adults give speeches. They become wiser because they try, misjudge, feel the impact, and then revise their behaviour with guidance. Digital life accelerates this learning loop and makes the stakes feel sharper, because mistakes can be recorded, shared, and replayed. The child does not just learn from the mistake. They learn from what happens when the mistake is discovered.

Fear makes learning brittle.

A family can respond to a digital mistake in two broad ways. It can respond as if the mistake proves something about the child's character: they are careless, rude, irresponsible, untrustworthy. Or it can respond as if the mistake is a learning event: something happened, it had an impact, and we can build a better plan for next time. The first response produces shame and secrecy. The second produces accountability and competence. This is not indulgence. It is pedagogy. Children will misjudge tone. They will overshare. They will click the wrong thing. They will forward without thinking. They will join group dynamics that they later regret. The question is not whether they will make mistakes. The question is whether the household turns mistakes into a hiding game or into a curriculum.

A typical example is an unkind message sent in a moment of frustration. The child may have been provoked. They may have been trying to be funny. They may have been copying the tone of peers. They may have been tired. The message lands badly. A screenshot circulates. The child feels a mix of shame and panic. The parent, discovering the message, feels a mix of anger and fear: anger at the cruelty, fear for the child's reputation and relationships, fear of what this says about the child. The named concept is *threat perception*. The explanation is that parents interpret the mistake as a threat to the child's future, and children interpret the discovery as a threat to their dignity. The implication is that both sides are primed to escalate, unless the family has a way to talk that lowers the temperature while still holding accountability.

A learning-first response begins by separating three things that families often collapse: the event, the impact, and the plan. The event is what happened in observable terms. The impact is what it did to other people, to relationships, to trust, to the child's reputation. The plan is what changes so the same pattern is less likely next time. Collapsing these creates chaos.

If a parent leaps from event straight to moral verdict, the child stops listening. If a parent leaps from event straight to punishment, the child focuses on the penalty rather than the lesson. The named concept is *sequenced reflection*. The explanation is that reflection works when it moves in order: facts first, meaning second, changes last. The implication is that families can discuss serious mistakes without a courtroom tone by keeping the conversation structured and specific.

This structure also protects honesty. When children think the primary goal of the conversation is to catch them out, they lie. When they think the primary goal is to understand and repair, they are more likely to disclose. The named concept is *disclosure incentive*. The explanation is behavioural: people tell the truth when telling the truth reduces danger. The implication is that the household must make honesty visibly safer than concealment, without turning honesty into a free pass. Accountability without fear means the child can admit what happened and still face proportionate consequences that teach and restore trust. Fear-based accountability teaches better hiding. Learning-based accountability teaches better judgement.

Digital mistakes have a distinctive feature that makes these conversations harder: permanence. A harsh word spoken in a playground might be forgotten or softened by tone and context. A harsh message can be preserved and re-shared. The show is the child's sudden realisation that a message is not a breath; it is an artefact. The named concept is *trace persistence*. The explanation is that digital communication creates records, and records change social dynamics because they can be shown to third parties. The implication is that a debrief after an unkind message is not merely a manners lesson. It is a reputational lesson. It teaches the child to slow down before publishing and to imagine the wider audience that a screenshot can create.

A named, checkable example from the platform world illustrates why this matters even when children are not intentionally misbehaving. In September 2006, Facebook introduced the News Feed in Menlo Park, California, normalising continuous social visibility: other people's reactions, updates, and posts arriving as a stream. The concrete outcome was a cultural shift towards constant awareness of what others are doing and saying. The named concept is *visibility pressure*. The explanation is that when social life is visible and rapid, people respond quickly to avoid being left behind or misunderstood. The implication is that children's mistakes often occur under speed pressure. A teen replies fast to avoid looking uncaring. A child copies a meme without understanding its tone. A group chat escalates because everyone is trying to perform. Families who treat the mistake as a solitary moral defect miss the role of speed and group dynamics. That does not excuse the behaviour. It makes the lesson more accurate.

The most powerful learning moments happen when parents and children can name the mechanism of the mistake without collapsing into blame. A child sent a harsh message because they were angry and wanted relief. The mechanism is impulsive publishing: feeling becomes text too quickly. A teen overshared because they wanted validation. The mechanism is social reward seeking: posting in search of reassurance. A child clicked a risky link because it was presented as exciting and urgent. The mechanism is cue capture: attention pulled by novelty. Naming mechanisms turns a moral drama into a solvable problem. The named concept is *mechanism literacy*. The explanation is that people change behaviour more reliably when they understand what triggers it. The implication is that the household can build practical safeguards: slowing down, drafting then pausing, checking audience, avoiding late-night messaging, turning off certain notifications, using shared-space check-ins. Again, these are educational discussions, not clinical advice.

A learning-first approach also includes amends, because digital mistakes often harm real people. Making amends is not humiliation. It is restoration. The show is the child recognising the impact and taking a specific step to repair, whether that is an apology, a clarification, or a commitment to change. The named concept is *restorative action*. The explanation is that character is built through repair, not through shame. The implication is that debriefs should ask not only "what did you do?" but "what do you need to do now to restore trust?" This matters for siblings too. A child who lashes out digitally often brings the same tone home. Repair teaches that relationships can be damaged and then rebuilt without denying the damage.

A second named, checkable anchor returns us to Bandura because it highlights why parental tone matters. Children learn through modelling. A parent who responds to a digital mistake with contempt models contempt as a legitimate response to stress. A parent who responds with steadiness models steadiness. The named concept is *modelling under pressure*. The explanation is that the moments that teach most are the moments under stress, because that is when people reveal what they truly believe is acceptable. The implication is that a parent's calm debrief after an unkind message is not only teaching the child how to behave online. It is teaching the child how to respond to mistakes in general: with accountability, with repair, and with a plan.

A credible limitation should be faced openly. Some mistakes feel so frightening to parents that calm becomes difficult. Parents worry about bullying, exploitation, reputational damage, and legal or school consequences in ways children cannot yet grasp. Parents are also sometimes dealing with their own histories of shame or social pain. The named concept is *parental flooding*. The explanation is that fear can flood the adult nervous system, making it harder to speak wisely. The implication is that families should not expect perfect calm in the first moment. They should aim for a predictable sequence: immediate safety first, then a pause to cool down, then a debrief when the adult can speak without humiliation. This is not about being soft. It is about being effective. A panicked conversation teaches children to hide; a calm conversation teaches children to bring problems early.

Reconciling this limitation requires one crucial discipline: avoid making the child's mistake into the parent's identity crisis. Parents often hear a child's unkindness as proof they have failed morally. That interpretation intensifies shame and fuels harshness. The named concept is *self-blame spiral*. The explanation is that adults become punitive when they feel judged, even by their own internal voice. The implication is that a learning-first response demands adult self-regulation: focusing on the child's behaviour and the repair plan rather than on the parent's fear of being a "bad parent". Children do not need a perfect parent. They need a stable one.

The motif that unifies this subchapter is the screenshot. Not as a threat, but as a reality check. A screenshot represents the way digital moments can travel beyond their original context. It also represents the way a mistake can become a teacher. When a child understands that their words can be copied and replayed, they begin to develop a useful hesitation. Hesitation is not cowardice. It is judgement.

The forward test is this. When the next digital mistake happens, and it will, what will your child expect from you: an explosion that makes disclosure dangerous, or a structured debrief that makes disclosure worthwhile? And what will you expect from them: perfect behaviour, or honest accountability and repair? The answer determines whether the household becomes a place where digital mistakes are hidden until they become crises, or a place where mistakes become learning events before the screenshot writes the story for everyone else.

## Modelling the rules you want

In 1961, at Stanford University in Palo Alto, California, Albert Bandura's Bobo doll experiments demonstrated a concrete fact about human learning: children imitate what they observe, especially when the observed behaviour seems effective or rewarded. The outcome was not a tidy parenting manual, but a durable warning. If adults model aggression, children learn aggression. If adults model calm problem-solving, children learn that too. Screens make this lesson sharper because the behaviour is so visible and so habitual. A child may not remember your speech about boundaries. They will remember where your phone was during dinner.

Normal beats noble.

Families often hope children will follow rules because rules are announced. Children rarely do. They follow what feels normal in the home. Normal is not what adults say they value; it is what adults repeatedly do when nobody is performing. A parent who asks a child to stop scrolling while repeatedly checking work messages in the same conversation is teaching a deeper rule: screens outrank people. A parent who forbids phones at the table while keeping their own phone on the table is teaching a different rule: rules are about power, not values. Children are excellent at detecting these contradictions. They may not have sophisticated language for them, but they have a precise word: unfair.

The central tension here is that adults often need devices for legitimate reasons while also trying to protect children from the device's pull. Work, caregiving, scheduling, and emergencies are real. Pretending otherwise makes adults dishonest and children cynical. Yet claiming adult exception without accountability makes adults hypocritical and children resistant. The household needs a more dignified stance: adults can have exceptions that are clearly bounded, honestly explained, and visibly constrained, while still modelling the core rules the family expects children to live by. This is not about adults pretending to be teenagers. It is about adults acting like adults: using tools deliberately rather than being used by them.

Begin with the smallest, most consequential behaviour: where the phone sits during shared moments. The show is the family meal where one phone lies face down on the table "just in case", and another follows, and soon the table becomes a charging dock for attention. The named concept is *ambient availability*. The explanation is that a phone in reach is a phone that will be checked, because checks are cheap and cues are constant. The implication is that "no phones at the table" is not enforced by scolding. It is enforced by the environment adults create. If adults remove their own devices from the table, the norm becomes simpler to maintain and harder to argue with. If adults keep their devices there, children will treat the rule as theatre.

Notifications are the next small behaviour that carries disproportionate weight. Notifications are not content. They are commands delivered by someone else's priorities. When an adult allows notifications to interrupt conversations, children learn that interruptions are normal and that response speed is more important than presence. The named concept is *interruptive norming*. The explanation is that norms are set by what is tolerated, and children notice what adults tolerate in themselves. The implication is that one of the fastest ways to reduce "but you do it" arguments is for adults to take ownership of their own notification environment: fewer audible pings, fewer visible badges, fewer reflexive checks. This is not a purity test. It is a legitimacy test. A household cannot credibly ask children to resist cues that adults visibly obey.

Work boundaries are the most sensitive part because they involve real consequences and real fears. Adults fear missing something important. They fear being seen as unresponsive.

They fear losing control of work demands. These fears can be justified. They can also be used as excuses for constant availability. The show is the parent answering emails at bedtime while insisting the child stop messaging. The named concept is *double standard drift*. The explanation is that adults often frame their own use as necessary and children's use as frivolous, even when both are driven by similar mechanics: social obligation, fear of missing something, cue capture. The implication is that children learn to dismiss adult rules as self-serving unless adults can demonstrate restraint in their own "necessary" use. Restraint might mean defining certain hours as truly protected, or at least modelling that messages can wait during meals and bedtime routines unless there is a clear, rare reason.

A named, checkable example helps show how the broader culture has attempted to formalise the tension between work and personal life. In 2017, France expanded what is often referred to as the "right to disconnect" through provisions in the Labour Code, requiring certain employers to negotiate policies about after-hours digital communication. The named concept is *availability governance*. The explanation is that when communication tools become constant, boundaries must be negotiated deliberately or they disappear. The implication for families is not to import labour policy into the home. It is to recognise that adults are also vulnerable to the always-on pull, and that children can see when adults have no boundaries. If the parent cannot disconnect, the child will doubt the legitimacy of being asked to disconnect.

The most common adult mistake is to try to model restraint through denial: "I'm not on my phone," said while on the phone. Children do not need adults to pretend. They need adults to be honest. Honesty about adult exceptions is therefore part of modelling. The show is the parent who says, calmly, "I'm checking one work message, then I'm putting it away," and then actually puts it away. The named concept is *bounded exception*. The explanation is that exceptions do not destroy rules when they are bounded and visible. The implication is that adults can maintain legitimacy by making exceptions rare, specific, and completed quickly, rather than vague and endless. Endless exceptions are not exceptions. They are the real rule.

This is also where "monitoring without spying" becomes credible. Children accept oversight more readily when they see adults living under some of the same household norms: devices have homes, shared spaces have expectations, bedtime has protections. If adults treat the home as a place where any screen use is permissible at any time, then monitoring feels like a power play rather than a safety plan. The named concept is *shared constraint*. The explanation is that shared constraints reduce resentment because they signal that the rule exists to protect a household value, not to control a child. The implication is that adult modelling makes child monitoring easier, not through authority, but through fairness.

A second named, checkable anchor returns to the tools themselves. In September 2018, Apple released iOS 12 in Cupertino, California, and Screen Time made it easier for users to see patterns of use and reduce their own triggers. The concrete outcome was not only parental control; it was also adult self-awareness. The named concept is *self-monitoring*. The explanation is that people change behaviour more easily when they can see what they do repeatedly. The implication is that adults who use tracking or quiet settings for themselves demonstrate that boundaries are not punishments for children. They are strategies for humans living with persuasive technology. Children recognise this quickly. They may not praise you for it, but they lose the hypocrisy argument, which is the point.

A credible limitation must be faced. Some adults have jobs with genuine on-call requirements or caring responsibilities that require responsiveness. Some parents are single parents who must coordinate constantly. Some households have emergencies more often than they would like. In such cases, adult modelling cannot look like perfect disconnection. The named concept is *non-negotiable availability*. The explanation is that some roles demand it. The implication is that modelling should focus on what is still within control: where the phone rests when not in use, how exceptions are bounded, how notifications are managed, and how adults return attention to the child after the interruption. A parent who must check a phone can still model a clean return: "I'm back. Tell me again." That return teaches presence as a practice, not a mood.

Reconciling this limitation is also a matter of tone. Adults should avoid using "because work" as a blanket justification that ends discussion, because that teaches children that power does not need to explain itself. A better stance is transparent and respectful: adults can explain that some responsibilities are different while still acknowledging the child's perception of unfairness. The named concept is *legitimacy maintenance*. The explanation is that people comply more readily when they believe the system is fair, even if it is not identical for everyone. The implication is that adult exceptions should be explained with the same clarity adults expect from children: what, why, when it ends, and what happens next.

The motif that holds this subchapter together is the phone on the table. It is simple. It is also brutally diagnostic. A phone on the table announces that the family moment is provisional and interruptible. A phone off the table announces that the moment has priority. Children follow these announcements more than they follow posters about family values. The table becomes the classroom for attention.

The forward test is uncomfortable because it turns the lens back onto adults. The next time you tell your child to put their device away, what will your hands be doing? Will you be modelling the same boundary or breaking it? And when you need an adult exception, will you make it bounded and honest, or will you treat your own scrolling as invisible? Children do not need perfect parents. They do need parents whose behaviour makes the household rules look like a coherent system rather than a one-sided demand.

# Chapter 12
# Review, Reset, and Grow Up

A family makes a clear rule, sticks it on the fridge, and enjoys a brief calm. The first week feels promising. The arguments soften. Bedtime improves. Then life happens. A grandparent visits. A school project requires a device. A child gets invited into a new group chat. A parent has a work deadline and breaks the table rule "just this once". Nothing explodes. The plan does not fail dramatically. It simply loosens. By the end of the month, the household is back in low-grade bargaining, not because anyone chose to abandon the plan, but because drift is what systems do when nobody checks them.

Drift is the default.

Families often imagine that the hard part is making rules. Making rules is easy. Keeping rules coherent as children grow and circumstances change is the real craft. A family plan that is not reviewed becomes either brittle or irrelevant. Brittle plans snap under pressure. Irrelevant plans are ignored. Both outcomes return the household to the same daily battles, only now with a layer of cynicism: "That plan never works." The aim of this final chapter is to turn the plan into a living agreement rather than a one-time crackdown, and to do so without reopening every debate each week.

The central tension is between stability and growth. Children need stability: predictable boundaries, consistent defaults, and clear non-negotiables that protect sleep, attention, and connection. Children also need growth: more autonomy, more privacy, more responsibility, and room to become themselves. Families often get trapped because they treat stability and growth as enemies. They tighten rules to preserve stability, and children push back because growth is being blocked. Or they loosen rules to respect growth, and stability collapses into drift. The household needs a third posture: stability in core protections with planned, reviewed expansion of freedom in exchange for demonstrated responsibility. That posture requires reviews, not because families love meetings, but because leaving growth to improvisation produces conflict.

This matters because children do not grow in a smooth line. They hit milestones that change the digital stakes overnight: new schools, new phones, new social platforms, new homework demands, new peer cultures. Each milestone increases both the child's capability and the child's exposure. A plan that worked last term may fail next term not because the child is suddenly bad, but because the environment has changed. Reviews prevent families from mistaking environmental change for moral collapse. They also prevent children from mistaking every request for more freedom as a confrontation. When the family has a predictable channel for renegotiation, children have less incentive to argue nightly, because they know the conversation has a place to land.

It also matters because adults are not static either. Adults get tired. Adults get distracted. Adults break their own rules and then avoid mentioning it, which teaches children that rules are performative. Reviews bring adults back into the plan without drama. They allow the household to acknowledge reality: "This part slipped," "This part worked," "This part needs adjusting," without turning it into shame or a courtroom. A plan without review is a plan enforced through mood. A plan with review is a plan enforced through shared expectations.

The stakes are not only behavioural. They are relational. A family that reviews and resets teaches a child a rare skill: how to live inside agreements. Modern life is full of agreements, explicit and implicit. People who can renegotiate agreements without manipulation, who can accept feedback, who can adjust behaviour in exchange for more freedom, are better prepared for adulthood than people who only comply under supervision or rebel under pressure. Reviews are not about perfect control. They are about teaching governance: how to manage a system over time without constant conflict.

The movement through this chapter is simple and disciplined. It begins with predictable reviews that are short enough to be realistic and structured enough to stop drift without turning the household into a parliament. It then turns to the deeper question of maturation: how freedom expands, how safeguards remain, and how parents let go gradually without abandoning their duty of care. The order matters because freedom without review becomes drift, and review without a growth pathway becomes stagnation. Children stop engaging when they believe nothing will ever change.

A quiet motif can anchor this final stretch: the calendar. A calendar is not a moral object. It is a reality object. It holds school terms, weekends, holidays, birthdays, deadlines, and the seasonal shifts that affect sleep and mood. A family plan that does not live on a calendar will be defeated by the calendar. A family plan that uses the calendar as a rhythm keeper becomes more credible. When a review has a predictable place on the calendar, renegotiation becomes normal rather than adversarial. The calendar makes the plan less personal and therefore less combustible.

There is also an adult psychological benefit that should not be overlooked. Reviews reduce the need for constant judgement in the moment. When adults know there is a review coming, they can hold a boundary calmly and say, truthfully, that questions will be heard at the agreed time. This lowers daily temperature. It reduces accidental bargaining. It reduces the way small conflicts metastasise into big ones. Children argue less when they believe the channel for change exists. Adults shout less when they are not forced to improvise policy while hungry and tired.

The unresolved question that drives this chapter is not whether you can maintain the plan exactly as it is. You cannot.

The question is whether you can maintain the plan as a coherent system while it changes. When your child asks for more freedom, will you treat it as a threat that must be resisted, or as a signal that the plan must evolve and be reviewed? And when the household slips, as it will, will you quietly abandon the plan out of discouragement, or reset it through a predictable process that keeps dignity intact and growth on track?

## Monthly reviews that prevent drift

In October 2016, the American Academy of Pediatrics in Itasca, Illinois, released its Family Media Plan tool, and the concrete outcome was a public invitation to treat digital life as something families manage over time rather than solve once. The tool's deeper message was not "set stricter rules". It was "review what you have set". That difference matters, because most families do not abandon their screen plans deliberately. Plans fade. They erode at the edges through exceptions, fatigue, school demands, visitors, and the quiet belief that next week will be calmer.

Drift is not disobedience.

Drift is what happens when a system is not checked. A household can begin with clear boundaries and still end up in constant negotiation a month later, not because anyone has become worse, but because the plan has become porous. One exception becomes precedent. One late night becomes a new normal. One busy period becomes a justification for convenience. Children are not stupid; they notice these shifts immediately, and they adapt. Parents notice too, but often later, usually when the arguments return. By then, adults feel angry and children feel entitled, and both think the other side changed first. A monthly review interrupts this story. It turns "you always" fights into "what actually happened" conversations.

A review is not a family court. It is a maintenance check. That distinction is everything. Many parents avoid reviews because they fear reopening every debate, inviting bargaining, or rewarding complaining. Those fears are real in households where reviews are unstructured. Unstructured reviews become a place for accumulated resentment to spill. Structured reviews do the opposite. They contain the spill. They make discussion predictable, time-limited, and anchored to observable outcomes rather than to moods. The named concept is *scheduled governance*. The explanation is that governance works better when it happens at a predictable time, in a predictable format, rather than erupting at the point of conflict. The implication is that a short review can reduce the daily need to negotiate because the child knows there is a legitimate channel for change.

The first purpose of a monthly check-in is to stop the boundary debate from happening nightly. Children argue in the moment because they want influence and because they fear there is no other time to be heard. Adults argue in the moment because they are trying to enforce and renegotiate simultaneously. That is a terrible combination. A review separates enforcement from renegotiation. The rule is enforced during the week. The discussion about whether the rule still fits happens at review time. The named concept is *channel separation*. The explanation is that when discussion is moved to a specific channel, the child has less incentive to keep the argument alive all week. The implication is that the household can hold boundaries more calmly because it can say, truthfully, that concerns will be heard later without needing to bargain now.

The second purpose is to replace moral heat with evidence. "You're always on your phone" is a sentence built for war. It is vague, accusatory, and impossible to falsify. "We noticed bedtime drift on three nights this week" is a sentence built for adjustment. It is specific, observable, and actionable. The named concept is *evidence-based language*. The explanation is that specificity reduces defensiveness because it does not require the child to defend their whole character. The implication is that a review should ask for concrete observations rather than general complaints, because general complaints invite general counter-complaints. This is not about turning family life into spreadsheets. It is about replacing the fog of impressions with the clarity of patterns.

Patterns are the real object of review. Families do not need to chase every incident. They need to identify which patterns are driving conflict and which patterns are protecting the family's non-negotiables. The show is a household discovering that most arguments cluster in one time window, or that one app triggers most meltdowns, or that bedtime rules crumble on weekends. The named concept is *pattern detection*. The explanation is that once patterns are visible, families can adjust a small number of levers rather than fighting constantly. The implication is that a review is a diagnostic tool. It prevents the common error of tightening everything when only one part of the system is failing.

A named, checkable example from outside family life helps normalise the idea that short, regular reviews prevent larger failures. In 1986, the first release of the Scrum framework for managing complex work emerged in the software world, and one of its defining practices became the retrospective: a short, regular review of what worked, what did not, and what to change next. The named concept is *iterative improvement*. The explanation is that complex systems improve through small, frequent adjustments rather than through rare, sweeping reforms. The implication for families is not to import corporate language into the living room. It is to recognise that family screen rules are a complex system: changing children, changing platforms, changing school demands, changing adult capacity. Iteration is more realistic than perfection.

The third purpose of a review is to create a credible pathway for fairness. Children often accept restrictions better when they can see how freedom grows. Adults often hold restrictions better when they can see how responsibility earns trust. A monthly review is where this exchange becomes legible. Not in the sense of bargaining for more minutes, but in the sense of noticing competence: clean bedtimes, respectful behaviour in conflicts, honest disclosure of mistakes, reliable completion of responsibilities before screens. The named concept is *earned expansion*. The explanation is that freedom can expand without undermining the plan when expansion is linked to demonstrated behaviour rather than to pressure. The implication is that reviews turn "you never let me" into "what would count as readiness", which is a far more useful conversation.

What to ask in a review is therefore less about rules and more about impact. Did the household protect sleep? Did conflict reduce or move to a more manageable form? Did the child feel included socially without late-night spirals? Did homework and morning routines hold? These questions anchor the review to the family's values rather than to an abstract ideal of screen discipline. The named concept is *values alignment*. The explanation is that values determine what the family protects, and protection is what rules are for. The implication is that when a child argues "other families allow it", the review provides a stronger reference point: "Our plan is built to protect what we protect; did it do that this month?" That is hard to dismiss because it is grounded in outcomes.

The way adjustments are made is as important as the fact of adjustment. A review that reopens everything becomes exhausting and invites manipulation. A review that forbids all changes becomes pointless and invites resentment. A useful review makes small, specific changes that are easy to implement and easy to measure next time. The named concept is *bounded adjustment*. The explanation is that bounded changes prevent the review from turning into a referendum on the entire family plan. The implication is that the household can evolve without losing coherence. It can tighten a rule in one zone, loosen a choice in another, adjust a routine in a vulnerable hour, or alter a setting on an app, while keeping core protections stable.

A credible limitation must be faced: some families will find reviews awkward at first. Children may treat them as an opportunity to demand everything. Parents may treat them as an opportunity to lecture. Teens may treat them as patronising. The named concept is *review friction*. The explanation is that any new household ritual feels artificial until it becomes normal. The implication is that the review should be made brief, predictable, and emotionally low-heat. It should not be scheduled at a time when everyone is hungry or exhausted. It should not be used to rehash the worst fight of the week. It should be treated as maintenance, which means it ends even if the conversation is not perfect. The perfection impulse is a form of drift too; it delays action until everything feels ready.

Reconciling this limitation returns us to the simplest advantage of a monthly review: it gives the family a place to put questions so they do not spill into every day. The calendar becomes part of the plan. The child learns, over time, that negotiation has a legitimate channel and that shouting is not required to be heard. The adult learns that boundaries can be held calmly because change is not forbidden; it is scheduled. The named concept is *predictable hearing*. The explanation is that people calm down when they believe they will be heard. The implication is that reviews reduce daily arguments not by silencing children, but by giving them a safer forum.

The motif worth holding is the calendar square. A review that lives on the calendar is harder to forget and harder to avoid. It becomes part of the family's rhythm in the same way bedtime routines and device-free zones do. A blank calendar square invites drift. A marked square invites maintenance.

The forward test is sharp and practical. Over the next month, will your family try to enforce a plan through constant micro-negotiations, or will it contain negotiation in a predictable review so the rest of the month can be lived? And when drift begins, as it will, will you treat it as evidence that the child is unmanageable, or as evidence that the system needs a small adjustment before low-grade arguing becomes the house's new background music?

## Updating rules as children mature

In 1762, Jean-Jacques Rousseau published *Emile, or On Education* in Paris, arguing that education should change as the child changes, with freedom increasing alongside demonstrated capability rather than being granted as a ceremonial right. The concrete outcome was not a universally agreed curriculum but a durable educational insight: rules that do not evolve become either tyrannical or irrelevant. Digital rules are especially prone to this failure because childhood shifts quickly and platforms shift faster. A rule that protected an eight-year-old can humiliate a thirteen-year-old. A rule that felt generous for a twelve-year-old can be dangerously naive for a fifteen-year-old.

Growth changes the bargain.

Families often treat screen rules as if they were house rules about shoes: set them once and enforce them forever. Devices do not behave like shoes. They are portals into social life, status, identity, and risk. Children also do not behave like shoes. They develop new capacities and new vulnerabilities, often in the same month. Updating rules is not "going soft". It is governance. It is the process by which a household keeps its core protections stable while widening freedom in ways that teach responsibility rather than trigger rebellion. If rules never loosen, teens learn that honesty has no payoff. If rules loosen without conditions, drift takes over. The middle is conditional expansion: more freedom in exchange for demonstrated responsibility, reviewed and revised as circumstances change.

Begin with the moments that force updates even in families who avoid them. A child moves to a new school, and suddenly homework platforms, group chats, and social schedules change. A child gets a new phone, and the device is more powerful, more private, more portable. A new social platform becomes the place where peers congregate, and the child feels excluded without access. These milestones often trigger panic-based governance: adults either clamp down or surrender. The named concept is *milestone shock*. The explanation is that abrupt change makes adults fearful and children demanding, and both react strongly. The implication is that families benefit from treating milestones as planned renegotiation points rather than as emergencies. Planned renegotiation reduces conflict because it moves the discussion into daylight, when dignity can be preserved.

The core of updating rules is to separate what must remain stable from what can change. Every family needs a small set of non-negotiables that protect basic functioning: sleep, respectful behaviour, school focus, and the right to be together without constant interruptions. Those goods do not become less important as children age. If anything, they become more important because adolescence multiplies demands and risks. The named concept is *core protections*. The explanation is that some boundaries are there to protect biology and relationships, not to control entertainment. The implication is that the family can say, with credibility, that certain protections remain stable across ages, while the details of how freedom is expressed within those protections will expand.

Expanding freedom is easiest to discuss when it is framed as a skill exchange rather than as a power struggle. Many teens hear restrictions as an insult: "You think I'm a child." Many parents hear demands for freedom as entitlement: "You want everything your way." Both are partly wrong because they are treating independence as status rather than as competence. The named concept is *competence framing*. The explanation is that competence is observable, while status is arguable. The implication is that a household that ties freedom to observable behaviours reduces bargaining. Behaviours such as charging devices in the agreed place, keeping phones out of bed, ending sessions without drama, managing group chats without late-night spirals, and disclosing mistakes early are not moral trophies. They are evidence that the child can handle more autonomy without the household collapsing.

A named, checkable example helps show why "evidence" matters in modern digital governance. In September 2018, Apple released iOS 12 in Cupertino, California, introducing Screen Time tools that allow families and users to see patterns of use and apply more granular controls. The concrete outcome, when used thoughtfully, is that debates can shift from "I think" to "I notice". The named concept is *feedback-informed adjustment*. The explanation is that adjustments based on patterns are easier to justify and easier to accept than adjustments based on adult anxiety. The implication is not that families must use any particular tool. It is that rule updates should be based on observed outcomes: sleep quality, conflict frequency, school functioning, mood stability, honesty, and respect. Evidence stabilises negotiations because it reduces the sense that rules are arbitrary.

New platforms create a special challenge because platform access is both social and reputational. A child may want a platform because peers use it. A parent may fear the platform because they have heard alarming stories. Both positions can be true without producing a workable household plan. The named concept is *platform migration*. The explanation is that children's social worlds migrate, and families cannot freeze them in place. The implication is that "no new platform ever" tends to become either a lie or a war. A more realistic approach is to treat new platforms as trials with defined safeguards: timing protections, privacy expectations, conduct expectations, and a review point. Trials avoid the false choice between blanket bans and open doors.

A second named, checkable anchor can help ground the idea that rules evolve with capability. In 1948, the World Health Organization was established in Geneva, and its broad definition of health has long included mental and social wellbeing. The named concept is *whole-life impact*. The explanation is that digital rules are not merely about content; they are about the child's functioning in sleep, relationships, learning, and emotional regulation. The implication is that updates should not be negotiated purely around "fairness" or "what other families allow". They should be negotiated around impact: does this new freedom support wellbeing or undermine it? When impact becomes the metric, the family's conversation becomes more mature and less tribal.

Updating rules also requires letting go, and this is where many adults feel grief they do not name. Letting go is not surrendering care. It is accepting that a teen's life will increasingly happen beyond parental view and beyond parental control. A parent can control a young child's device use by controlling the device. A parent cannot control a young adult's device use by controlling the device, because the young adult will eventually leave the house. The named concept is *handover anxiety*. The explanation is that adults fear the moment when safeguards cannot be enforced externally. The implication is that the purpose of rule updates is not to cling to control longer. It is to increase internal capability in the child so that external control becomes less necessary. The family plan, at its best, is a training programme for adulthood.

A credible limitation must be acknowledged. Some children mature unevenly. Some are trustworthy in one domain and reckless in another. Some families face stresses that make gradual expansion harder: inconsistent schedules, shared custody, limited time, high school pressure, mental health challenges, or social instability. The named concept is *uneven readiness*. The explanation is that readiness is not a single trait; it varies by context, stress, and skill. The implication is that rule updates must be tailored, and tailoring can still be fair when the logic is clear. Fairness here means "what you can handle safely" rather than "what your sibling gets". This is particularly important in households with multiple children, where comparisons can become a constant source of conflict if the family cannot articulate why freedoms differ.

Reconciling these limitations requires consistency in the process rather than sameness in the outcomes. The process can be stable: regular reviews, clear criteria for expanding freedom, clear protections that do not change, and a predictable response when a trial goes badly. The named concept is *procedural fairness*. The explanation is that people tolerate unequal outcomes better when they trust the procedure that produced them. The implication is that children and teens are more likely to accept different freedoms if they believe the household's process is honest and predictable, not driven by mood or favouritism.

The motif that holds this subchapter together is the set of keys. Keys signal access. They also signal responsibility. A child does not receive keys to a car because they want them; they receive keys because they can demonstrate, through practice and guidance, that they can use them without endangering themselves or others. Digital access is similar. It is not a prize. It is a responsibility with consequences. When families treat access as a key that can be earned and managed, rather than as a toy that must be confiscated, the whole emotional tone changes. Teens resent being treated like children. They respond better when they are treated like apprentices to adulthood.

The unresolved tension is that children will always want more freedom slightly before they are ready for it, and parents will often want to hold freedom slightly longer than is wise. That tension does not vanish. It must be governed. The forward test is whether your family can update rules without turning each milestone into a battle: when the next new platform appears, the next phone upgrade arrives, or the next school transition changes the digital landscape, will the household respond with panic and improvisation, or with a process that expands the keys of freedom in exchange for demonstrated responsibility while keeping the core protections locked in place?

# About the Author

Reema Sanzari writes for families who want calmer homes in a noisy world. Her work is rooted in a simple belief: boundaries are not about control; they are about care, attention, and the daily conditions that help people treat each other well. She is especially interested in the small, repeatable choices that change a household over time - the tone of a reminder, the placement of a charger, the wording of an agreement, the decision to protect one shared meal.

Like many parents and carers navigating modern childhood, Reema has watched screens shift from occasional entertainment to ever-present infrastructure: homework portals, class chats, family calendars, friendships, and downtime, all in the same pocket. She brings a practical, non-alarmist voice to the question families quietly ask: how do we keep the benefits of technology without letting it set the rhythm of our lives?

Her approach is shaped by a cultural memory that is not so distant: evenings when the telephone stayed in one place, photos were printed, and a family could be temporarily unreachable without it signalling an emergency. She uses that thread not to romanticise the past, but to recover what still matters now - sleep, conversation, play, and the dignity of growing up with guidance rather than constant surveillance.

9 789376 551200

Printed at Repro India Ltd.